Monograph 6?

THE AMERICAN ETHNOLOGICAL SOCIETY

Robert F. Spencer, Editor

THE HERERO OF WESTERN BOTSWANA

Aspects of Change in a Group of Bantu-Speaking Cattle Herders

FRANK R. VIVELO

WEST PUBLISHING CO.
St. Paul • New York • Boston
Los Angeles • San Francisco

Library of Congress Cataloging in Publication Data

Vivelo, Frank Robert.

   The Herero of Western Botswana.

   (American Ethnological Society. Monographs; 61)

   Bibliography: p.

   Includes index.

   1. Hereros. I. Title. II. Series.

DT797.V58   309.1'68'103   76-44453

ISBN 0-8299-0057-8

When goods manufactured by the industrialized nations with modern techniques become available through trade to aboriginal populations, the native people increasingly give up their homecrafts in order to devote their efforts to producing specialized cash crops or other trade items in order to obtain more of the industrially made articles.

Murphy and Steward, 1956:353

*

Foreword

The anthropological importance of the Herero is due to a number of unusual cultural features and conditions of their life and location. First, they are the most exclusively pastoral of all the Bantu peoples of the southwestern African cattle-herding zone where they share this mode of life with the non-Bantu Nama (Hottentots). It is well established that East Africa is the major region of pastoralism in Africa south of the Sahara and its borders, and the presence of a comparatively few pastoral groups in southwestern Africa, isolated from their presumed East African homeland by a belt of tsetse infested tropical forest and bush, therefore poses some engaging culture-historical puzzles. The location of their ancient region of origin and the nature of their ancient culture, the era and route of their migration, the degree to which their present pastoral specialization was brought with them or was developed in adaptation to a new environment, and the extent to which they have exchanged cultural features and a mode of life with their neighbors—all are questions that have engendered speculation on the part of cultural historians, but speculation backed by very little historical and no archeological evidence. Indeed, no really thorough comparative linguistic and ethnographic studies have been offered in support of the solutions proposed for these problems. The few fragmentary legends that were recorded by early students of Herero culture are contradictory and may even be interpreted to suggest the possibility of a multiple origin and convergent routes of migration from both the north and the east.

The term "Herero" is applied as an ethnic label in various senses to certain peoples of southwestern Africa. Most strictly it is the name of the largest division of the Herero-speaking peoples, a division that is definable culturally though formerly, at least, it was not unified politically. In a more general sense the term includes also the Mbanderu or Eastern Herero who are culturally very similar to the Herero proper but may have a separate origin in part. In a still broader sense it includes the cattleless Tjimba who were formerly to be found in small isolated groups in some northern parts of South West Africa. Some of the Tjimba were Herero who had lost their cattle through wars, famines, or pestilence and had reverted to a hunting and gathering mode of life. Many of these have now reacquired cattle and consider themselves to be Herero again. But other Tjimba recently found living in a remote mountainous region of the Kaokoveld (the northwestern corner of South West Africa) appear to be the descendants of a people who never kept domestic animals for food, who contrast physically with the Herero, but who nevertheless speak a dialect of the Herero language (MacCalman and Grobbelaar, 1965). It is my guess that these latter Tjimba will be found to be related to the Kwisi or Bergdama. The cultural exchange that may have taken place between the pastoral Herero and the non-Bantu peoples of southwestern Africa—the Twa (including the Kwisi and Bergdama), the Kwepe, the Bushmen, and the Hottentots—is a matter needing careful exploration.

Lingustically and culturally, the closest relatives of the Herero are the Himba who today occupy the basin of the lower Kunene River, below Ruacana Falls, and who enter the historical record in 1617 if they are indeed, as Fr. Carlos Estermann judges, the descendants of the pastoral "Maquimbes" mentioned by Cereveria Pereira, the founder of the presidio at Benguela (Estermann, 1960:22). From this it appears that pastoral Bantu peoples have been present in Angola for more than 350 years. The Himba share not only a way of life with the Herero, though they are today somewhat more agricultural, but they also share the double set of clans and the combination of patrilineal and matrilineal descent, which is a second feature making these Herero-speaking peoples of anthropological interest.

More distantly related, but still falling within what Fr. Estermann (op. cit.) considers to be the Herero cultural division of the southern Bantu peoples, are several small ethnic units that practice a mixed herding and cultivating economy in favorable locations

in the western valleys of the Chela range and the semi-arid plains below them as far north as 14° south latitude. These—the Kuvale,
Ngendelengo, Hakawona, Zimba, and Tjavikwa peoples—appear to
be exclusively matrilineal and share some matri-clans with the Himba and Herero. Still more distantly related by culture to the Herero
and Himba are two other groups, the Ovambo tribes of the mid-An-
gola-South West African border and the Nyaneka-Nkumbi peoples
settled in the lands drained by the middle Kunene and its tribu-
taries. Though cattle breeders to various degrees, they all depend
more upon the cultivation of grain for their livelihood. The relationship of these various ethnic units to one another and to the Himba
and Herero is a problem to which some answers might be proposed
when adequate comparative linguistic studies have been carried
out.

Being cut off from East Africa by a zone where cattle cannot be
kept, the southwest African cultural area provides one side of a kind
of anthropological laboratory where theories of adaptation and acculturation developed in the study of peoples in the one region
might be tested by comparison with those developed in work done in
the other. Here we have another reason for finding the southwestern
Bantu people, and the Herero in particular, as the best known and
most exclusively pastoral group, of interest for more modern kinds
of anthropological research.

It is of special importance to the student of African cultures to
know that the Herero of South West Africa are one of the better reported peoples of Africa, the number of works dealing with them in
some way numbering well over 500, though the majority of these are
not professional anthropological studies. Most of the older works
bearing upon Herero culture were written by German missionaries,
explorers, traders, government servants, and military officers, or
settlers in South West Africa, and most, of course, are in the German language.*

While the Herero were embroiled in a series of greater and lesser
wars throughout most of the nineteenth century, it was their uprising in 1904 against the German government of South West Africa that had the most severe effect upon their culture and society.

*Because this literature is so important as a basis for modern studies of the Herero
and of the cultural changes they have undergone in recent time, the writer has translated some of the more useful studies and has fostered the translation of several
others that are also of anthropological value. These translations have been made
available to the Human Relations Area Files for duplication and distribution.

Though at first successful in their revolt, they eventually succumbed to German military strategy and force; the Herero fighting strength was destroyed, thousands were slain, and many of those remaining were dispersed. In their defeat the surviving Herero became divided into two groups—those who fled across an arm of the Kalahari Desert into Botswana, and those who remained in or eventually returned to South West Africa. This separation produced a situation in which the Herero living in the two regions came into contact with different indigenous African and colonial European cultures and made adjustments to different habitats, different political systems, and different economic forces. The isolation of the two sections from one another has not been complete, however, for there has been a small movement of visitors and migrants across the border in both directions. Thus in any study of culture change in one of the two regions the possibility of influence from the other must be entertained. Though recent censuses do not provide information on peoples by tribal affiliation, from older reports it may be estimated roughly that there are some 40,000 or more Herero in South West Africa, and about 6,000 in Botswana, most of whom live in the western part of the country.

The conditions of Herero life before the uprising of 1904 and the subsequent separation are rather well documented in the older literature. Now some modern anthropological accounts of the Botswana Herero half a century and more after the separation are available, Frank Vivelo's treatise constituting an important addition to these materials. And some attention has been paid to the Herero of South West Africa in the past quarter century by anthropologists of the German school (Lehmann, Wagner, Köhler, and Schlosser) and most recently by an American (Pendleton). While these studies make a good beginning in providing information useful for a comparison of the courses of cultural change in the two regional branches of the Herero, much remains to be done. Indeed, it is important to have periodic studies in both countries, as more rapid acculturation may be anticipated with the acceleration of political evolution: independence was achieved by Botswana in 1966 and seems likely to come in some form to South West Africa in the near future.

As one who some 25 years ago took advantage of the fact that Herero refugees from South West Africa had established themselves in Botswana (where the cultural restraints upon them were much less severe) and saw this as an opportunity to study the life-ways of this anthropologically classical Bantu pastoral people, I enthusiastically welcome Frank Vivelo's further work on the Botswana Herero and their progressive adaptation to changing conditions. This is the sort of study that, with its extensive documentation, leads us from the realm of soft data and easy speculation to that of hard fact and well attested conclusions.

Gordon D. Gibson
Smithsonian Institution

REFERENCES

Estermann, Carlos
    1960   *O Grupo Étnico Herero.* (Vol. 3 of *Etnografia do Sudoeste de Angola.* Memórias da Junta de Investigações do Ultramar, No. 30.) Lisbon.

MacCalman, H. R., and B. J. Grobbelaar
    1965   "Preliminary Report of Two Stone-Working OvaTjimba Groups in the Northern Kaokoveld of South West Africa." *Cimbebasia* 13: 1-31.

OTHER LITERATURE CITED

Köhler, Oswin
    1956a   "Ahnenkult der Herero." *Afrikanischer Heimat Kalender 1956* 80-86.

    1956b   "The Stage of Acculturation in South West Africa." *Sociologus* n.s. 6: 138-153.

    1958   *A Study of Karibib District.* Ethnological Publications, No. 40. Pretoria: South Africa, Department of Native Affairs.

    1959a   *A Study of Gobabis District.* Ethnological Publications, No. 42. Pretoria: South Africa, Department of Native Affairs.

    1959b   *A Study of Omaruru District.* Ethnological Publications, No. 43. Pretoria: South Africa, Department of Native Affairs.

    1959c   *A Study of Otjiwarongo District.* Ethnological Publications, No. 44. Pretoria: South Africa, Department of Native Affairs.

1959d   *A Study of Grootfontein District.* Ethnological Publications,
         No. 45. Pretoria: South Africa, Department of Native Affairs.

Lehmann, F. Rudolf
    1950   "Einige Spannungs- und Ausgleichserscheinungen in der
            Sozialen Organisation Mittel- und Südwestafrikanischen
            Völker." In *Beiträge zur Gesellungs- und Völkerwissenschaft*
            (Festschrift Richard Thurnwald), pp. 245-270. Berlin: Verlag
            Gebr. Mann.

    1951   "Die Häuptlings-Erbfolgeordnung der Herero." *Zeitschrift für
            Ethnologie* 76: 94-102.

    1955   "Das Häuptlingtum der Herero in Südwestafrika." *Sociologus*
            n.s. 5: 28-42.

Lehmann, F. Rudolf
    1963-65   "Ejuru. Sprach- und religionswissenschaftliche Anmerkungen
               zum Himmels-Begriff der Herero." *Journal of the South West
               African Scientific Society* 18-19: 48-64.

    1965-66   "Die Bedeutung der Wörter zera und tapu." *Journal of the
               South West African Scientific Society* 20: 101-128.

Pendleton, Wade C.
    1974   *Katutura: A Place Where We Do Not Stay.* San Diego: San
            Diego State University Press.

Schlosser, Katesa
    1955   "Die Herero im Britisch-Betschuanaland-Protektorat und ein
            Besuch in einer Ihrer Siedlungen: Ncwe-le-tau." *Zeitschrift für
            Ethnologie* 80: 200-258.

    1958   *Eingeborenenkirchen in Süd- und Südwest-Afrika.* Kiel:
            Mühlau.

    1962   "Die Sektan der Eingeborenen in Süd- und Südwestafrika als
            Manifestationen des Gegensatzes zwischen Weissen und
            Nichtweissen." *Afrikanischer Heimat Kalender 1962.* 101-107.

    1965   "Profane Ursachen des Anschlusses an Separatistenkirchen in
            Süd- und Südwestafrika." In Ernst Benz (compiler), *Messian-
            ischen Kirchen, Sekten und Bewegungen im Heutigen Afrika.*
            Leiden: Brill.

Wagner, Günter
    1952   "Aspects of Conservatism and Adaptation in the Economic
            Life of the Herero." *Sociologus* n.s. 2: 1-25.

Wagner, Günter, and Oswin Köhler
    1957   *A Study of Okahandja District.* Ethnological Publications, No.
            38. Pretoria: South Africa, Department of Native Affairs.

Preface

This is a study of social change among a group of Herero cattle herders residing in western Botswana, Africa. Previous descriptions of the Herero are compared herein with observations made by the author in 1973. Based on these comparisons, major transformations in Herero society are reported and interpreted.

I attribute most changes in Herero social institutions and patterns of social behavior to their adoption of the practice of selling formerly sacred cattle. In turn, the adoption of cattle sale is interpreted as a result of Herero reliance on new resources, mainly of European provenience, after their wealth in herds was severely depleted by war. Thus, it is suggested that endogenous change among the Herero was precipitated by exogenous factors. The influence of exogenous stimuli to change is especially apparent in the political sphere, where contact with foreign nation-states produced significant transformations in Herero political organization.

In preparing this volume I considered my primary obligations to be a description of the Herero as I observed them in 1973—since they are so little known ethnographically—and an account of the changes Herero society has undergone over the last century. Accordingly, I applied myself to sticking closely to the ethnographic data within the body of the text and to limiting discussion of theoretical issues to the Introduction and Conclusion and to a few paragraphs and footnotes within the text. During the course of this study, however, several implications emerge that are pertinent to the study of social change in general. Among these, two stand out and, though by no means revelatory or novel, are worthy of mention. These are: 1) that changes in a group's overall organization of social relations frequently rest on adjustments in the primary economic activities of the group's members; and 2) that social change may not be explicable if analysis is restricted to the group in question without reference to its relationships to other groups with which it is in contact. Other implications are discussed in the Conclusion.

Departing somewhat from tradition, I reserve for the Introduction which follows my expressions of gratitude to all those friends and colleagues who, through their support, encouragement, criticisms, and suggestions, helped to make this study what it is—though all responsibility for its contents rests with me.

An especially well-built Herero house, with pole fence in front and small structure for storing maize (right background). At the time I left Makakun, the owners of this house were planning to have a plank roof installed.

Contents

FIGURES

TABLES

PHOTOGRAPHS AND SKETCHES

THE HERERO OF
WESTERN BOTSWANA

Aspects of Change in a Group of
Bantu-Speaking Cattle Herders

†

Introduction

BACKGROUND

This is a case study[1] of a human dilemma, often referred to as social change. It concerns the Herero, a group of Bantu-speaking cattle herders in south-central and southwestern Africa.[2]

The Herero are described in previous literature as having a system of double descent, as practicing ancestral veneration, as being nomadic or semi-nomadic, as treating their cattle as ritually important property that are at the center of all economic, social, religious, and political activity.

The first descriptions recorded deal with the Herero living in South West Africa around the middle of the nineteenth century and were written primarily by German missionaries, as were most later accounts.[3] (For example, the major work on the Herero to date is Irle's [1906]. The German works are being translated by Gordon Gibson and by others and are now being processed for inclusion in the Human Relations Area Files at Yale University.)

The Herero are said (e.g., by Vedder 1928:156) to have migrated westward from the lacustrine area of eastern and central Africa and entered South West Africa from the north. Vedder (1938:152–3) estimates that the Herero entered the area known as the Kaokoveld in northern South West Africa around 1550. After remaining in the Kaokoveld for about 200 years, they began a gradual push south into north-central and central South West Africa around 1750.[4]

1

In their diffusion through South West, the Herero came into conflict with other native occupants of the territory, most notably the Hottentots.[5] From about 1825 to 1892 a state of war existed off and on between the Herero and Hottentots, with first one group maintaining the upper hand and then the other.

By 1870 the Herero had established their supremacy over the Hottentots. In that year a treaty was signed and a relative peace existed in South West Africa during the next decade. In 1880, however, hostilities again erupted between the Herero and Hottentots.

In 1884 South West Africa became a German territory, and the German authorities used the disunity and intertribal conflicts to help them establish their authority. They favored the Herero against the Hottentots. They planned to use the Herero to subjugate the Hottentots and then to disarm the Herero.

In return for German "protection" the Herero ceded mineral rights in their land. At the same time, European farmers and tradesmen were moving into South West Africa and settling the land. By the 1890's, when the Hottentots had by and large been subjugated, the Germans had adequately established themselves in the territory. They then turned their efforts more directly toward domination of the Herero. Plans were made for native reserves. The Herero were to be disarmed. Through fines, excessive interest on debts, and so on, the Herero cattle were to pass into German possession (see Leutwein, quoted in Goldblatt 1971: 120ff.).

The culmination came in January 1904 when the Herero rose up against the Germans. At the battle of Waterberg, in August 1904, the Herero were decisively defeated. Two or three thousand managed to escape eastward into what was then Bechuanaland (now Botswana).[6] During their flight through the Kalahari Desert, they lost all their cattle. It was among the descendants of these escapees that I conducted fieldwork and it is these Herero that I mean when I refer to "the Herero."[7]

The Herero-speaking peoples actually consist of four major divisions: the Mbanderu, the Himba, the Tjimba, and the Herero proper, the last being the "true" Herero because of their wealth in cattle. There are many references in the earlier literature to the four subdivisions.[8] It would serve no useful purpose, however, to list here the various opinions regarding the origins of these groups. The truth of the matter may be lost to us, as it is lost to the Herero themselves. They have only vague and indistinct notions of the differences. It approximates the native Herero view to sum up in these terms: the Herero and Mbanderu look upon themselves as brothers of the same parents, while the Himba are thought of as very distant cousins and the Tjimba as even more remote relatives. All that can be said with any certainty is, "The Herero, a Southwestern Bantu people, have been divided into three geographically distinct tribes called Herero, Mbanderu, and Himba since before their first contact with Europeans" (Gibson 1956:111). Today Gibson recognizes that some Tjimba are Herero who have lost their cattle and that others appear to be formerly non-Bantu hunting-and-gathering peoples who have adopted the Herero language (see the foreword to this volume, as well as Vedder 1928:156 and 1938:135).

The Herero in Botswana today differ considerably from what one might expect from the descriptions in the earlier literature. The ancestors are no longer included by the people in their daily affairs; traditional religious organization is almost nonexistent; descent has decreased in importance as a referent for behavior; camps are more sedentary than they are nomadic; but most significant is the fact that the Herero now sell their formerly "sacred" cattle on a regular basis. This study is an attempt to understand how these changes came about.

INFLUENCES IN HERERO SOCIAL CHANGE

The purpose of this case study is to explicate social change among the Herero of western Botswana—simply: what changed and why.

I interpret the changes recorded in the institutions and overall social patterns of the Herero as due to changes in the resources they rely on. The resource upon which the Herero formerly relied was cattle as ritual (nonsale) property. The new resources on which the Herero rely are cattle as sale commodities and European goods. Simply stated, the change in orientation from cattle as ritually important to cattle as an exchange commodity has led to a reorganization of social relations generally.

I further hypothesize that the change in economic orientation was precipitated by the loss of cattle when the Herero fled from South West Africa to Botswana after the German-Herero war of 1904. In particular, when exogenous stimuli in the form of nonlocally available resources impinged on Herero society, the Herero use of cattle changed to exploit these resources.

After the 1904 war, the defeated Herero were deprived of the vast herds upon which their livelihood depended, and they fled to Botswana. During the thirty years in Botswana while they accumulated new wealth in herds, they made their living by hiring their labor to the Tswana, and were subject to influences not only from the Tswana but also from Europeans. Continued culture contact with Europeans[9] and Tswana during this period further eroded the already weakened traditional social institutions. The social institutions were already weakened because they were dependent on the possession of ritually important cattle, and the Herero no longer possessed cattle. Herero participation in European and Tswana-dominated interaction, which included cattle sale for the acquisition of other goods, served to undermine further the old ways. Thus, when the Herero reorganized themselves around the new herds they had slowly amassed, they began to incorporate this major new element, the sale of certain ritual cattle, which was inimical to the old system in which sale was prohibited.

In short, the organization of social relations is changing (the process is not complete) because the economic basis on which it depends has changed. In turn, the economic organization changed because stimuli to change from outside Herero society were present at a time when the Herero herds had been destroyed by war. Neither the war nor the new influences (European goods) would have been sufficient in themselves to produce a drastic reorientation in economy—that is, as long as the Herero possessed large herds. The Herero had been subjected to similar influences from Europeans in South West Africa yet had not abandoned their traditional ways.[10] Missionaries and traders alike were unsuccessful in inducing the Herero to give up their ritually important cattle. It was only after the Herero herds had already been lost through war that foreign economic practices (i.e., the regular sale of cattle for other goods) began making inroads on the Herero. The war which destroyed the old economy in combination with the subsequent contact with European economy during the period of Herero impoverishment together are interpreted as sufficient to account for the change.

The Herero, however, did not abandon their former ways suddenly. The transition from an economic orientation that viewed cattle as ritually important to one that capitalizes on their value as a market commodity was not swiftly accomplished. The changeover is only now being realized, seventy years after the Herero entry into Botswana.

Pastoralists, especially African cattle herders, are famous for their "conservatism." They strongly resist efforts of Europeans to induce them to give up their ritually important, skinny, low-milk-yield cattle. This is because cattle are more than just economic commodities to them. Their social relations, prestige, religion, and their sense of identity are tied to these cattle. Too much is invested in their cattle for the people to renounce them. And to such people, selling ritual cattle is tantamount to renouncing them. A developed taste for sugar, for sunglasses, or for European cloth is not sufficient to explain the sale of cattle, even though Europeans willingly pay for milk and beef. White preachers may teach that it is immoral to consider cattle as religious objects and to venerate ancestors (from whom the cattle are believed to be sacred trusts), but normally such arguments would have little weight. The costs are too high.

But if a people have lost their cattle, and thus the *raison d'être* for the traditional institutions and their justifications, and then, over a thirty-year period, are subjected to these foreign influences, they are more likely to become gradually dependent on sugar, to grow accustomed to the look and feel of European clothes, and to regard money as a means to acquire these things. They no longer have the old investments to give up for these luxuries; they have *already* lost them. And they are more likely to accept the white man's religion (to "join the missionaries," as my informants say) because it is seen as efficacious. That is, the Europeans teach certain things about God and good, and the Europeans are perceived as wealthy. "If we," the people might argue, "adopt European ways, including their religion, we too will be wealthy. We were wealthy once, but we lost our wealth. Perhaps this is due to the errors of our previous ways, including our belief in the ancestors." Since the people have already lost their herds, they now have little to lose. It is, in short, worth a try. The costs are negligible. And so, when they reaccumulate their herds, they redefine their relationship to them—that is, they begin to put their herds to new uses, to exchange cattle for other goods to which they have become accustomed.

I do not mean to suggest that the changeover is either as conscious or abrupt as the above might imply. It happens slowly and it happens without explicit articulation. The Herero case suggests that it is gradual indeed. It also suggests that it is psychologically painful to those who were socialized during the time when the traditional social organization was still flourishing. Although younger Herero (those born in Botswana, their present home) experience little or no conflict over their new relationship with the resource base, older Herero (those born in South West Africa, their former home) do.

This is the elders' dilemma. The old ways, the former organization of social relations which turned on cattle as ritual property, remain real to elderly Herero. It was the way they were taught. They internalized its values. But the exigencies of the new economy, the revised definition of their relationship to their cattle and the practice of selling cattle, do not require these values. Elderly Herero repeatedly expressed their sense of guilt over this. They say, "We did a bad thing," referring to the sale of formerly ritual cattle and the adoption of Christianity. This guilt leads them to deny themselves certain things. For example, though they do sell cattle that were ritually important (and, hence, were not to be sold) and the milk from these cattle, they will not drink the milk of the cattle. Younger Herero do so without compunction.

Religious ideology for the faithful tends to take on a reality of its own. This, especially in the case of a society in change (where the impartial observer may conclude that a persistent religious form is no longer appropriate to emerging organizations of labor), can be seen as psychologically, rather than sociologically, based. I mean by this that adults who have been socialized according to one ideology generally find it difficult to abandon that ideology even when the economic and other social relations in which they participate have altered and seem to require it. Abruptly abandoning an old ideology is highly traumatic because it is so intimately tied to the individual's sense of identity. To deny the ideology is, in a sense, to deny oneself. To admit the irrelevance of the old values is to admit the irrelevance of one's life.

Young people can more easily deny the old values because they have not invested years in living by them. Less intensely socialized in the old ideology and aware from an early age of the discrepancy between ideology and behavior among their elders and more firmly anchored in the new economy, they find it easier to reject previous ideologies and to embrace those which more successfully legitimate the existing social institutions.

But the pending loss of the former ideology as an integral part of a society's organization can result in severe feelings of guilt in older members because of their psychological attachment to it. Instead of abandoning the older ideology and embracing one more appropriate to the changed situation, they tend to separate religion and religious ideology from their other spheres of behavior in an attempt to retain the old values. In the Herero case, the elders were trying to keep the old values, which asserted the ritual importance of cattle, by reestablishing the former religious practices that involved cattle in their rituals. In other words, they were trying to retain a ritual treatment of cattle in one sphere at the same time they were treating cattle as sale items in another. The two did not fit. Gradually the economic importance of cattle overshadowed their religious importance. Hence, I say religious practices changed for economic reasons.

This brings me to a consideration of Gordon Gibson's reports on the Herero. Gibson conducted field research among the Herero in 1953 and in 1960–61. His reports, which all refer to the period of his first field trip, show that during that time Herero society evidenced a much greater similarity to pre-1904 Herero society than it does today. If all this change was in process, why did not Gibson find Herero society to manifest it more than it did? Why was it not until after Gibson's visits that the change became so apparent? Because, I hypothesize, the elders were still in control.

More broadly, the answer I think lies in the balance or tension created between the forces of conservatism and the impetus toward change that a slow transition permits. The change in people's orientation to their resources does not automatically and abruptly change the entire social fabric in one swift sweep. Rather, people gradually accomodate their institutionalized activities to the new economic base. Among the Herero, the source of conservatism, the influence that inhibited the abrupt abandonment of the old institutions, is to be found among the elders. They are the ones who had internalized the now inapplicable values (which legitimated the former institutions which, in turn, depended on the former economic orientation).

When sufficient cattle were accumulated by the Herero to enable them to separate (about 1934) from the Tswana for whom they worked, an attempt was made by the elders to revitalize the old institutions. Sacred fires were rekindled, the ancestors were reinstated, the former rituals were resumed. Enough older men were still alive to remember the old ways, to value them, to want them back. Now that they had their cattle back, they wanted to resume their former relationship to them. To that end, they revived the former institutions which supported that relationship. But that relationship was undergoing redefinition. They sold some cattle for foods that were not home-produced, although they tried to limit the sale of ritually important or "sacred" cattle.

This, I speculate, was the state of things when Gibson visited the Herero in 1953, when, he says (1962:617), they were beginning to sell ritually important cattle. There were still a number of old men alive who controlled the disposition of cattle and who valued the old traditions. Though they were beginning to sell ritually important cattle, they did so reluctantly. They were trying to effect a compromise between the former traditions and the sale of cattle. For them, the relationship to their resources had not been thoroughly redefined.

But it had for younger Herero who had grown up in Botswana and had been associated all their lives with the European- and Tswana-dominated situation. They had never had the former economic orientation to cattle that their elders had. For them, growing up in a condition of poverty, without cattle and divorced from the old institutions, cattle were a means for making a living. They were items that could be sold (as that is what the Tswana and Europeans did) for other things they had come to value. Cattle were, and are, to them a market commodity. Thus, the former organization of social relations that were based on the old economic foundation—especially descent and religion—is neither necessary nor useful any longer. It is no exaggeration to say that for the younger people they do not even exist.

Data supporting this interpretation constitute the body of this case study. Another piece of information I consider supportive of this view is the occurrence of a revitalization movement among the Herero during the 1960's (Gibson, Richard B. Lee, personal communication). I interpret this as a last-ditch effort to revive the old ways or to institute a new ideology which incorporated some traditional beliefs and that it failed because it emphasized values that were incompatible with the new economic orientation toward cattle.[11] By 1973 the revitalization movement had died, the old institutions were in their death throes, and the elders were nearly all dead. Control of cattle is passing into the hands of middle-aged men who ignore the former traditions.

EXPLANATORY FRAMEWORK

Since the aim of this study is to describe and to offer an explanation for the major aspects of social change among the Herero, I sought to apply a theory which best accounted for the Herero ethnographic facts as I knew them.[12]

The theoretical framework upon which my interpretation is based is one suggested by Yehudi A. Cohen. Elements of his theory from which my interpretation is derived appear in several of Cohen's publications (especially 1968 [and 1974], 1969a, and 1971), but the theory is nowhere set down in its entirety except in manuscript form and is not yet available to a general audience. It is therefore beneficial to provide a summary overview of those aspects of the theory that are relevant here.

The premises upon which Cohen's theory builds are that the social organization of an adaptive unit is dependent on its "boundary cultural relations"[13] and "that changes in human culture and social organization are exogenous, that is, such transformations have their principal sources outside a society's boundaries" (ms., ch. 4).

. . . Every adaptive unit [read, in the present instance, Herero society] is, in its entirety, a unique organization of productive labor activities . . .

. . . Each of an adaptive unit's institutions is a link in its organization of productive labor; every institution, in other words, is itself an organization of labor within the society's overall mobilization.

Corollary: An organization of labor changes whenever there is an alteration in the sources of harnessed energy and in the technology employed so that effective use may be made of them [ms., ch.2].

What are generally referred to as persistence and change are continuations and transformations in an adaptive unit's institutional building blocks regarded as organizations of labor.

Corollary: We may say that social change has taken place or is occurring when there are alterations in the criteria of recruitment to an organization of labor, when there is a change in the categories of personnel who have control over the resources on which the adaptive unit relies, when there are reorganizations of personnel in the institutional links themselves, and when the distribution of authority in task units is reallocated. The four criteria of social change that I offer are not exclusive; instead, they are interdependent and overlap with each other [ms., ch. 3].

Let us turn now to a closer look at the theory and apply it to the Herero. I will start in the middle, with Cohen's four criteria of social change (ms., ch. 3). In considering these, I will touch on all other relevant points.

Social change has been completed in a society or institutional building block only when all criteria have been met. Social change does not refer to any one phenomenon or event; it is, instead, a complex process that is composed of many elements. Moreover, social change is a gradual process in which one criterion is met here and now and another then and there . . . Thus, social change has only *begun* to occur when less than all four criteria have been met throughout the society—or in a sector of it in a complex one like a nation-state—and it may only be said that there *has* been a transformation in an institutional link after all four criteria have been met . . .

First, we may say that social change has begun when there has been an alteration in the criteria of recruitment to the adaptive unit's organization of labor . . . But the criterion of recruitment does not refer only to roles within the organization of extractive labor; it pertains also to criteria of recruitment to other institutional building blocks, such as marriage and religion. For instance, a change in rules that allows marrying persons to contract their own marriages in place of arranged unions or one that allows members of different racial or ethnic groups to marry in place of one that confined people to racial or ethnic endogamy also signifies that social change has begun. Likewise with the organization of religious behavior. A rule that permits clerics to marry in place of a requirement of celibacy or an alteration in ritual or ceremonial roles of priests and laity denotes the onset of social change in the religious sphere. Each of these changes is a transformation in the criteria of recruitment to an organization of marital or religious labor.

The Herero of western Botswana fit this conceptualization of change in a number of ways. Religion, which has changed drastically, will serve as an example. Recruitment to formal positions of religious leadership was based on seniority in a descent-ordered unit (a lineage or sib) and inheritance of the symbols of such leadership (such as the "sacred hearth") from one's predecessor. Today this traditional form of leadership has all but disappeared, as have its symbols. There is no longer recruitment to the position. In addition, where the position still exists, it is entirely separate from political leadership. This is notable because under the old system the roles of religious and political leader were vested in one person.

Moreover, the various rituals an ordinary Herero underwent during critical periods in the life cycle have also disappeared. These ceremonies were formerly conducted at the sacred hearth in the context of religion. They emphasized an individual's "connection with his ancestors" and his obedience to them. Today the "connection" has been broken, and the rituals have gone.

Social change has begun when there is a significant alteration in the categories of personnel who have control over resources on which the adaptive unit relies in its adaptive strategy. . . .

illustrates another point of Cohen's, that "those who speak in the name of the state represent a source of energy in the habitat of local groups").

In summary, the Herero sought to use the resources of their inside or local habitat as a means of tapping resources in the habitat of the outside or boundary culture.

Cohen postulates two types of habitats (ms., ch. 6):

> The first is an adaptive unit's own territory; it may be referred to as the local or inside milieu which provides resources that are locally available. An inside habitat is not only defined in terms of space, resources, or topographic ranges and natural divisions, though these are important. An inside habitat is also conceptualized socially . . . This is the physical area in which allegiances are given, in which life moves. This is the territory beyond which people rarely go . . . The second type of habitat is made up of the milieus of other groups with whom an adaptive unit is in contact and which provide resources, goods, and skills that are not locally available for those outside its bounds. This is the habitat of boundary culture.
>
> *Corollary:* Every significant expansion or contraction in a society's boundary cultural relations alters the sources of energy on which inside occupational roles depend.

Seen in this light the sale of cattle is a means of obtaining commodities that are not locally available at the same time that cattle are the primary resource of the inside or local culture. Cattle sale, then, becomes a means or a kind of technique aimed at tapping new resources. And, as Cohen states (ms., ch. 2), "every technology as well as every resource requires an appropriate organization of task groups" and that change results "when a unit's members find, though not necessarily aforethought, that the ways in which they do their work in some spheres of activity and the associations formed to achieve their ends are incompatible with other organizational modes with altered habitational conditions, with new means of production, or with newly introduced resources."

In this study I am concerned with describing changes in Herero social institutions and interpreting them as due to the adoption of exogenously stimulated cattle sale. The exogenous influences that stimulated cattle sale in the first place will be a secondary concern.

But another aspect of exogenously produced change among the Herero, which began before the practice of selling cattle was initiated, concerns political organization. Therefore, in regard to Herero political change, exogenous influences will be primary considerations. Unlike other aspects of institutional change among the Herero, which are due to exogenous influences filtered through the medium of cattle sale, political change resulted directly from exogenous factors. It is, in other words, of the same order as cattle sale (both having resulted from outside stimuli) and not dependent on cattle sale (as, for instance, changes in religious practices are).

Three time periods can be identified in analyzing changes in Herero political authority. The first concerns the development of local leaders who had arisen because of their control over valued resources. Since they were first to settle near permanent water sources, they exerted limited control over access to the resource. Other Herero who wished to settle in the same area in order to utilize the resource became, therefore, dependent on these first arrivals and submitted to their authority in return for access to the resource.

But if a leader became overbearing and his followers felt ill treated, they could simply pack up and move off. The leader had no means to compel others to loyalty. They could relocate near a resource elsewhere without interference. But when Europeans began settling in Hereroland in South West Africa and occupying formerly open areas, they thus limited land available to the Herero. Consequently, the authority of a leader was strengthened because his followers' freedom of movement had been curtailed. This led to the development of what I call incipient chiefdoms.

The next two phases in Herero political change resulted directly from Herero contact with a state society. Another element of Cohen's theory comes to the fore here. He says (ms., ch. 8):

> . . . The state is the most important group in a nation-state; all other groups in the society must adapt to it . . .
> *Corollary:* Those who speak in the name of the state represent a source of energy in the habitat of local groups.

The development toward a paramount chieftaincy in South West Africa and the changes in political authority among the Herero in

Botswana can only be understood in these terms, that is, that the changes were the result of exogenous influences or stimuli produced by contact with a state.

The development of increased political authority among the Herero in South West Africa was due to the influence of the Germans and other Europeans when they were establishing themselves in Herero territory. Several attempts were made by Europeans to install a paramount chief among the Herero in order that they (the Europeans) might have a single native spokesman to deal with. The Germans, during the period of their occupation of the country, made the greatest efforts in this direction. By the beginning of the twentieth century, an incipient paramountcy was emerging. But it came crashing down with the defeat of the Herero in the 1904 war.

In Botswana the changes that local authority underwent are explicable only in terms of the fact that the Herero emigrated to a country that was already under the control of a state bureaucratic apparatus. They were subject to the authority of the Tswana chiefs who, in turn, were subject to the British. The position of leader among the Herero was transformed into one of local level representative of the state.

PRESENTATION OF DATA

To document social change among the Herero, it is necessary to attempt to reconstruct the traditional organization of social relations founded on the ritual importance of cattle and to ascertain what factors impinged on this system and how their influences contributed to Herero society as it appeared in 1973.

A good way to get into a discussion of Herero society as an integrated organization of social relations is to begin with a consideration of residential units and community composition. This is discussed in chapter 1. Since in former times these were phrased in terms of descent, a discussion of Herero lineages and sibs is also introduced in chapter 1. In chapter 2, economics—making a living being the empirical basis for people living together—is examined. The final chapter moves on to political organization: the maintenance of order and control among people living together. This requires an examination of leadership and authority, which, in turn, requires the introduction of considerable historical material. The former religious aspects of political organization provide a contrast with the current bifurcation of these spheres, and suggestions are offered regarding the reasons for this.

Each chapter is primarily descriptive in that the concern is to demonstrate the occurrence of change, though the interpretation emerges in the course of description. A brief summary section of each chapter outlines how the material in that chapter relates to the interpretation. A general summary then draws the present work to a close.

Finally, the approach to the data here is decidedly "etic." Nevertheless, some of my phraseology has an "emic" cast. This is for simplicity. For example, I speak throughout of the Herero "connection with the ancestors." This is to be read as "the connection (or relationship) the Herero conceive to exist between themselves as living members of the society and their deceased forebears." I use the abbreviated phrase as a convenient shorthand, for to repeat the longer one throughout the presentation is awkward and unnecessarily cumbersome.

FIELDWORK: GENESIS AND EXECUTION

The choice to conduct research among the Herero was a result of several factors, most important of which was a general interest in pastoral nomads. That I chose the Herero in preference to any other pastoral group was due in part to accident. At the time I was formulating my research project, I was associated with Richard B. Lee at Rutgers University. Since Lee had conducted research among the !Kung Bushmen in Botswana, Yehudi A. Cohen, a close friend who has had a powerful influence on me both personally and professionally, suggested I consult with him about the feasibility of doing research among the Botswana Herero because of Bushmen-Herero relationships frequently mentioned by Lee in conversation. Lee was enthusiastic and encouraged me to explore the subject further.

After reading Gibson's three published papers on the Herero, I became intrigued with the possibilities of fieldwork among these people. The Herero of Botswana are unusual in that they are in contact not only with hunter-gatherers but also with cultivators and representatives of a nation-state. They have a system of double descent while most, if not all, other pastoralists are described as having single unilineal descent. The Herero have a long history of conflict—conflict with other tribal groups as well as with Europeans. These and other factors that are less easily articulated made me determined to work among the Herero.

Originally, my research plans called for a period of two years in the field, but circumstances compelled me to shorten it to roughly one-fifth that time. In June 1973, my wife, my five-month-old daughter, and I flew to Maun, Botswana. Immediately it was apparent that I had been seriously misinformed about facilities in Maun. There were no accommodations available for my family. Clearly I could not wander about the Kalahari Desert with an infant.

In addition, there was no possibility of renting or purchasing a motor vehicle in Maun. I therefore determined to travel to Francistown or Gaborone to try to find some form of reliable transportation. The research would have been totally impossible without it. I decided, however, to remain in Maun for a short time in order to make contact with the Herero, explain my purposes to them, and make some beginning of the research.

It was not long, though, before my daughter became seriously ill. The medical attention she received in Maun was deplorable. Finally, after several days tending her day and night, we realized (though the doctor did not) that she was dying. Naturally enough, I was more concerned about my daughter's well-being than I was about the research. I rushed her to Johannesburg and there found adequate medical care. The doctor there told us that one more day would have been too late.

As soon as she was well enough to travel, my wife and I took her back to the United States to her own doctor. She quickly recovered under his care.

Once she had regained her health, it seemed only practical that I return to Africa—this time without my family—and complete my

The main street of Maun, capital city of Ngamiland District. On the left are Tswana huts. The white building in the background is the post office.

research. I had already made something of a beginning; additionally, all my camping equipment and research material were still in Africa.

This time, however, I made arrangements to rent a Land Rover before entering Botswana. Through Irven DeVore of Harvard University I contacted Dr. Trefor Jenkins of the South African Institute of Medical Research in Johannesburg. He had been of help to DeVore in the past and offered to assist me in obtaining a motor vehicle. Since no arrangements could be made in Johannesburg, he referred me to Miss Cynthia MacIntyre in Windhoek, South West Africa. I flew to Windhoek and, through Miss MacIntyre's indefatigable efforts, was finally able to rent a Land Rover from her personal friend Georg Heye (for the commercial leasing companies will no longer allow their vehicles to be hired for the hazardous journey from Windhoek to Maun). Without Miss MacIntyre's help my research could never have been conducted.

Moreover, fieldwork in Botswana would have been much more

arduous than it was without the companionship and assistance of Robert G. Bone. Because of the unpleasant experience during my first trip to Botswana, I had determined not to return alone.

I had sought a companion but found in Bone a sensitive field-worker. He had, so to speak, come along for the ride but ended up occasionally driving. Not the least of his contributions was map drawing. All the homestead diagrams and the map of Makakun found in this study are primarily his work. While he trudged about under the hot sun, meticulously recording the placement of huts and corrals, I sat in the shade conducting interviews. For the time he saved me and for the privilege of working with him in general, I will always be grateful.

I also owe thanks to Harold de Kock, a former hunter and safari guide who is now a construction contractor. This business requires him to travel throughout Botswana. Whenever I was in trouble, no matter where I happened to be in the country, he would suddenly appear to lend a helping hand. I do not know why he chose to adopt me, but I am grateful that he did.

The author with a three-year-old Herero girl named Tjavanga.

It was through him that I made my first fruitful contact with the Herero. Unlike many other whites in Botswana, his respect for the Herero and their ways was evident, and the Herero recognized this and reciprocated. In Maun, he introduced me to Joas Konobiwa, with whom he had served in Europe during World War II. Konobiwa, in turn, introduced me to other Herero. I resided at his homestead while working in Makakun.

I chose Makakun as my main research site because it was the earliest and largest settlement of Herero in Ngamiland District. I chose Ngamiland because both Gibson and Lee had worked there, so it was the area about which I had most prefieldwork information.

I first set up camp, however, near Dauga because it is a small settlement east of Maun, and Joas Konobiwa suggested that it would be best for me to start my work close to Maun before settling in a remote community such as Makakun.

He sent for his nineteen-year-old son Uakondja Joas, who was attending school at Mahalapye, to come to Maun and serve as my interpreter. Uakondja spoke English well and his quick intelligence and ready grasp of anthropological concepts made him an invaluable asset to my research.

After about ten days near Dauga, Bone, Uakondja Joas, and I returned to Maun for supplies and then pushed on to Makakun. For nearly three months I resided at Joas Konobiwa's homestead while gathering data throughout Makakun.

A standard operating procedure soon developed. I had designed a rather lengthy questionnaire with which I began each interview. Though this provided some structure and formality for the first hour or two with an informant, it was of limited research value and served primarily as an icebreaker. While I concentrated on filling in the questionnaire, Bone mapped the homestead. About the time the questionnaire was completed, Bone would be finishing his task and would join me and the informant.

Uakondja Joas would have already explained to the informant that I had come to learn about the history and customs of the Herero. After completing the questionnaire I asked the informant to tell me whatever he could remember of Herero history. While the informant spoke and Uakondja Joas translated, Bone and I would separately take notes. As the informant related the history as he re-membered it or as it was told to him,[14] he would touch on various aspects of social organization, and I would interrupt him and ask him to elaborate on a specific subject—for example, marriage, re-ligion, or cattle management. Only in this way was I able to obtain information on social organization.[15] On those few occasions when I began by asking for information about a specific topic, the interview session was not as productive as I would have liked.

By midafternoon the informant would be too tired to go on, and he would either call a halt to the session (which would then be con-tinued the next day) or switch roles with me and begin questioning me about life in the United States. Perhaps my most gratifying moment during fieldwork came when one old gentleman, after several such sessions, declared that thenceforward he would call me *omuatje* ("child") and that I could call him "father."

At the end of a day, after returning to camp and cooking a meal, Bone, Uakondja Joas, and I would discuss the information learned that day. Bone and I then compared notes, and I typed up a com-plete version of the day's interview based on both sets of notes. In the evening Uakondja Joas gave us language lessons or we joined the people of the homestead to talk casually. I played recorded music for them and taped their singing.

Fieldwork was also conducted in Makunda in Ghanzi District. On the drive from Windhoek to Maun to retrieve the equipment I had left there during my first trip, I met a gentleman from the Kgalagadi tribe named Mothoosele Modisapitse in Ghanzi who in-troduced me to some Herero. These Herero were from Makunda but were in Ghanzi to visit the doctor. I spent two days in their com-pany, and they invited me to come to Makunda and work there. So after I left Makakun I drove to Makunda.

On the way, Bone and I stopped again at Ghanzi (Uakondja Joas had by this time returned to school in Mahalapye) and stayed a few days at the hotel there. We went over our notes many times, looking for gaps in the data and formulating some specific questions. By the time we got to Makunda, therefore, we knew precisely the kinds of information we needed to complete our notes.

In Makunda we received permission from Richard Kambura, the local headman, to set up camp near his homestead. Kambura spoke

English very well and quickly understood the nature of my investigations. In fact, he understood so well that two days after our arrival in Makunda, he came to my tent one morning and said, somewhat mysteriously, "Come with me."

The ethnographer at a meeting of homestead heads in Makunda. Richard Kambura, the community headman, is recording information in the ethnographer's notebook. (See Introduction and footnote 16 for explanation.)

We drove a couple of miles to a neighboring homestead where a small crowd was gathered. Kambura explained that he had sent a message to all the older homestead heads in the area to convene there and wait for us. When we arrived he informed the old men who were there that we were Americans interested in the Herero and that we had some questions to ask. I offered them some tobacco, and they passed it around while I asked questions and Kambura translated.[16] By the end of the day, I had answers to most of the questions on my list. Kambura's initiative had saved me about two weeks of traveling from homestead to homestead to consult with each of the men individually.

Bone and I remained a few more days in Makunda, unhurriedly ordering our field notes, before driving back to Windhoek in South West Africa. Most of this time was spent in the company of Richard Kambura, and I am grateful for his hospitality and assistance.

I owe debts of gratitude to so many others it is impossible to mention them all. There is no way I can adequately express my gratitude and affection for Yehudi A. Cohen. Without his guidance, friendship, and encouragement I might now be making rope-sole shoes. To others—notably Robin Fox, Gordon D. Gibson, Vera Green, and Lionel Tiger—I am grateful for suggestions regarding the presentation of my data. I also acknowledge Warren Shapiro, who—though unconnected to the present project—has been an important influence on my anthropological perspective.

In addition, I want to recognize here the cooperation of the government of the Republic of Botswana. The freedom with which I was allowed to pursue my investigations is deeply appreciated.

Lastly, there are the Herero themselves. It is with sincere gratitude and heartfelt affection that I acknowledge the assistance of the Herero people in making this work not only possible but highly enjoyable as well. My indebtedness to them is immeasurable. They welcomed me warmly into their communities and their homes. They gave generously and unstintingly of their time and energy, demonstrating infinite patience through long, tiring hours of interviews, and good-naturedly enduring the awkwardness and improprieties of one new to their ways. I thank them all for everything they have done for me and for making my stay among them one of the most pleasant and memorable experiences of my life.

NOTE OF THANKS TO THE HERERO

Embo ndi ra raisiua, otja purapuira, ko muhoko uo tji herero. Nandarire mo usupi ue mbo ndi, otja mo marorero aehe, uo ku ungura oukohoke ko ngaro no tjivara tji ko uherero, ka pena muano uarue uo kuhungira otjinjo no tjinjo pendje nembo. Na peri nao mba ungura o uini me jandja o hange mou rizemburuka uo kutjanga embo ndi ndi mba utira oua herero mo me ndjitoorero uao ua naua. Tjinga pari no uhatoi ku ku heri kuami uriri nauina kuene kutja ongaro indjo nguru jari a maijanda. Mo mariangero uandje mokati kenu, muatjaterererue tjinene mo mapurira uandje muene. I ja mutjiua kutja ovakuru tjiva za no kuta uina omiana omikuru mavijanda. Mua jandja e muma rokutja tjipeha karere embo ro mbutiro jo u herero, ovanatje vo vanatje venu ka maa ve ku kara no ndjiviro jo mbutiro jo u herero. Nambano me jandjere embo ndi ko ruuano ruandje no ndjevirero jo ndunge jo tji herero otjikuru, nandarire o miano no tuzo ka tji mavi jenene.

Pamue no ndangi jo ko mutjima me itavere oua tjiri uo mbatero jo va herero mo tji ungura tji pamue no ndjato mutjo. Ondero jandje muene ka maa ijanda. Mue ndji ja kurire naua mo ku kara kuenu no mo zonganda zenu. Mua jandja oire o hara no ndjito no masa uenu o ku raisa o ua tjiri no ku hinotjiruejo no mapurira o mare no u ua uo ku toora, omundu omupe mo miano vienu. Mue ri jandjererere o ku zira no ku kondja o ku ndji zuuisa naua tjiri tjiri.

Me tja ndangi kuene amuhe ku ngamua a tjihe tji mue ndji ungurira no ngaro jandje mburukiro tjo ku kara kuandje. Nu mezeri kutja matu uana tjimanga rukuao.

NOTES

[1]Research for this study was conducted from May to October 1973 and was sponsored by the National Institute of Mental Health and the Wenner-Gren Foundation for Anthropological Research.

[2]Field research was undertaken among the Herero of western Botswana, primarily in the northwestern district of Ngamiland (in the Herero communities of Makakun, west of Lake Ngami, and Dauga, just east of Maun, the district capital), but also to a limited degree in Ghanzi District farther south (in the Herero community of Makunda, near the border of South West Africa). (See Appendix A for maps.)

A greater number of Herero are found in South West Africa (also known by the United Nations designation Namibia), where their way of life has been severely altered under the political system of that country. Other

Herero-speakers live in southern Angola, but we have no descriptions of them in English. Gordon D. Gibson, who previously did fieldwork among the Botswana Herero, conducted research among the Herero-speaking Himba in Angola in 1973 which overlapped with mine in Botswana. Gibson has also recently completed translating Estermann's (1956–60) ethnography of Herero-speakers in Angola, which until now was available only in the Portugese original.

[3]The Herero are often referred to in the literature as Dama or Damara, from the Hottentot name for them, and the area they occupied in north-central South West Africa is called Hereroland or Damaraland. The appellation Damara for the Herero must not be confused with that of Berg-Damara, the name applied in the early German literature to the Bergdama. According to von Francois (1896:101): "The Hottentots called the immigrant Herero Gamaba-Daman, Cattle-Damara, in contrast to the Berg-Damara, who are designated Khaub-Daman, Dirt-Damara (expressed mildly)." Vedder says (1928:157) that the Hottentots called the Herero 'Gomacha-Dama,' that is, 'Damaras rich in cattle' in contradistinction to the Bergdamaras."

[4]For further information on the origins and migrations of the Herero, see, for example, Dannert (1906:3): Hahn (1869:229–31); and Vedder (1929:156, 1938:134ff.).

[5]The main accounts concerning the diffusion of the Herero throughout South West Africa are Brincker (1899:131–2); Hahn (1869:227–31); Vedder (1928:157, 166; 1938:135–56); and von Francois (1896:100–1).

[6]Bechuanaland was a British protectorate until its independence in September 1966, when it became the Republic of Botswana. Throughout I speak of Botswana, regardless of whether I mean pre- or post-1966.

Setswana is a Bantu language of the dominant group residing today in the Republic of Botswana. Setswana-speaking peoples are known collectively as Batswana. The Tawana (or Batawana) are the numerically predominant subgroup of the Batswana living in Ngamiland in northwestern Botswana. The Tawana are the particular Batswana people with whom the Herero historically have had most contact. For simplicity, I refer to "the Tswana" when I mean any of the Setswana speakers.

[7]Strictly speaking, *Ovaherero* is the correct term for the Herero, for *ova-* is the prefix designating "people." (Thus, for instance, *Ovambo* is the same

as Ambo people.) *Omuherero* is one Herero person. For simplicity I use the term *Herero* throughout to refer to a population of people and to a single member of that population. *Otjiherero* is the language of the Herero people.

[8]See, for example, Brincker (1899:131–2); Hahn (1869:485); Vedder (1928:155–6, 1938:135); and von Francois (1896:101).

[9]Herero contact with Europeans in Botswana was not extensive until around 1930. But European influence, especially concerning economic transactions, began for the Herero in South West Africa and continued in Botswana, where the Herero were further exposed to European luxuries. The reason that exposure to European goods seems to have had little effect on the Herero in South West but was influential for them in Botswana is taken up shortly.

[10]This is clear from the literature and from a number of my informants' statements; see especially the text on p. 162 in chapter 3.

[11]That is, revitalization movements may be seen in part as attempts to put the cart before the horse. Such movements try to retain or reinstate a former ideology in an effort to abandon existing social conditions and to return to the old ways. That these movements are usually unsuccessful offers support for the view that ideologies are dependent on organizations of social relations and not vice versa.

In the Herero case, according to Gibson (personal communication), "prophets" had arisen who tried to combine Christianity with aspects of traditional Herero religious organization. It may be inappropriate to call such an attempt toward syncretism in religion a revitalization movement. It might just as appropriately be seen as a transitional movement that eases the passing of traditional ways. Richard Lee, however, who was in Botswana in the mid and late 1960's characterizes it as a pan-Herero revitalization movement with back-to-South-West-Africa overtones (personal communication).

[12]Since in part my interpretation attributes causal priority within a society to the economic sphere, it may be said to be in the tradition of such approaches as those of Nimkoff and Middleton (1960), Oliver (1962), Steward (1955), Leslie White (1949, 1959), and others. But I refer in detail only to Cohen's theory because my own analysis of the data led me to an interpretation of Herero social change that was more compatible with

Cohen's theoretical framework than with any others with which I am familiar. I therefore decided to use Cohen's theory to introduce my interpretation. It must be emphasized, however, that my purpose is not to illustrate the theory with the Herero case but to explicate the Herero case in terms of the theory. This is in accord with my intention to restrict the scope of this study to Herero social change, for this work is a specific ethnographic study and not a comparative one. Implications for the study of social change in general, though mentioned at the end of this work, are not emphasized. I have therefore chosen not to present a critical review of possible alternative interpretations of social change.

[13]The concept of boundary culture was first used by Murphy (1964). He suggests that societies cannot be understood as isolated units: "Ethnographically, it is manifest that nearly all human societies have relationships of some kind with another society, and usually with more than one" (p. 847). He introduces the term boundary culture to refer to the area of interrelationship between societies in contact: "We may loosely describe societies in contact by drawing two partially overlapping circles, the common area representing the sphere in which roles and groupings interrelate" (p. 850). It is to this that Cohen refers when he speaks of boundary cultural relations.

[14]Informants were always precise about what they had only "heard about" and what they themselves witnessed.

[15]It was by the consistency of responses to my inquiries that I judged the accuracy of the information I collected.

[16]At one point Kambura, tired of translating my questions from English to Otjiherero and translating the responses from Otjiherero to English and then having to spell words for me, simply took my pen and notebook and recorded the information himself.

1

Locality and Social Structure

THE HOMESTEAD[1]

The primary residential unit among the Herero is the "homestead" (*onganda*, pl. *ozonganda*). This consists of a number of huts or houses, called *ozondjuo* (s. *ondjuo*), arranged in roughly circular form or, what is more likely nowadays, in an arc, around the livestock enclosures or corrals.

The number of corrals varies, depending on the numbers and types of livestock kept. But generally there are three cattle corrals: the primary corral where cattle are habitually kept; a milking corral adjacent to the primary corral where cows are taken (separation from the calves facilitates milking); and a spare milking corral. The Herero explain that the spare milking corral is used only when the ground in the other milking corral has been trampled into mud during the rainy season. Since it is difficult for the women to carry out their milking tasks under such conditions, the milch cows are moved to the spare milking corral where the wet ground has not been walked over continually.

One or two additional corrals are usually found in a homestead. If the number of sheep and goats is exceptionally large, two enclosures will be erected, one for adults and one for the young. Normally, however, there is only one corral, in which are kept all the small stock.[2] (In the latter case, the animals invariably arrange themselves in a

29

standard manner when shut in for the night. The females and young huddle in the center of the corral, while the males encircle them and face outwards.)

The corrals are constructed by arranging branches of thorn bush in a circle. Within the homestead the corrals are placed in a roughly north-to-south line. Thus, if all five corrals are present, they are arranged in the following manner, beginning at the extreme north and running south: the spare milk corral, the primary or general corral, and the milk corral forming one cluster, then the sheep and goat corral and the lamb and kid corral forming a small cluster.

There is no standard size for any of the corrals since this depends on the number of animals a corral must accomodate. A range of 30 feet to 140 feet (with a mean of about 80 feet) was calculated for eight general cattle corrals that were measured at their widest points (since the corrals are more elliptical than circular).

Typical goat corral (left foreground) and cattle corral (right background). Corrals are more or less circular and are constructed of thorn bush. (See Chapter 1 and Appendix B for information on layout of Herero homesteads.)

Just to the east of the main cattle corrals (the primary or general corral and the main milking corral) were found in former times an ash heap or "sacred hearth" (*okuruo,* pl. *omaruo*) and an upturned bush symbolizing the revered *omumborumbonga* tree.[3] Today there is only one extant *okuruo* in all of Makakun, the oldest Herero settlement in Botswana. The *okuruo,* once the locus of all important activities and the quintessential symbol of Herero society, is all but gone.

To the east of the *okuruo* was the hut of the senior or "great wife" of the homestead head. This head is called *omuini,* which means "owner."[4] Earlier reports (e.g., Gibson 1952:130; Vedder 1928:192) state that the *omuini* has no hut of his own but rotates among his wives (for the Herero are polygynous), ideally staying an equal length of time with each. Though women are the primary builders (but men do help in construction), my informants claim adamantly that a man holds equal and joint ownership in all huts built by his wives.

Gustav Kandjii's *okuruo* ("sacred hearth"), the last in Makakun. In former times, a fire burned continuously before the upturned *omuvapu* bush, and all important rituals were conducted at the *okuruo.* (See Chapters 1 and 3.)

It is likely that both versions are correct and that this is simply another aspect of change among the Herero, for it is consonant with the increased emphasis on agnation and the decreasing importance of matrilineality. It will be seen later that the *ovondjuo* (the people of the hut) comprise the smallest uterine unit in Herero society (Herero descent terminology also allows it legitimately to be called the smallest segment in the lineage system), and decreasing attention to matrilineality thus permits a greater assertion of patrilineal or agnatic authority in this sphere.

Formerly huts were made of branches and skins and were partially portable.[5] The walls and floors were smeared with cow dung. A small opening was left in the wall and covered by skins. Entrance and egress were effected by crawling on hands and knees through the opening. A depression was made in the center of the hut floor for a fire, and a small hole was left in the roof through which smoke escaped. Cowhides were spread on the floor of the hut for sleeping. These hides, or sheep-or goatskins, were also used as blankets. The hut contained clay and wooden cooking and eating utensils and storage vessels. The only furnishings were small wood and thong chairs that the Herero made.

Huts today are still circular but are permanent. The walls and floors are made of clay hardened by the sun. Many have glass windows (the glass having been obtained from derelict motor vehicles that dot the stark Kalahari landscape like the fossil remains of prehistoric beasts). There is a full-sized door, made of wood and sometimes covered with scrap metal. The roof is usually thatched, but more and more Herero today are hiring laborers (mainly Tswana) to construct plank roofs for them. No longer do hides and skins cover the floor for sleeping. Instead one finds a metal-framed, Western bed, mattress, pillows, and blankets acquired through traders. No fires are made inside the hut. Furnishings and utensils are more often commercial than homemade. For instance, though the little wood and thong chairs of traditional Herero manufacture are still found, most chairs are commercially produced and acquired at town stores. Only a few Herero today are adept at making the old style chairs.

The ideal *onganda* or homestead is comprised of a series of huts extending in northwesterly and southwesterly arcs from the senior

Examples of Herero houses *(ozondjuo)*. Within each "yard" there is a sun-dried mud enclosure where cooking is done over an open fire. (See Chapter 1.)

wife's hut and extending around the central portion where the corrals and fire are located. In such an arrangement, the northern arc consists of the huts of other wives and concubines of the *omuini,* the southern arc consists of the huts of his married male agnates and unmarried boys, and the extreme western section consists of remoter relatives and servants. Though not one existing Herero homestead conforms to this design, it is generally the configuration described in the earlier literature and confirmed as ideal by my informants.

The senior wife's hut was always located on the eastern side, with the opening of the hut facing westward, that is, toward the center of the *onganda.* All other huts also open toward the center. Some earlier sources (e.g., Vedder 1928:168) say that the senior wife's hut was larger than the others. Today all dwellings are approximately the same size.

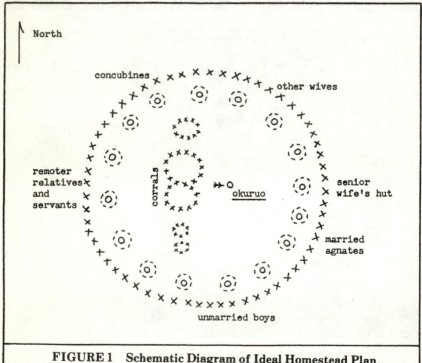

FIGURE 1   Schematic Diagram of Ideal Homestead Plan.

In earlier years the entire homestead was surrounded by thorn bush (though no homestead today is—reflecting the absence of raiding and thus no need for defensive structures), just as the individual household clusters within it were enclosed by pole fences (fenced "yards" are still occasionally found today).

Figure 1 depicts this ideal plan.

This is the general plan, in idealized form, for the physical layout of Herero homesteads. We can now discuss who is supposed to be living in them, after which we can examine who is actually living in them. By examining a homestead plan of twenty years ago supplied by Gibson and several present-day homesteads and comparing them with earlier descriptions, we will be able to see the changes in homestead configuration over time.

In the idealized version, the main residential units of the *onganda* are the matricentric household groups (or clusters, or yards since they are usually each surrounded by a pole fence) which consists of a woman's hut, in which she resides with her young children, and other huts alongside hers for cooking, for guests, and for older unmarried sons. The woman's hut is called *ondjuo,* and the same term is applied to the larger household cluster. (The term *ovondjuo,* "those of the house," is applied to the residents collectively.) The *ondjuo* is named after the mother.

Each of the homestead owner's wives with her offspring occupies a separate *ondjuo* within the homestead. "In the case of sororal polygyny the secondary wife may build her hut close to that of her elder sister, and the sisters and their children then form one household" (Gibson 1956:113).

Other household clusters are also found within the homestead. There are those of the wives of the *omuini's* younger brothers and those of the wives of his married sons. "The *onganda* is thus an economic and social unit formed around a patrilineal extended family practicing virilocal residence" (Gibson 1956:112).

Also attached to a homestead may be found remoter relatives (i.e., those claiming a matrilineal or affinal relationship to the owner and who, for various reasons, find it to their advantage to reside in his homestead), poor and elderly agnatic or uterine relatives, and even unrelated poor Herero (who herd for the *omuini* in return for milk).

In addition to the actual homestead itself, there may also exist extensions of it called *ozohambo* ("cattle posts," s. *ohambo*). These are manned by close agnatic relatives, brothers or sons of the *omuini*. They are little more than cattle corrals with a makeshift shelter for the herdsmen. They serve to distribute cattle over wide areas, thus exploiting large tracts of pasturage.

How does this ideal-typical homestead plan compare to actual homesteads? The homestead described by Gibson, which he found in Ngamiland in the early 1950's, conforms generally to this plan. Figure 2 is based on Gibson's diagram (1956:114).

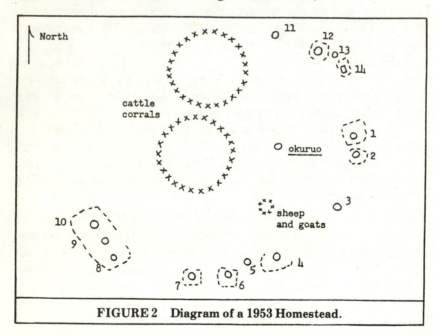

FIGURE 2   Diagram of a 1953 Homestead.

Table 1 indicates that hut 1 is that of the *omuini's* senior wife; hut 2 is that of the *omuini's* deceased older brother's wife. The senior wife (of the former *omuini* and now of the present *omuini*) occupies the easternmost hut, as dictated by the ideal plan. Huts 3 and 4 are those of close agnates' families. This, too, conforms to the plan. Huts 5 through 10 are those of "remoter relatives" related to the owner or one of his agnates either through a uterine or affinal relationship. (The fact that these huts are not located to the west of the corrals is probably due to the absence of a greater number of agnates to fill out the southern arc.) Huts 11 through 14 are those of junior wives and their descendants. They are located in the northern arc as prescribed.

TABLE 1   Key to Diagram of 1953 Homestead

Number	Identification
1	Hut of senior wife;
2	Hut of widowed daughter of owner's deceased elder brother;
3	Hut of owner's classificatory son (married, no children);
4	Hut of owner's eldest son and chief heir, the son's wife and children;
5	Huts "occupied by widows related to the owner of the village through his father's matri-clan but also related matrilineally to his chief wife and to his sons by marriage";
6	
7	
8	Huts of matrilineal relatives of owner: an elderly male, a classificatory sister's son to owner, and this man's sister's daughter and granddaughters, who are widowed, divorced, or unmarried;
9	
10	
11	Hut of owner's most recent wife and her granddaughter by an earlier marriage;
12	
13	Huts of descendants of owner's junior wife.
14	

The *okuruo* is situated in the proper location, as are the cattle corrals. The sheep and goat corral is perhaps too far east to conform exactly to the ideal. But, nevertheless, this homestead conforms generally to the plan earlier reported (see, e.g., Luttig 1933:33 and Vedder 1928:181). Since Gibson (1956:113) calls this "a fairly typical homestead," we may conclude that it reflects the general pattern of Herero homesteads in Ngamiland for the early 1950's. As such, it does not indicate a great deal of change from the older, "traditional" layout. The homesteads that I observed in 1973, however, indicate a great deal of change.

Eight homesteads in Makakun were scrupulously mapped. A detailed consideration of some of these will be helpful. Five homestead diagrams are shown in Figures 3 to 7 and explanations are provided in Tables 2 to 6. Diagrams for the remaining three homesteads not discussed here appear in Appendix B.

Homestead A (Fig. 3, Table 2)

This is an uncommonly small *onganda,* especially when one considers that the *omuini* is one of the wealthiest Herero in Ngamiland. Part of the explanation, however, lies in the fact that this individual is highly acculturated in the sense that he functions exceedingly well in the Botswana state system. (He sits on the Tawana Land Board, which is charged with the reviewing of applications for and the apportioning of land within the district.) Although he has a large herd of cattle, most of which are in his younger brother's care at a cattle post some fifteen miles from the homestead, he also keeps a reserve of cash on deposit at a bank. His nineteen-year-old son is away most of the time at school in Mahalapye and will soon start university training. The *omuini* served in World War II and spent a considerable amount of time in Italy. His knowledge, by no means extensive, of the old, traditional ways is yet greater than many his age. His son, however, is almost completely ignorant and often derisive of the old ways and beliefs.

The homestead configuration reflects little of the ideal plan. There is no *okuruo.* His only wife's hut is situated more to the south of the corrals than to the east. Though his son's hut is southwest of this hut, his brother's hut is northeast of it. His elder sister's hut is in the northeast where the ideal plan would position his other wives if he had any.

Except for the fact that the huts open to the west and that the corrals are placed in a generally westerly location, the *onganda* is set up in a rather haphazard fashion.

Homestead B (Fig. 4, Table 3)

Whereas homestead A was small, this homestead is large. This, aside from the *omuini's* wealth in cattle, is due to the fact that he is

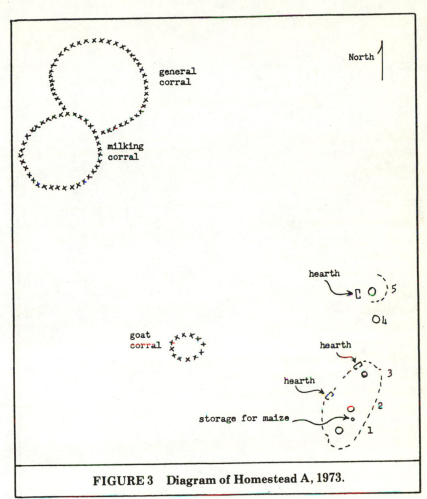

FIGURE 3 Diagram of Homestead A, 1973.

TABLE 2 Key to Diagram of Homestead A

Number	Identification
1	Hut of son. (Ego in all cases is the *omuini* of the homestead.)
2	Hut of *omuini* and wife.
3	Hut of yB, yBW, and two children.
4	Abandoned hut (belonged to ZD, who has gone to South West Africa).
5	Hut of eZ.

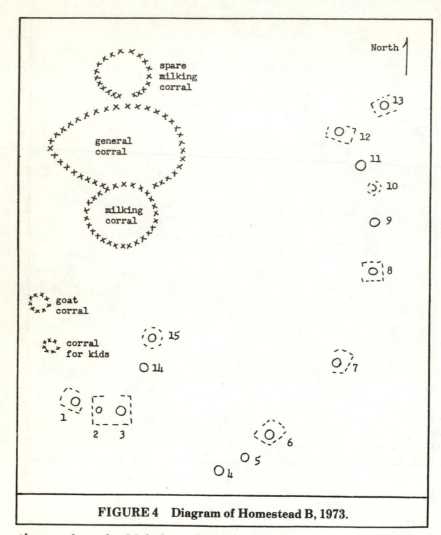

FIGURE 4   Diagram of Homestead B, 1973.

the *omuhona* for Makakun. *Omuhona* refers today to a headman, a person of authority who adjudicates local disputes, who is theoretically the local spokesman for the community vis-á-vis the national government, and who is also the local spokesman for the national government vis-á-vis the community.

Once again, there is no *okuruo* at this homestead. The homestead lacks the traditional focal point and consequently does not evidence the traditional configuration called for by the ideal plan.

The first wife's hut is located directly south of the corrals. The second (and now only) wife's hut is situated more to the east, yet it still lies south of the corrals. Nonrelatives' huts are scattered throughout the arc and are not located to the west of the corrals. These nonrelatives consist of a scribe, school children, and some Bushmen. The scribe is paid a salary by the central government to assist the *omuhona* in writing reports (which must be in English). There are two separate huts for the children, without their parents, who reside at the homestead during the school year in order to be near the school (by government order the homestead of the *omuhona* must be located near the school). And the Bushmen are hired herdsmen and laborers who are paid in kind and cash. Wives' huts, those of married agnates (a FyB and family, the wife and child of a deceased yB), that of an unmarried agnate (FyBS), and those of the aforementioned nonrelatives are interspersed in random fashion. The *omuini* also has two children by a concubine who live in his homestead with his wife (the concubine resides in her natal homestead).

TABLE 3   Key to Diagram of Homestead B

Number	Identification
1	Hut of *omuini's* first wife; no children.
2	Storage hut.
3	Hut of scribe.
4	Hut for children of a woman (unrelated to *omuini*) who does not live in this homestead.
5	Storage hut.
6	Hut of wife of deceased yB and small child.
7	Hut of second wife and five children.
8	Hut of eD (unmarried).
9	Same as hut 4.
10	Hut in construction; will be storage for hut 11.
11	Hut of FyB, FyBW, and children.
12	Hut of FyBS.
13	Hut for hired Bushmen workers.

Once more, the only resemblance this homestead bears to the ideal pattern is that the corrals are situated more or less to the west of the huts.

Homestead C (Fig. 5, Table 4)

TABLE 4   Key to Diagram of Homestead C

Number	Identification
1	Hut of eBS (and eBSW until she died) and five children.
2	Hut of eBS, eBSW, and children.
3	Hut of eBS, eBSW.
4	Hut of eBS.
5	Hut of eBW (and eB until he died) and children.
6	Hut of second wife's daughter.
7	Storage hut for huts 6 and 8.
8	Hut of second wife.
9	Storage hut for hut 10.
10	Hut of yB, yBW, and yBS.
11	Formerly first wife's hut (deceased); now "*okuruo* house."
12	Hut of FyBS, FyBSW, and FyBSS.
13	Storage hut.
14	Hut of "FBM" (quotation marks indicate a classificatory relative).
15	Hut of third wife and nine children.
16	Storage hut.
17	Storage hut for hut 18.
18	Hut of Z.

This homestead belongs to an individual the Herero refer to as one of the last "true Herero" (*omuherero katjiri*). This *omuini* has an *okuruo,* and his advice is sought on those very rare occasions when knowledge of traditional practices is desired. The presence of the *okuruo,* the last functioning *okuruo* in all of Makakun, and the *omuini's* sense of responsibility as a vessel of tradition for his people lend to his *onganda* a more traditional character (that is to say, a configuration approximating to a greater degree the ideal pattern).

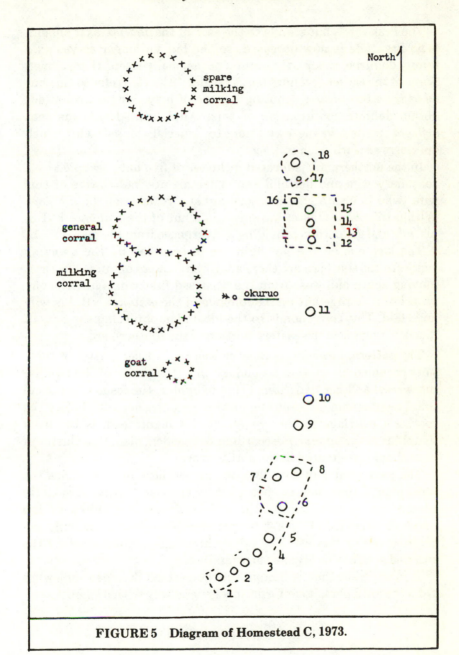

FIGURE 5   Diagram of Homestead C, 1973.

The first wife's hut stands to the east of the *okuruo,* as it should. (The first wife is now deceased, so the hut no longer serves as a family domicile, though the *omuini* occasionally sleeps there alone.) Some of the earlier accounts (e.g., Vedder 1928:168) refer to this hut as *otjizera* or *otjizero,* denoting a place of holy things. I could not obtain definite confirmation of this. All I could learn was that *otjizera* in some vague way refers to "special things" with which outsiders are forbidden contact.

In the northern arc is located a cluster of five huts occupied by a secondary wife and her children, a female uterine relative of this wife (who is also a classificatory agnatic relative of the *omuini*). Within this same cluster, however, is a hut of the *omuini's* FyBS, his wife and child, thus providing a divergence from the plan.

The last hut on the northern are is occupied by the *omuini's* sister. In the southern arc there are three clusters of huts. The first, moving south and west from the deceased first wife's hut, is comprised of a storage hut and a domicile of the *omuini's* yB, his wife and child. This corresponds to the ideal plan of placing the huts of married agnates in the eastern portion of the southern arc.

The pattern, however, is then broken by another cluster of three huts occupied by another secondary wife (the senior of the two living wives) and her daughter. (This daughter, the issue of a concubinal relationship between the mother and another man before the mother's marriage to the *omuini* of this homestead, is the legal daughter of the *omuini*.)[6] According to the ideal plan, this cluster of huts should be situated in the northern arc.

The next cluster of five huts on the southern arc resembles the ideal plan in that they are occupied by agnates. The most easterly placed hut is occupied by the wife and young children of the *omuini's* deceased eB. Next to this stands the hut of the only unmarried son of this eB. The other three huts are occupied by the married sons of this eB and their families.

It is apparent that, although this homestead diverges somewhat from the ideal plan, it conforms in a general way to that plan.

Homestead D (Fig. 6, Table 5)

This *onganda* exhibits none of the characteristics of the ideal pattern. There is no *okuruo*. All of the huts, except one, are occupied by
uterine or affinal relatives of the *omuini*. The exception is that of the
omuini's FB, an elderly and somewhat senile gentleman who has

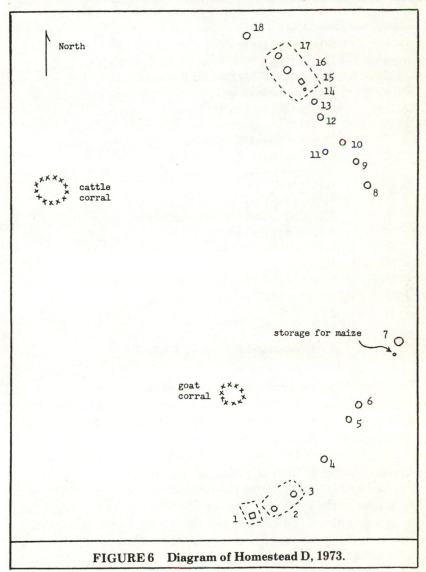

FIGURE 6   Diagram of Homestead D, 1973.

more or less retired from the vital affairs of the homestead. His hut, located on the tip of the northern arc, reflects this.

TABLE 5   Key to Diagram of Homestead D

Number	Identification
1	Storage hut for hut 2.
2	Hut of MeZ.
3	Hut of MyZS, MyZSW, and one child.
4	Hut of D (unmarried).
5	Storage hut for hut 6.
6	Hut of MZS.
7	Hut of *omuini* and wife.
8	Hut of M (recently deceased).
9	Abandoned hut.
10	Hut of MyZ.
11	Storage hut for hut 10.
12	Hut of second wife and two children.
13	Storage hut for hut 12.
14	Storage hut for hut 15.
15	Hut of MZD.
16	Storage hut for hut 17.
17	Hut of MZS.
18	Hut of FB.

Homestead E (Fig. 7, Table 6)

This homestead reflects the poverty and lack of social status of its *omuini*. He owns few cattle (about twenty head), may have contracted an inappropriate marriage,[7] and is physically deformed—all of which sets him somewhat apart from his fellows. The four dwellings are all occupied by close agnates and are not arranged in any conceivable pattern. There is, of course, no *okuruo*.

It is unnecessary to describe the remaining homesteads in detail. They appear in the appendix, and, as is evident from the diagrams, they do not conform to the ideal pattern of old. A new pattern may be emerging, however, suggested by the southward shift of the senior wife's hut; but this is not a conscious reorganization and there is not enough information yet to confirm this as a new pattern.

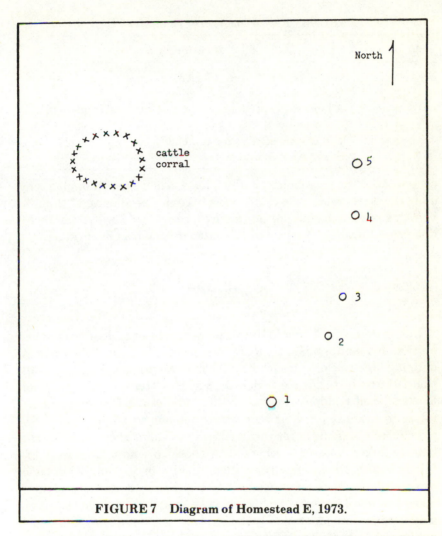

FIGURE 7   Diagram of Homestead E, 1973.

What the data do seem to indicate is that the lack of an *okuruo* means an absence of a physical focus in the layout of the homestead. And the fact that the homestead configuration lacks a physical center reflects the loss of the central core of traditional Herero society. The *okuruo* formerly epitomized the essence of what it meant to be Herero; it symbolized the connection with the ancestors and the ritual importance of cattle. The old sacred connection with the an-

TABLE 6   Key to Diagram of Homestead E

Number	Identification
1	Hut of yB, yBW, and children.
2	Hut of *omuini*, W, and one child.
3	Abandoned hut (formerly hut of eBS, who has left the homestead).
4	Hut of eBS, eBSW, and one child.
5	Storage hut for hut 4.

cestors, with the time-honored ways, has been broken (though a tenuous thread remains) and cattle have become "secularized" though vestiges of their former ritual importance linger. I will attempt to document these assertions and this interpretation as I continue.

RESIDENCE

Before going on, I should like to provide a brief addendum to this section. In an unpublished paper Gibson described the difficulties in defining "the rule or rules from which one can predict or generate all the patterns of residence which do occur in Herero society, at all levels of their residential organization" (1959b:2). For instance, he refers to persons residing with other persons to whom they were patrilineally linked, others with those to whom they were matrilineally linked, and still others with those to whom they were affinally linked. He also mentions the difficulty in deciding what level of coresidence is of significance for analysis: "does [coresidence] mean residence in the same hut, or in the same yard, or in the same side of a homestead, or merely in the same homestead, with or without its associated cattle-posts, or only in the same chiefdom?"

It was my hope to unravel the hidden residence rules with the aid of the relatively recent decision-model approach.[8] But it appears from the foregoing that Herero residence practices do not conform to a set of well delineated rules. Certain broad generalizations can be enunciated, but like all such generalizations their value is limited. For example, we may say that a woman upon marriage leaves her natal residence and goes to live with her husband (i.e. virilocal residence). Her husband is generally expected to reside, and usually does reside, where his father resides or resided (i.e. patrilocal residence). Thus, the term *patrivirilocal residence* may be applied to both the pattern and rule of residence for newly married couples. But the term amounts to an empty phrase. What of widows and widowers, young unmarried adult males and females, young children, children of divorced parents, children of unwed parents, and so on?

It is impossible to construct a systematic set of rules of residence for the Herero, since for many individuals several alternatives are available and equally appropriate. In order to supply at least a generalized account of residence options, the following guide is provided.

Preteenage children of either sex, whether born in or out of wedlock, normally reside with their mother. If the child is the issue of a recognized marital union, and the parents are not divorced, the mother and children live together in the same hut in the homestead where the father resides. If the father is monogamous, he too lives in this hut. Otherwise he shares the huts of his several wives. Children of divorced parents reside while they are young with their mother, who, after divorce, usually returns to her father's (i.e., her natal) homestead, although she may live in a brother's homestead if the natal homestead has segmented, or she may even live in a homestead with a married sister. Anytime after infancy the children go to live in their father's homestead, to be cared for by another wife of the father or even by one of his female uterine relatives if she lives in his homestead. The same holds for children of concubinal unions, provided the genitor (the biological father) has become the pater (the legal or sociological father) through the payment of childwealth, for a man's concubines need not reside in his homestead. In addition to these options, children may be lent to friends or relatives, who have few or no children, or may be away at school; but these are temporary arrangements.

A married woman lives in the homestead of her husband. A divorced or widowed woman may live in her natal homestead or one of its derivatives, usually headed by a brother, if it has fragmented. But she may also elect to remain in the homestead of her former or deceased husband since, if she has male children there, she knows she will be cared for. A concubine nowdays usually lives in her natal homestead and is visited there by her consort, but she may also live in his homestead. If childwealth is not paid, her children remain with her and take on the patrilineal affiliation of her father (which, of course, is the same as her own). There is no stigma of "illegitimacy" attached to such children. If the mother later marries another man not the genitor of her children, and the genitor has not paid childwealth, the children belong to her new husband by virtue of his having paid bridewealth to her father.

A married man usually lives in his natal homestead with his close agnates (his brothers or father). A widowed or divorced man usually does not change his place of residence.

Technically, a very poor person may attach himself to any homestead that will have him. But no case of this was found in Ngamiland in 1973. There are few poor Herero, but even the poorest family encountered elected to set up its separate homestead and struggle on its own rather than become dependents in more affluent homesteads. (Actually the family was not entirely on its own, for other Herero in the vicinity occasionally lent aid.)

The picture would be incomplete without mention of the towns, though only a very small number of Herero are found in them. The Herero one encounters in towns are primarily transients. They come for one of two reasons: to trade or to obtain medical care. Herero today make extensive use of the limited medical facilities in Botswana. They may come in small groups or large ones to a town with a hospital.[9] While in town they set up makeshift shelters constructed of cardboard, brush, and cloth arranged randomly where there is space. These visits usually last only a few days. But in the case of serious illness requiring hospitalization, a husband or wife might remain in the area for months until the loved one recovers. (In such a case, food and even money will periodically be sent to the individual by relatives in the bush.)

Herero also come to town to trade. A man may take one or a few oxen to a trading store to sell, or several men may drive a number of animals in for sale. But my informants also reported to me that some Herero make beer and sell it in town, though I observed no actual cases of this. (See also Gibson 1962:630.)

Trading stores are generally owned and run by Europeans or Tswana. But there is one store near Makunda that is managed by a Herero. He spends most of his time in the town of Charles Hill where the store is located and maintains a residence there. Yet he still has a place in the nearby Herero bush community of Makunda as well. This is true of all Herero encountered in towns. Regardless of how long or for what reason they are in a town, they think of their "homes" as being in the bush. Somewhere there is a homestead with a hut that is theirs.

LINEAGE AND SIB

In Herero society descent is reckoned both patrilineally and matrilineally. Every Herero person is linked to a series of male ancestors through his or her father and to a series of females through his or her mother. At birth each child is simultaneously a member of

Some Makunda Herero in Ghanzi to see the doctor. (See Chapter 1, footnote 9.)

two socially recognized sociocentric (as opposed to egocentric) units, one by virtue of his relationship to his father and the other by virtue of his relationship to his mother. These units are named and put to different social uses. Such a system of reckoning descent has been called double descent (or double unilineal, dual, duolineal, or bilineal descent): "the utilization in one society of both patrilineal and matrilineal principles of affiliation resulting in two lineage systems cross-cutting each other" (Gibson 1956:109).

It is unnecessary to attempt to resolve here the longstanding theoretical issue of what constitutes double descent, nor need we even delineate the various arguments.[10] For our purposes we need only clarify the position taken here on one of the main points of the controversy. It has been stated (e.g., by Fox 1967:132) that true double descent exists only where both patrilineal and matrilineal groups are present. Murdock (1949:15), to take another example, says that double descent "combines patrilineal and matrilineal descent by assigning the individuals to a group of each type."

This criterion is rejected in this presentation. Instead of only descent *groups,* the qualification is expanded to include descent *categories* as well, and the term *unit* (or "descent-ordered unit"; see Scheffler 1966:548) is employed to comprehend both. Thus, we may paraphrase Murdock and say that double descent combines patrilineal and matrilineal principles of descent and simultaneously assigns an individual to a unit of each type by virtue of his descent and/or his filiation to each parent.[11]

The largest, named, descent-ordered units in Herero society are the *otuzo* (s. *oruzo*) and the *omaanda* (s. *eanda*). An *oruzo* consists of males and females who are agnatically related. It is internally differentiated into several demonstrable agnatic descent lines or continua related to locality (at least in the past). These subdivisions of the *oruzo* may therefore be termed "patrilineages." The patrilineage founders are said to be descended from a single ancestor. Usually the original ancestor is unnamed and precise genealogical connections from him to living members cannot be traced. The *oruzo,* therefore, conforms to Murdock's (1949:46) definition of a sib, and the *otuzo* will be referred to here as "patrisibs."[12]

An *eanda* consists of males and females who are uterine relatives. It is internally differentiated into several matrilineal descent lines.

Though in the case of the *eanda* subdivisions actual genealogical relationships to the founders of these lines cannot be
traced, the term "matrilineage" will still be applied to them in order
to parallel the terminology used in reference to *otuzo* and their subdivisions. The *eanda* will be called a "matrisib." (This choice of
terms is supported by the native Herero terminology.)

A Herero belongs to the *oruzo* or patrisib of his father and to the
eanda or matrisib of his mother. All the earlier reports on the
Herero agree on this, and it is still true today. What the social correlates were for these units in the past, however, is decidedly unclear.
The various accounts often contradict each other and are even internally inconsistent. Part of the difficulty stems from imprecision
of terminology. A single author, such as von Francois (1896), might
use "group," "family," "tribe," "relatives," "sib," or "gens" to
mean *oruzo*, and he might also use the same term to refer to a homestead. One is rarely sure to what a German author is referring unless
he uses the native Herero term. Instead of trying, therefore, to force
the earlier literature into a unified account and then to depict the
situation as found in western Botswana in 1973, it will be clearer to
present the current reality and to refer in the course of this description to previous literature.

It was found in 1973 that agnatic differentiation among the
Herero in western Botswana consisted of 21 patrisibs,[13] each internally subdivided into several lineages. The lineages are called in
Otjiherero *ozonganda* (s. *onganda*), which is the same term applied
to homesteads. This is because what are now lineages are said to
have come into being originally as new homesteads. In addition, the
patrisibs are categorized into six, unnamed, larger entities I shall
call "phratries."

The Herero explain this patri-organization by origin myths. The
following is the myth I obtained for the *oruzo* called Ongueuva from
one of its members. This is the only *oruzo* for which a founder is
named. It is well represented in Ngamiland, for the Herero identified later in this study as belonging to the lineage Otjiseu (a large
segment of which emigrated from South West Africa to Botswana)
were members of Ongueuva.

At one time all the Herero were one people. There were not divisions into different *otuzo*. All the Herero people ate the same foods. But as time progressed and conditions of the environment fluctuated, causing variations in food supply, the people had to choose among available edible animals, assigning some to be eaten by certain people and disallowing the consumption of these to other groups of people. The food was apportioned among all and each person knew what he could and could not eat. Thus food restrictions came into being, and these provided the bases upon which *otuzo* are distinguished.

At that time, when the Herero were undivided as to *otuzo*, there was a man named Gueva. Gueva had two sons. These sons grew up in hard times. They were poor and food was scarce. One day the brothers came upon some hornless sheep of a certain color (*ondovazu:* spotted gray with white and black).[14] There were not many. The elder brother and younger brother decided that the elder would take the sheep, keep them, and eat them. But the younger brother would move elsewhere to settle and would not eat such sheep, reserving them for his brother. The elder brother became the founder of Otjiporo *oruzo*. The younger brother, who did not eat the sheep, became the founder of Ongueuva *oruzo*. To this day his descendants do not eat hornless sheep of that color.

This younger brother, the founder of Ongueuva, had several sons. During a time when they were poor, they happened upon a bull. The eldest brother decided, because of his poverty, to take this bull and start his herd; while the younger brothers forbade themselves such a bull and went elsewhere to settle. The eldest brother who took the bull as his became the founder of Okanene *oruzo*.[15]

Among the younger brothers it came to pass that one grew very sick. He consulted a man who was known as a successful curer of illnesses. He treated this brother. As part of the treatment, the curer, whose name was Ndjiva, proscribed certain foods to the brother. The brother grew well from not eating such foods. Because these food proscriptions contributed to his healthy recovery, his descendants decided to continue them. Thus the brother became the founder of Ondjiva *oruzo*, named after the curer who treated him.

There still remained, however, four brothers who were the
sons of the man who started Ongueuva. These brothers, who
were named Seu, Ngura, Munjo, Murangi, all continued to
follow the same food restrictions as their father, not to eat
hornless sheep of a certain color. So Ongueuva ceased to be
divided.

Nevertheless, the brothers decided to set up separate
ozonganda apart from each other, though not at great distances. Thus they each came to found an *onganda;* and all
Ongueuva homesteads to this day are the descendants of these
four brothers.

This is why today the Ongueuva, Otjiporo, Ondjiva, and
Okanene *otuzo* consider themselves so closely related. They all
sprang from ancestors who were kinsmen. At their beginnings,
they were located at not great distances from one another.
They offered each other help in time of need; they fed each
other's hungry; they lent cattle among themselves; they cured
each other's sick; and they kept conflict among themselves to a
minimum. Even today, though the *ozonganda* of the various
otuzo have become dispersed with time, they maintain a feeling
of relatedness among themselves, still cure each other, still
offer mutual help, and still try to keep disputes within the overall group and out of the courts (though today cases are taken
more often to a court of law).

As this legend indicates, there are proscriptions and prescriptions
for each *oruzo,* and these serve as the patrisib's identifying characteristics. Today these pertain to the type of livestock the members of an *oruzo* may not keep, those they may keep, and those they
should keep.[16]

In order to discuss these restrictions, however, it is necessary
first to record the cattle categories distinguished by the Herero.[17]
There are four of these categories.

Ozongombe Ozonzere (s. Ongombe Ondere)

These are "sacred" or "special" cattle. They are not particular to
the *oruzo* but to a lineage. This is evidenced by the fact that the
ozonzere cattle are designated by the homestead founder (who in
time becomes the founder of a lineage) and not by the current home-

stead *omuini.* A cow is selected by the founder as *ondere.* Thereafter
its offspring are known as *ozonzere* cattle. Technically, no Herero
may eat the meat of *ozonzere* cattle. (In former times, when an
ondere animal died, its carcass was placed outside the homestead
for the dogs and Bushmen to eat.) Today, however, the Herero do
consume these cattle. They also sell them, which at one time was
also forbidden. It was once believed that *ozonzere* cattle were the
leaders and guides for the herd, always able to locate water and
grazing wherever they might be.

Ozongombe Za Oruzo

These *"oruzo* cattle" are also "sacred" or "special." Each *oruzo* is
enjoined to keep certain, specified cattle as a symbol of the *oruzo*
and to refrain from keeping certain, but not all, others reserved for
other *otuzo. Oruzo* cattle are identified by their colors. (Formerly
horn conformation was important as well but is no longer today. In
fact, dehorning is a growing practice among present-day Herero.
Without horns, cattle are less likely to injure one another.) Like all
tribal cattle herders, the Herero distinguish a great variety of cattle
color-types which are indistinguishable to the unpracticed eye of the
outsider. My informants identified thirty-six color-types for me,
and I was able to take color photographs of thirty of these. It was
by the number of *oruzo* cattle that wealth was measured in the old
days. (Today wealth is measured by the total number of animals, regardless of the category to which they are assigned.) Finally, *oruzo*
cattle may be eaten by the members of the *oruzo* and by members of
all other *otuzo* to whom the color-type is not specifically tabooed
(izera).[18]

Ozongombe Za Ka Uriri

These are literally "general cattle." It is probably these cattle
that previous authors mean when they refer to "secular" cattle.
These are all cattle which are not *oruzo* or *ozonzere* or *izera*
("tabooed") cattle. These may be eaten or sold freely.

Ozombunda

These may be glossed as "victory" or "war" or "prize" cattle. They were cattle obtained through raiding. More precisely, they were cattle selected from among those acquired in a raid to commemorate some feat or exploit of the victor during the encounter which netted him the prize cattle. The rest of the cattle then joined the "general" herd or, if they were of the specified color-type, the *oruzo* cattle. My informants' memories conflict about *ozombunda* cattle. Some say the selected *ozombunda* cattle could only be eaten by older males. Some say they could be eaten by all males, young or old. Others say that the victor could only designate *some* of the selected *ozombunda* cattle for male consumption, while the rest could be eaten by anyone. Since raiding is no longer practiced, there no longer are any *ozombunda* cattle among the Herero, so these questions cannot be resolved. (It may be that there is no single resolution, that treatment of *ozombunda* cattle varied from group to group within the society.)

Appendix D lists the twenty-one *otuzo* and their restrictions. (Some information, however, is missing. This is indicated in the table by a question mark.) In general, it confirms the ecological interpretation offered by a native informant that the food restrictions serve to distribute resources over the whole population. The *otuzo* of a phratry tend to have similar restrictions. This lends some support to his assertion that the related patrisibs—and not only related lineages within a patrisib—at one time were more geographically compact than they are today. (This matter is considered again, from a different angle, in chapter 3.)[19]

In present-day Herero communities in western Botswana one finds homesteads, whose agnatic core members belong to the same patrisib and even to the same lineage, dispersed over wide areas. Scattered among them are homesteads affiliated with many other patrisibs which are often members of different phratries.

Let us turn our attention, then, to the process of homestead segmentation which, in turn, gives rise to lineages among the Herero.

At the death of an *omuini* his cattle are divided among his sons and, to a lesser extent, his sister's sons. If relations among the sons

are amicable, and the pasturage is adequate, they may elect to remain in a single homestead. In that case the eldest son becomes
omuini of the homestead—though, as Gibson (1956:116) points out,
the herd is divided in title if not in fact. If the brothers decide to
separate, one takes his herd and family and establishes a new homestead elsewhere. The owners of these homesteads, however, continue to regard themselves as close relatives. After several generations of such segmentation, the homesteads are scattered over a
wide area, though they still recognize their kinship with one
another. Eventually the founder of the original parent homestead is
regarded as the founder of a *lineage,* which is now comprised of the
scattered homesteads. So when one asks a man the name of his
onganda ("lineage") but not the place where he now lives (homestead), he replies with the name of a homestead founder four to six
generations removed from him.

Gibson (1956:116) reports a similar finding, as well as an additional level of segmentation. After stating that following separation
and the establishment of independent homesteads, the male
founders of these daughter homesteads continue to recognize their
close relationship to each other and to the parent homestead and
they apply the same term *(onganda)* to this larger social grouping
that they apply to the individual homestead, he goes on to say:

> This wider social *onganda* therefore includes the patrilineal de-
> scendants of an ancestral homestead several generations in the
> past and is named for its deceased owner. The descendants of
> this ancestral *onganda,* whose depth may be from three to six
> generations may be called a patri-lineage. Often two levels of
> *onganda* or lineage segmentation are recognized, several lower
> levels being combined into a wider *onganda* of still earlier origin
> which is in turn called by the name of its patrilineal founder. In
> such a case the two levels of segmentation may be dis-
> tinguished by designating them minor and major patri-
> lineages, following the use of Evans-Pritchard (1940:195ff.). As
> a rule a Herero is able to recount his patrilineal ancestors back
> ten to fifteen generations, reaching back beyond the founder of
> his minor patri-lineage, but generally not reaching to the
> founder of his major patri-lineage without admitted gaps.

I found that the Herero no longer recognize that level of lineage
segmentation Gibson calls a major patrilineage. (This is not to say

that I doubt that they did so in the past. On the contrary, I accept that they did and take the present situation as another manifestation of change among the Herero in western Botswana.) Today, informants simply omit a major lineage instead of recognizing it: either they state they have forgotten previous ancestors or they date the founding of the *oruzo* closer to the present. For example, to stay with Otjiseu *onganda* of Ongueuva patrisib, both responses were received. In the above myth, Seu, actually the founder of a minor patrilineage in Gibson's terms, is asserted to be only one generation removed from the founder of the *oruzo*. Thus, all the ancestors preceding Seu are, in effect, denied. Other informants questioned about this responded that they had forgotten Seu's predecessors.

I was repeatedly given the genealogy as it appears in Figure 8 for Otjiseu, the lineage or *onganda* founded by Seu (individuals whose names are italicized were my informants).

Although this chart is by no means complete (my intention was simply to record the genealogical relationships among some of my informants), it agrees with the genealogy given by Schapera (1945:11ff.) for Otjiseu—except, that is, for the ancestors of the founder Seu. Schapera's data were collected over thirty years ago, and his informants remembered several of Seu's ancestors whom mine have forgotten (see Fig. 9).

How do we explain this change in a society whose traditional form of religion is ancestral veneration? For the time being, we may say that since the connection with the ancestors has become so tenuous, it is of less importance to maintain knowledge of their identities. (Young men today do not even know the names of their deceased grandfathers!) What apparently caused the break with the ancestors will be taken up later.

To illustrate this lack of traditional knowledge about progenitors and to illustrate as well the process of segmentation, the following case is provided. Three homesteads, all situated near each other, were visited in Makakun. The heads of these homesteads all belong to Otjiporo *oruzo*. In fact, they are "brothers" in Herero kinship terminology (biologically, only two are brothers and the third is their patrilateral parallel cousin). Though they are all members of the same lineage, they did not know its name since the founder has

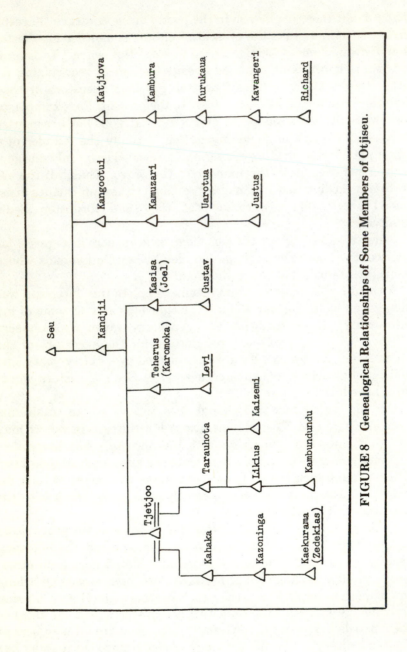

FIGURE 8   Genealogical Relationships of Some Members of Otjiseu.

been forgotten. This is by no means a singular case; indeed, it is normal. Otjiseu is the exception in that it has some very old members still alive who can remember four or five generations back. (Be-

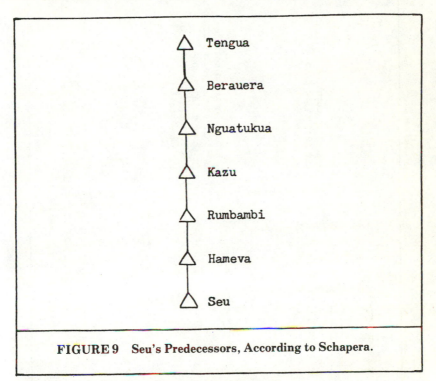

FIGURE 9   Seu's Predecessors, According to Schapera.

sides, it is the oldest and numerically predominant lineage in Ngamiland.) My Otjiporo informants (whose names are italicized in Fig. 10), however, were both born in Botswana.

Finally, completing this outline of Herero patri-organization, are the largest categories that are based on a notion of agnatic relationship—which I have chosen, following Gibson (1956:116), to call phratries. Gibson says these phratries are sometimes recognized, but I found no case in which they are not. Though they function only minimally today, they still serve as devices for classification, and all patrisibs are assigned to these six phratries.

The reason they function minimally is that their existence is predicated on the fact that each phratry's member *otuzo* share common

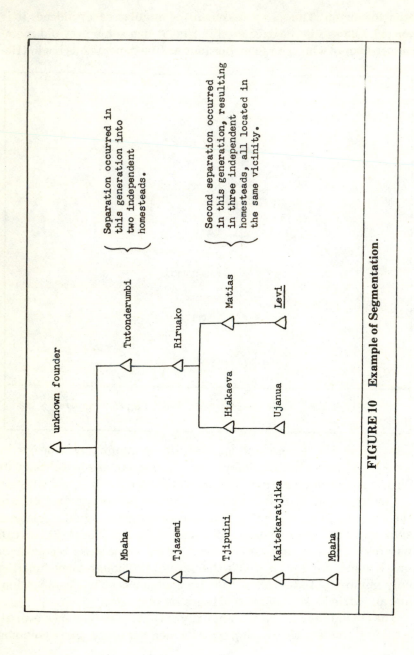

FIGURE 10 Example of Segmentation.

ancestors. A decreased emphasis on ancestral veneration (which will be documented) has thus led to the decreased importance of phratry activities, which were primarily religious occasions. Once again, further consideration is deferred until later.

Let us turn now to an overall description of Herero matri-organization. The same procedure was employed for identifying *omaanda*, Herero matrisibs, during field research as was used for confirming *otuzo*. A master list was compiled from earlier sources[20] and informants were asked whether or not the listed items were recognized matri-units.

The number of *omaanda* reported in the previous literature total ten (though individual sources report from six to nine *omaanda*). The actual number is nine and is unchanging. This was repeatedly confirmed by informants, as indicated in Appendix E. (The reason that the master list contained ten *omaanda* is that some earlier authors list "Omuekuenjata" and "Omuekuendata" as two separate matrisibs. These are actually two misspellings of one *eanda*, Omuekuendjata. Another point of confusion in the previous literature results from the fact that some sources show what are actually themselves full-fledged *omaanda* as subdivisions of others.)

Not only the number of *omaanda* but their major internal differentiation is fixed as well. Just as patrilineages are derived from homesteads, matrilineages are derived from houses within homesteads. And just as the term for patrilineage and homestead is the same (*onganda*), the term for matrilineage and house or hut is the same (*ondjuo*).

The majority of informants insist that each *eanda* is divided into a "big house" (*ondjuo nene*) and a "little house" (*ondjuo katiti*).[21] According to Herero folklore, all *omaanda* were founded by women, and two major houses, big and little (which I shall refer to as "major matrilineages"), were founded by daughters (eZ and yZ respectively) of the matrisib founders.

Segmentation continues below the level of the major matrilineage to subhouses (which I shall term "minor matrilineages").[22] Although genealogy cannot be traced to the level of the major matrilineage, it was in the past at least traceable for minor matrilineages. This is no longer true today. Women can always name their minor matrilineage but cannot trace the genealogy from the founder to themselves. Men, unless they are elderly, rarely know the name of their major matrilineage and may not even know their *eanda.*[23]

At the level of the minor matrilineage, the number of segments is not fixed. Since minor matrilineages are of shallow genealogical depth and are descended from actual huts or houses that are named after their women owners, it is understandable that their number is continually changing.

An example of the internal differentiation of one *eanda* or matrisib is provided in Figure 11.

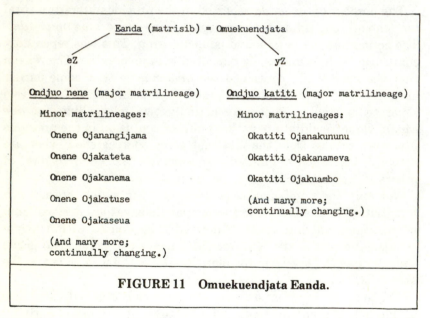

FIGURE 11   Omuekuendjata Eanda.

As is the case with *otuzo*, there is also in Herero matri-organization a level of affiliation beyond the *eanda* level. Though there are six phratries for *otuzo*, there are only two for *omaanda*. Informants could give no rationale for this; this is simply the way things are they say. The scraps remembered of the origin myths for *omaanda* offer no clue; neither do the putative genealogical ties between *omaanda* founders help. As regards influencing specific behavior, the matrilineal phratries are insignificant. These phratries exist today primarily as classificatory devices. It is impossible to determine, either from the earlier literature or from living informants, the social-behavioral functions, if any, of matrilineal phratries in the past.

To indicate the extent to which the phratry level of matri-organization defies systematic analysis, the following data are provided. I attempted to collect origin myths for all *omaanda*.[24] The few informants who remembered anything, remembered only the barest outline. In the list below, the *eanda* name appears on the left and whatever information was obtained is shown opposite it.

1. Omuekueuva.   Founded by a child (eZ to 2) born in sunshine.
2. Omuekuenombura.   Founded by a child (yZ to 1) born in rain.
3. Omuekuatjivi.   Founded by the only surviving child (a female) of 1.
4. Omuekuauti.   Origin unremembered.
5. Omuekuendjata.   Founded by a daughter of 2. She went to a river and drank only a little bit of water, just a little drop, so she took the name Omuekuendjata, indicating "drop of water."
6. Omuekuendjandje. Founded by a woman who married a son of 2. The name means "generous."
7. Omuekuahere.   Founded by a daughter of 2.
8. Omuekuatjiti.   Origin unremembered.
9. Omuekuenatja.   Origin unremembered.[25]

If we plot the relationship among the *omaanda* on a genealogical chart (omitting, of course, 4, 8, and 9), it looks like this:

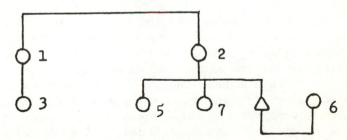

A neat dual division immediately suggests itself: one unit might consist of 1 and her descendants ("sun people"), the other of 2 and her descendants ("rain people"). Unfortunately, this is not how the *omaanda* are categorized. I therefore offer the ethnographic fact that Herero *omaanda* are distributed (as shown below) in two larger divisions I call phratries and provide no interpretation for this since analysis reveals none and my informants could offer none.

┌─ PHRATRY ─┐   ┌─ PHRATRY ─┐

1   5
2   6
3   7
4   8
                        9

I have stated that kinship and descent have decreased in importance as referents for social behavior. It remains now to offer evidence to support this. An example will be drawn from in-phratry activities. Formerly, according to informants, these abounded. The activity for which I have the most data is reciprocal curing among patrisibs within a phratry. (To my knowledge, the institutionalized curing relationships described here are not reported in detail anywhere else.) The absence, or near-absence, of this activity today is considered to be indicative of the shift from descent-based interaction to individual, impersonal interaction for services; for the traditional curing activity has by and large been replaced by visits to a Western physician.

In regard to in-phratry activities, Gibson (1956:122) makes the following comments:

> The members of a phratry do not gather for joint activities, and their priests do not meet in consultation over matters concerning the phratry. . . . In general, little notice is taken of the relationship between members of various *otuzo* within a phratry. It is only in the treatment of sickness resulting from the displeasure of the ancestors that the unity of members of different *otuzo* within the same phratry sometimes receives social recognition. When sickness is determined by divinition to be due to the displeasure of the ancestors, resulting either from failure to observe the restrictions of the *oruzo* or from failure to provide a customary sacrifice for the ancestors, an ap-

peal to the ancestors and a propitiatory sacrifice must be made
by a priest at his sacred hearth on behalf of his afflicted clans-
man. Normally the sufferer would appeal to the priest of his
particular patri-lineage to perform the rites for him, but priests
of related patri-lineages within his *oruzo* may also act on his
behalf. If, however, the sufferer is far from a priest of his own
oruzo, as when traveling, or if his priest himself is absent, a
priest of any of the related *otuzo* within the phratry may perform the rites. In this connection it is interesting to note that a
priest does not appeal to the oldest ancestors known to him by
name or call upon ancestors held in common by himself and the
sufferer, but he calls only upon certain of his own forefathers
recently dead, those of the past three or four generations, for
only they may be influenced by their living descendant, the
priest, and are therefore responsive to his appeal.

The account of traditional curing procedures given by my informants differs from Gibson's in several ways. To begin with, the
standard practice was to seek out an *omurangere* (pl. *ovarangere*, a
religious leader; see chapter 3) who was *not* in the sufferer's own
patrisib but was a member of a patrisib of the same phratry as the
sufferer's. Any such *omurangere* would do, the final choice of curer
being based on personal preference and distance to be traveled to
reach him.[26]

But going to an *omurangere* was not the first step when a person
was ill. Before going through the formal curing ritual, at which an
omurangere would officiate, the sick person first visited an
onganga.[27] An *onganga* was a diagnostician who was also skilled in
the use of medicinal herbs and roots. He (or she) would determine
the nature of the ailment. If the problem was a minor one not caused
by the patient's transgression of the ancestors' will (for instance, by
his eating tabooed food), the *onganga* would treat it himself. If the
malady was more serious or due to the ancestors' wrath, the afflicted person would be sent to an *omurangere*.

Some of my informants said that only one *omurangere* presided at
the formal curing ceremony, while others maintained that all the
ovarangere of the phratry came together to perform the ceremony.
The Herero's confusion over this matter only serves to illustrate the
extent to which traditional practices, such as curing, have fallen

into disuse. The different opinions regarding the number of officiating *ovarangere* at the curing ceremony may also be influenced by the fact that there is only one *omurangere* alive today in Makakun.

In any event, the ritual proceeded as follows, The *omurangere* first slaughtered some *oruzo* cattle and then collected a few sticks. He smeared *omaze* (fat) from the slain cattle on the sticks and then rubbed the sick person with them. During this last act, the *omurangere* called upon the ancestors—all the ancestors of the phratry as a collective body—and asked them to heal their afflicted child. If it was their decision that the patient should die of his affliction, they were implored to accept him into their midst. The entire ceremony was, of course, conducted at the *okuruo*.

Today the traditional curing rite is passing away along with the *ovarangere* and *omaruo*. Informants explained that the curing procedure described above was performed "if you believe it," that is, if one still had faith in the ancestors and the traditional ways. Very few Herero have this faith nowadays. Instead they consult a Western physician. Even elderly Herero visit European doctors. They have little choice since there are so few *ovarangere* in Botswana to perform the ritual.

The significance of this example for the present work is that it demonstrates a turning away from the ancestors and a lack of faith in their effectiveness. It illustrates the decreased importance of common descent as a basis for interaction and a preference for a European-influenced solution to the problem of sickness.

According to my informants, in-phratry activities used to be numerous. In addition to curing, they consisted of giving gifts of cattle to needy fellow phratry members, extensive visiting and mutual hospitality, and lending assistance whenever it was requested.

Gibson's informants, however, painted a different picture. He says (1956:134):

> Early in my field work I put the question, "How do you treat a stranger who belongs to your own *oruzo*?" and was surprised to hear the answer, "We chase him away to his home." The informant explained, "When we meet a stranger we ask him his *eanda,* and when he tells us we send him to people of that *eanda*

and they take him in." Later observation showed that one has little obligation toward distant relatives of his patri-clan but many obligations toward distant relatives "through mothers."

I cannot explain this discrepancy between Gibson's report and mine. In a sense, however, the discrepancy is irrelevant, for the fact remains that neither situation obtains today. Significant change has occurred. Regardless of what existed formerly, present practices indicate the decreased reference to descent for behavioral purposes.

This is so in the case of matrilineal phratries as well. Though previous accounts indicate the former importance of matrilineal relatives for some activities, especially vengeance (see, for example, Dannert 1906:10–11 and Vedder 1928:198–9), present-day Herero say they pay little or no attention to a person's *eanda* affiliation. In only one case do the Herero act in reference to their matrilineal descent. When an individual dies, persons from each *eanda* in the deceased's phratry are entitled to take an ox from his herd and slaughter it. Though this still occasionally occurs, informants say it is no longer a systematic practice.

Marriage is another sphere of activity that could be employed as an illustration of the declining use of descent criteria for behavioral purposes and as an indicator of social change. Gibson remarks (1956:124):

> The Herero of Ngamiland assert that the influence of the ancestors extends only to a "true Herero," i.e., to those born of Herero *mothers* and to those who have not renounced their belief in the power of the ancestors. . . . In olden times captive women from foreign tribes might be taken as concubines by the Herero, but they were never formally married because they were not eligible to carry the fire to the sacred hearth and their sons were not eligible to inherit either the priesthood and its fire or the sacred cattle. If the child of such a union were to steal milk from the sacred vessels, his tongue would swell and he would die. Even today, for this reason, Herero men in Ngamiland rarely if ever take the women of other tribes in formal marriage.

My informants claim that today Herero may freely intermarry with non-Herero and that no stigma is attached to such unions. I can offer no evidence to support this assertion, for none of the 28 marriages for which I have data was contracted with a non-Herero. One marriage, however, occurred between a Herero man and an Mbanderu woman. The children are considered "true" Herero, entitled to inheritance just as their full-Herero half-siblings are. This seems to indicate a definite change if we accept as accurate Brincker's statement (1899:132) that the Herero considered the Mbanderu "foreigners and unequal to them; because of this marriages between them and the Mbanderu are unpopular" As I have pointed out in the introduction, a shift from ethnic endogamy to intergroup marriage is one of the indications of social change.

COMMUNITY

Now that the basics of Herero descent-ordered affiliation have been introduced, discussion of locality beyond the individual homestead, as well as some homestead-related considerations previously omitted, may proceed.

How nomadic the Herero were in the past cannot be definitively determined. That they were migratory—or, more precisely, that their movements resembled the "migratory drift" described by Stenning (1959:206ff.) for the Fulani—is indicated by the early German literature. At least this seems to have been the case until they reached central South West Africa when continued freedom was limited by the presence of the Hottentots and then by Europeans.

But "migratory shift" refers to a displacement or shifting of a pastoral orbit gradually over time. What kind of seasonal or short-term nomadism did the Herero practice? What was the character of their "pastoral orbit"? What kind of settlements resulted?

Hahn (1869:247) says the Herero were constantly on the move: "the Herero generally live a constantly nomadic life, like the Bedouins. They move from place to place with their herds, depending on the condition of the pastures." Similarly, Brincker (1899:131) calls them "inveterate nomads." Buttner (1883:550–1) asserts that the Herero "never built permanent houses before the arrival of Europeans and even now only the fewest do it" and also recognized that the term *onganda* connotes "a place where milking is done" and not a permanent residence.

The following passage from von Francois (1896:165) is quoted here because it sums up the view of Herero nomadism found in the early literature and because it contains information to which reference will be made again when leadership and authority are discussed.

> The Herero are nomads and as such, not tied to settled places. They chose them with regards to the demands of their property, their domestic animals. Since, however, the quality and quantity of the forage, as well as of the water, changes in the same place according to year and season, the herders are forced to change living and herding places. Only in a very few watering places, where the whole year through, nature offers plentiful water and grass, are permanent settlements found. In these cases, it is not only a single family, or a few, but often several hundred inhabitants, who constitute the population of such a place.
>
> The establishment of a mission, and the advantages which a mission establishment guarantees, contribute to the stabilizing of such a settlement. Stone houses are built, from a watering site develops a housing site, a settled place.

It is safe to conclude, based on the early German sources and on my informants' insistence, that in pre-European times the Herero were a highly mobile, nomadic people. The kind of semi-desert land they moved through, in which resources—except for a few isolated spots and along waterways—were scarce and unpredictable, also lends support to this view.

Consequently, homesteads or camps would probably have been small, temporary, and insubstantially constructed. This is corroborated by the previous sources. It also suggests that homesteads would have been widely scattered over large areas in order to exploit the limited resources more efficiently.[28]

Gibson, referring to the Botswana Herero of 1953, speaks of their "pastoral mobility" and "widely scattered residential units" (1962:618) and labels the Herero "semi-nomadic" (1959a:8). Since, however, he is concerned in these papers with other aspects of Herero society, he does not elaborate on these points.

The best way to characterize present-day Herero in western Botswana is to call them "semi-sedentary." They no longer move their camps about the countryside in search of pasturage and water. Homesteads remain on the same site for years. Permanent wells are dug nearby. When pasturage in the area of the homestead becomes scarce or poor, a cattle post is set up where grass is better and most of the herd is moved there. One or two residents of the homestead go with the cattle to the cattle post. The others remain at the homestead to tend a few cattle that provide milk and the small stock from which they occasionally pick a slaughter animal for meat.

Each homestead has access to two kinds of wells. Near every homestead is its individual well which provides drinking water and water for washing. For simplicity I shall call this the drinking well. Strictly speaking, the drinking well belongs to the homestead. But in practice anyone may drink from the well. Permission of the *omuini* is not needed, though it is considered a courtesy to request his permission. This is merely a formality, however, for permission is never denied. The Herero say, "You cannot refuse a thirsty person water from your well to drink. It is the same as if he came to your hut and asked for water. You could not refuse."

The attitude is entirely different for the other type of well: the livestock well. Not even the herdsmen seeing to the watering of the animals may drink here. The livestock well is not the property of a single homestead. Several homesteads—three to five—share it. It is their communal property, and no other homestead may use it. None of the homesteads using it will normally be located more than two or three miles from it.

While the drinking well is just a bucket-and-chain affair or windlass (the aperture being covered by logs and enclosed by a pole fence), the livestock well is more elaborately constructed. Though a few are hand-operated, many livestock wells today are pump-driven. They are divided into two adjacent sections, each surrounded by high thorn bush. One section, with an opening about ten feet wide, contains a trough from which the animals drink. The trough is made of wood or tin, is about eight feet long, a foot to a foot-and-a-half wide, and about one foot deep. Thorn bush or poles line one side of the trough, so access to the water from that side is impossible. Hence, the animals must line up to drink along the free side, and only five or six can do so at once. (This facilitates control of the animals by the herdsmen.) The trough is filled by a hose leading from a large reservoir tank in the other section. The well itself and the pump are also located in this section. One such livestock well is shown in Figure 12. Mention of the homesteads that use this well leads into a discussion of community composition.

The livestock well diagrammed in Figure 12 is located in the northwestern section of an area in southern Makakun known in Otjiherero as *orutjandja*. It is a flat, treeless area, a basin or pan, roughly oval in outline. This particular *orutjandja* is about two miles long and a mile to a mile-and-a-quarter wide.

Only two Herero settlements, a cluster of four homesteads on the northern side and a cluster of three on the southern side, are located around the *orutjandja* at its western end. (Other homesteads, primarily Tswana, are also located at this *orutjandja*.) Appendix F contains an outline drawing of their relative positions.

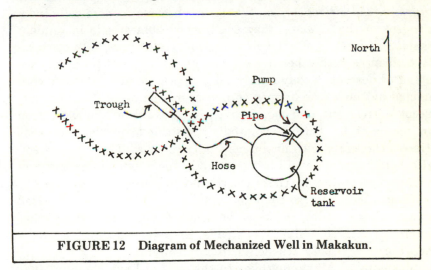

FIGURE 12   Diagram of Mechanized Well in Makakun.

The livestock well depicted in Figure 12 belongs to the four homesteads of the northern cluster. These are the ones identified above as homesteads A, D, E, and one other (homestead F in the appendices). A similar well is found for the southern cluster, which consists of the three related Otjiporo homesteads that served above as our example of a case of homestead segmentation. My comments here will concentrate on the northern cluster livestock well since more time in the field was spent there than at any other.

The four owners of the homesteads are members of three different patrisibs. Two belong to Ohorongo, one to Omakoti, and the last to Ongueuva. These represent three different phratries as well. Informants were questioned on this, since it was thought that related homesteads would be located near each other, as is indeed the case with the southern cluster of Otjiporo homesteads. It turns out that today this southern cluster is the exception. In fact, it is the only case in Makakun of a cluster being composed of only related homesteads. (Part of the explanation for the Otjiporo cluster is that it came into existence, that is, the original homestead segmented, relatively recently.)

The Herero claim that formerly it was related homesteads that formed neighborhood clusters.[29] The Herero who came to Botswana, however, were few in number, poor, and originally from various *otuzo* in South West Africa. When they became economically independent of the Tswana, they established homesteads in random fashion, regardless of patrisib affiliation, and entered into cooperative alliances with other homesteads on the basis of proximity instead of descent. Today nearly all cooperative activities are conducted by those who happen to live near each other. Common descent is irrelevant, and cooperative activities are no longer phrased in terms of it. This is pointedly illustrated by the fact that Herero cooperate with anyone, even Tswana, who live near them. (Economic activities will be taken up in the next chapter and provide documentation for these assertions concerning cooperation.)

Thus, a large Herero community such as Makakun is comprised of a number of widely scattered homesteads which cluster together in groups of three to five homesteads. Interspersed throughout the area are other tribal settlements, mainly Tswana.

Makakun (or Makakung) lies to the west of Lake Ngami.[30] It is the oldest of Herero settlements in Botswana, for it was to the area of Makakun that the earliest Herero immigrants came and it was here that a large percentage of the later immigrants settled. Makakun is estimated[31] to be about thirty miles north to south and about ten miles east to west.

According to informants Makakun, until recently, contained about ten or twelve homestead clusters, consisting on an average of four homesteads each. If each homestead is the residence for an average of fifteen people (the range of population for homesteads visited was from five to about 28 to 30), and thus 60 per cluster, we can estimate the upper population of Herero for Makakun's 300 square miles at about 600–720 souls. This is not the total population for Makakun, however, since other peoples, such as Tswana, Bushmen, Mbukushu, live in the area. (The Tswana live in villages or homesteads similar to those of the Herero, while the others are scattered individuals or small groups who hire themselves out to Tswana and Herero.)

Informants state, however, that because of the severe drought affecting the arid and semi-arid regions of northern and southern Africa at present, about half of Makakun's Herero population has moved. They have gone north to Shakawe where water is obtained from the Okavango River. Many Herero still in Makakun will then be in a better position to exploit the existing resources since they will have less competition for them. By dividing their herds between homesteads and cattle posts, a larger area is available for exploitation.

A similar process is occurring in Makunda, another larger Herero community in Ghanzi district near the border of South West Africa. About three years ago, before the drought came to Makunda, there were 100–150 homesteads in a dense array there. Today there are only thirteen, a drop in population of about 90 percent. The majority of the community has moved to an area some fifteen to thirty miles to the northeast of Makunda where wells are more productive and where formerly many cattle posts were situated.

But movement today is not as easy as it once was. The national government owns all land. Individuals or groups may lease it from the government but they may not own it. If the Herero wish to buy or sell leasing rights or if they wish to move their homesteads permanently, they must obtain permission from the district land board. In Ngamiland this is the Tawana Land Board. It is multitribal in composition, and one Herero is a member. According to informants, the land board has had jurisdiction over the Herero for only the past two years (it must be remembered that Botswana has been in existence as an independent country only a few years). Before that time, they say, they could settle pretty much anywhere they pleased without specific authorization. Today they can move their homesteads only temporarily without consulting the land board.

This fact, which is an illustration of Bates' (1971:109) contention that the state "is often a more critical factor in determining land use relations than the local ecology," enables us to understand more readily how the Herero have changed from the "inveterate nomads" of the earliest literature, to the "semi-nomads" of whom Gibson speaks, to the "semi-sedentary" Herero of 1973. The erosion of former nomadic ways seems to have resulted from the increased interference and constraints stemming from the larger or more powerful political entities with which the Herero have had to contend. To borrow from Bates (1971:127), their increased sedentism is "best intelligible as a political response to other communities and the state."[32]

SUMMARY

Changes in homestead configuration are outlined in this chapter. These changes are interpreted as due to the disappearance of a physical focus. This physical focus, the *okuruo* (or "sacred hearth"), is absent because the traditions which it symbolized and which were reinforced through ritual are passing away. The traditions are declining because the former relationship of the Herero to their cattle, which these traditions reinforced and legitimated, has been redefined, and this has led to a redefinition of the Herero relationship to the ancestors. The economic redefinition is of cattle as a market commodity, property that is sold (chapter 2). Thus, the effect of cattle sale on other aspects of social organization is suggested.

I have attempted to outline the Herero double descent system and suggest that its use as a referent for social behavior has diminished. This is exemplified by the absence of former descent-based activities such as reciprocal curing among patrisibs within a phratry. The interpretation, elaborated in succeeding chapters, for the decline in these descent-ordered institutionalized activities is that the use of descent as a referent for social behavior depended on a particular organization of labor revolving around cattle as ritually important property. That is, the former economic orientation toward cattle maintained that cattle were exclusive property to be kept within a group and not to be sold to outsiders. The religious ideology reinforcing this control over resources asserted that cattle were a gift from, and held in trust for, the ancestors. The group that shared the obligation of caring for cattle, then, were those who shared a set of ancestors—in other words, those claiming common descent. The sale of ritually important cattle is incongruent with this framework, for it introduces "strangers" into a formerly exclusive kinship relationship. So when cattle selling became the practice, the organization of social relations based on the former economy underwent an adjustment which brought it more in line with economic reality (chapters 2 and 3).

The de-emphasis of the matrilineal side of the double descent system is consonant with this shift in economic orientation. Since. cattle are now primarily individually owned and disposed of and the individual claim to rights over cattle, as opposed to group rights, is upheld by the non-Herero courts, especially regarding court decisions unfavorable to matrilineal inheritance, the claim to authority over the resource by matrikin has been eroded (chapter 3). Consequently, the position of matrilineage, matrisib, and phratry in the social organization generally has been weakened.

Finally, a description of community composition further underscores the unimportance among present-day Herero of descent and the idiom of kinship as organizational principles. Rather, the current situation does not invoke relatedness to stabilize interaction. Geographical proximity and a common interest in producing what is now conceived of as a marketable product (cattle) are sufficient in themselves to foster reliable cooperative relations (chapter 3). So once again the change to cattle sale is interpreted as responsible for further changes in social relations.

The scattering of descent-phrased units over a wide area also contributes, in conjunction with the impersonal relations engendered by a market orientation, to the erosion of descent as a behavior referent.

Fallers (1965:115) makes a similar point:

> It is apparent that where, as in Busambira, the local unity
> and continuity of the patrilineage has been broken, individuals'
> day-to-day social relations will be less structured in lineage
> terms. Where few or none of a person's neighbors are lineage-
> mates, the lineage can hardly loom large as a context for social
> interaction . . . It would seem likely that the persistence of an
> institutional norm as an effective part of an individual's social
> personality is, at least in part, a function of the frequency with
> which he has an opportunity to act in terms of it. If this is so,
> the motivation to follow lineage norms will tend to atrophy in
> the person who seldom sees his lineage-mates. Though it may
> be technically possible for him to maintain interaction with
> them, he will tend rather to be influenced by the easier and
> more frequent contacts which he has with his non-kin
> neighbors.

Lastly, the growth of a market orientation and the reliance on
specialists (as in the use of non-Herero laborers for such tasks as
roof construction) and in increased reliance on nonlocally produced
goods (such as commercial metal utensils, Western-style clothes,
and domicile furnishings) are also indicated in this chapter (ex-
plored further in chapter 2).

NOTES

[1] On the configuration of the Herero homestead, see Gibson
(1952:129–31; 1956:112–15); Vedder (1928:180–1); and von Francois
(1896:168–9).

[2] Many more goats than sheep were in evidence among the Ngamiland
Herero. Several homesteads had goats but no sheep at all. A count was not
made, however, and the Herero could provide no figures.

[3] Gibson (1956:123) identifies the *omusaona* bush *(Acacia detines)* as the
proper type for this use in Ngamiland, though Luttig (1933:26) mentions
the employment of the *omuvapu* bush as well in South West Africa.
Omuvapu was identified by Gibson (1956:123) as *Grevia sp.* The correct
spelling (Gibson, personal communication) is *Grewia*.

According to myth, Mukuru, the original Herero, sprang with his cattle from the *omumborumbonga* tree. For accounts of the Herero creation myth, see Brincker (1900:173–4); Dannert (1906:3–4); Hahn (1869:498); Luttig (1933:19, 25); Vedder (1928:165, 1938:131–2).

⁴Gibson had previously (1956) given the meaning "owner" to *omuini,* and my informants confirmed this translation. In an effort to make the term clear to me, an informant picked up my cigaret lighter and said, "Just as you are *omuini* to this, a man is *omuini* to his *onganda.*"

⁵For earlier descriptions of huts (including appearance, construction, contents, and furnishings), see Buttner (1883:490; 1884:386); Gibson (1956:112–13; 1959a:13); Hahn (1869:247–8); Vedder (1928:168–9, 181, 192, 199–200); von Francois (1896:166–7).

⁶Concubinage and childwealth have been previously discussed by Gibson (1959a:25–8). Today, the distinction Gibson notes between "concubinage" and "amour" seems to be fading, and the concubinal relationship for a married man tends to exhibit the more informal characteristics of "amour." The "concubine" (*omusuko,* pl. *ovasuko*) usually lives in her father's homestead rather than in her consort's. If children result from the union, genetricial rights are vested in the mother's father—and the child takes on the father's patrisib affiliation—unless her consort pays child-wealth for them. Childwealth consists of a "gift" offered to the concubine's father. (If this is not paid and the woman marries someone other than her consort, the bridewealth paid by the groom makes the children his.) The usual amount of childwealth nowadays in four heifers. I could elicite no term in Otjiherero for "childwealth" (which Gibson [1956:121 gives as *okatjivereko*), but there is a phrase: *ovina vio ku kuata omuatje* ("things," or a gift, "for taking a child").

⁷Material regarding marriage is not presented in this work, for it is difficult to determine its significance for social change. This is due primarily to the fact that the previous literature offers various reports regarding which units were exogamous and which were not. Since we cannot confidently determine from the available literature what marriage rules were for the Herero in South West Africa, it is difficult to evaluate what the present situation signifies in terms of change.

Thus I say the *omuini* of homestead E may have contracted an inappropriate marriage, for he married within his own *oruzo* (patrisib). On the other hand, because of a previous "inappropriate" marriage, his bride was in the appropriate genealogical relationship (that of *omuramue* or "cross-cousin") to him to be taken as a spouse. Not enough time was spent in the field on the subject of kinship and marriage for me to be able to classify this marriage with any confidence or to determine marriage rules generally from the data I collected on 28 marriages.

[8]Some literature relevant to this technique is: Geoghegan (1969, 1970a, 1970b, 1970c); Goodenough (1956); Howard (1963); Izmirlian (1969); Keesing (1967, 1970).

[9]Herero may travel miles over rough country to see a doctor. I met one man who had traveled with a larger group from their home in Makunda to the hospital in Ghanzi. From there he was going to travel across the Kalahari to Lobatse to consult an optometrist! (The Herero suffer from eye disease and discomfort caused primarily by the swarms of flies their cattle attract.)

[10]Examples of relevant literature are: Faris (1969); Forde (1950), Goody (1961); Leach (1962); Murdock (1940); Ottenberg (1968); and D. M. Schneider (1962). Scheffler (1966) provides an examination of the generic issues of descent, descent group, descent construct, and so on.

[11]I distinguish between groups and categories on the basis of whether or not the members act together for some purpose as members of these units. When people get together to do things together, I call such a collectivity of persons a group. It is an organized action-set of persons. (By organized is meant that there are principles by which the collectivity of persons structures itself for some purpose or purposes.) A category, however, is a classificatory device (a way of classifying persons), the members of which category do not act as a group for any purpose. My application of the term category here to descent-ordered units differs from the sociologist's category of "all people with red hair" (a statistical category) in that in the present case the categorization is based on some culturally shared notion or concept of descent (Scheffler's "construct") which implies some kind of recognized relationship among the individuals involved, rather than simply being based on a physical or other accidental characteristic.

Thus, my identification of Herero descent organization as a double descent system does not rely on the existence of actual patri- and matri-groups but on recognized units (groups or categories) which are based on principles of patrilineal and matrilineal descent.

In the present work, then, sib is generically defined (altering slightly the definition found in R. A. I. 1951:28) as a group or category of persons of both sexes, membership in which group or category is determined by uni-lineal descent or filiation (the latter criterion being intended to cover those cases in which sib membership is not determined by descent from a distant ancestor but is governed by the rule that a child is a member of the same sib of which his parent, father or mother, is a member), and which group or category is symbolically represented (by a name, a set of taboos, an emblem, etc.).

Based on this definition, we may describe a Herero *oruzo* as a patrisib (membership in which is directly determined by and is the same as one's father's—i.e., pater's—*oruzo* membership, and the internal differentiation of which is based on agnatic descent lines). It is asserted by informants that *otuzo* were once (though they are no longer) more or less localized on the basis of an agnatic construct (or notion of patrilineal relationship among the members). And we may describe an *eanda* as a matrisib (affilia-tion to which is directly determined by and is the same as one's mother's *eanda* membership). *Omaanda* are nonlocalized categories of uterine rela-tionship (i.e., based on a uterine construct or notion of matrilineal relation-ship), the individual members of which are geographically dispersed but re-tain the construct identifying them each with the others through common female relatives.

[12]Van Horn (1972:6) asserts that the Herero *oruzo* meets Murdock's (1949:68) criteria for "clan." I disagree, for Murdock's second specification is that a clan "must have residential unity," a qualification the *oruzo* no longer meets—if, that is, it ever did.

[13]The number of *otuzo* seems not to be fixed. This is due 1) to the fission of one *oruzo* into two or more segments which at first may be considered lineages of the same patrisib but after time attain *oruzo* status or 2) to the dying out of the male members of an *oruzo*, so that eventually it becomes extinct. The former process seems no longer to operate in Botswana be-cause of the small number of Herero there.

Several authors mention the names of some *otuzo* or provide lists of them: Dannert (1906:13ff); Gibson (1952:162ff., 1956:119ff.); Irle (1917:353–4); and Viehe (1902:110ff). From these sources and from Gib-son's unpublished field notes, I compiled a master list of 36 *otuzo* which I checked with my Herero informants. Appendix C presents the results in tabular form of my informants' responses to the question, "Is this a Herero *oruzo*?" An affirmative consensus was reached for only twenty and an additional *oruzo,* which to my knowledge does not appear in any of the earlier accounts, was uncovered. (See also ch. 3, p. 118, and note 6 for that chapter.)

[14]According to some informants, the two brothers came upon a *slaughtered* sheep. The older brother said he was hungry and would eat the sheep. The younger brother objected, saying such sheep should not be consumed. The two disagreed and went their separate ways, giving rise to different customs.

[15]A slightly different version is offered by some informants. While the brothers were searching out a suitable site to set up an *onganda* (homestead), they were offered an ox (by whom is unknown). The eldest brother accepted the animal and built his herd around it. The other brothers said that cattle of that type should not be reared and went their separate way.

[16]The earlier literature indicates that *otuzo* restrictions formerly obtained in other areas (such as taboos on plant foods) as well. This is no longer true today. For an orderly summary of what the earlier sources have to say regarding these restrictions, see Gibson (1952:162ff.).

[17]The Herero word for cattle is *ozongombe* (s. *ongombe*).

[18]For each *oruzo,* besides its specific *oruzo* cattle, certain animals (cattle, sheep, and even wild animals) are identified as *izera* ("taboo"). *Izera* animals may not be kept or eaten. This restriction is probably more consistently observed by present-day Herero than are any others, though breaches occur.

[19]By comparing the table in Appendix D with Gibson's summary of earlier sources (1952:162ff.), it can be seen that there are no really radical divergences, though there are some differences. Where these occur, I tend to trust my own data, since nearly two dozen informants contributed to their compilation.

[20]References for *omaanda* are: Dannert (1906:17–18); Gibson (1952:168, 1956:126–7); Hahn (1869:501–2); Irle (1917:352–3); Viehe (1902:113ff.); von Francois (1896:172).

[21]Two (out of about two dozen) informants dissent. They claim that only one *eanda,* Omuekuenombura, is so divided. This is in direct contradiction

to Schapera's statement (1945:26) that all *omaanda* have subdivisions *except* Omuekuenombura.

[22]This terminology is not original; Gibson (1956) employed it before me.

[23]This contrasts sharply with earlier reports (e.g., Viehe 1902:109, 112) that state emphatically that every Herero knew his *eanda* and his matrilineal descent.

[24]Viehe (1902:113ff.) provides the most detailed information on these myths. His versions are generally comparable to the information I received. I deliberately refrained from relating to my informants the myths he supplies in an effort to determine to what extent present-day Herero remember them. The answer provides another indication that the old ways are in their death throes. No men at all knew anything about the myths. Some women could supply a few fragments. (I was hampered in collecting data from women since, because I am male, my access to female informants was limited.)

[25]The matrisib Omuekuenatja indicates something to the effect of "an *eanda* that is not an *eanda*," just as the patrisib Omuhinaruzo means "without an *oruzo*." In response to the question of whether the members of these sibs might have been the offspring of whites or other non-Herero and Herero, informants were emphatic in their denial. They give no explanation for these sibs. (The members of Omuhinaruzo, incidentally, assume all the restrictions of Ongueuva *oruzo*.)

[26]Gibson reports (personal communication) that he actually witnessed in-sib curing, specifically at least two cases in which a father cured his own child. My informants' generalization that the *omuini* functioned as *omurangere* for his homestead (see chapter 3) also contradicts their assertion on other occasions that individuals sought out distantly related *ovarangere* when they were ill. The point to be emphasized, however, is that no matter what the former practice actually was, it no longer obtains today.

[27]Formerly, the Herero had several categories of shamans. For relevant information, see Brincker (1900:69, 71, 74, 86–8, 92); Buttner (1883:491, 1884:387); Dannert (1906:9); Gibson (1956:120); Hahn (1869:504–5); Irle (1917:359–64); Vedder (1928:173–5, 184); von Francois (1896:194, 200–1).

[28]Extrapolating further on the meager data available, it might also be contended that cattle posts, arms of the homesteads, arose primarily as the more mobile counterparts or extensions of homesteads that were established near some fairly constant water site.

[29]We will have occasion to discuss this subject again later, especially in chapter 3.

[30]Lake Ngami has been dry for many years, as Sillery (1952:20) has previously pointed out.

[31]Because of travel and other difficulties (including the high cost of gasoline) accurate measurements could not be taken. Appendix G contains a map of Makakun prepared while in the field.

[32]The local-level stimulus for the emergence of particular indigenous institutions and organizations of social relations may be sought in ecological influences or economic necessity in band and tribal society. In state societies or when dealing with so-called primitive societies being encroached upon by state societies, the state itself may be the crucial factor in understanding form and change in social organization and its institutional framework. Their "stimulus is political rather than economic or technological per se" (Cohen 1969a:676).

2

Economy and the Organization of Labor

The economic pursuits of the Herero are various. Hence, they are far removed from the somewhat romantic ideal image of the "pure pastoralist." Cattle herding historically has been, and remains today, their primary subsistence activity. Yet they also are engaged, in decreasing order of importance, in trading, hunting, and cultivation. Though none of these ancillary activities approaches pastoralism in importance, they nevertheless provide a diversity which contributes to the viability of the economic system.[1]

LIVESTOCK MANAGEMENT AND ANIMALS KEPT

Herding is still today a male activity, as it was in the past.[2] Men construct corrals and see to their maintenance; they herd and water the cattle; they perform castrations; they assist at births when necessary; and they do the slaughtering. The only cattle-related activities performed by females is the daily milking.

Herero cattle management may be characterized as laissez-faire. Except for the rainy season, which begins in late October or early November and lasts till early or mid-April, cattle are normally not shut in the corrals at night. Instead they spend the night in the pasture they have been grazing during the day. Herdsmen will occasionally travel, by horse or donkey, to the pasture to look over the herd, checking for injured or sick animals or for signs of predators, but rarely will they spend an entire day with it. It is enough for them to know what pasturage the animals are using at any particular time. When grass in one area has become so thin that the herd is beginning to wander too far in search of food, a herdsmen will scout around until he finds another unoccupied, suitable area and then lead the herd to it. If the new area is too far from the corrals of the homestead, then a new cattle post will be established or the old one relocated and a well dug so that the herd can return periodically (approximately once every two days) for water.

The entire herd, however, is not allowed to wander at will. Calves are kept in the corral. They are not allowed to move with the herd, nor are they watered in the morning with the other animals. Instead they remain in the corral until evening when their mothers return to nurse them. These cows return every night to their calves, regardless of whether or not the entire herd returns.

During the rainy season a close watch is kept over the entire herd. Unlike conditions during the dry season, when good pasturage tends to be found in isolated and fairly well-delineated areas (thus influencing the herd to remain in a group for grazing), more good grass is available over a wide area. Consequently, individual animals tend to stray from the herd and become separated from it. If an animal wanders too far, it may not find its way back to the herd, for tracks are easily obliterated in the wet season. (Buttner [1883:555] noted a similar observation for the Herero in South West Africa, as did von Francois [1896:259]: "herds usually stay together, except when there are heavy rainfalls.") Hence, cattle must be herded into corrals at night and herdsmen accompany them to pasture during the day to keep them from straying.

Cattle pastoralism in semi-arid lands requires the digging of waterholes, since naturally occurring surface water is almost nonexistent. Buttner (1883:530–2) provides the most detailed account of how wells were dug in former times. It was, to say the least, a laborious task requiring the cooperative labor of many men, for the well had to be dug deep and the water passed from bottom to top in hand-to-hand fashion.

Precisely how this task group was formed is never stated. Did the people involved in the labor itself or, perhaps more important, in control of that labor consider themselves relatives? Were they from the same homestead, the same lineage, related lineages of a sib, or related sibs in a phratry? From previous literature regarding spatial organization we have observed that community composition in prehistoric times probably tended to be phrased in terms of patrilineal descent, that common descent was probably invoked for behavioral purposes, and that the lower the level of segmentation, the greater the probability of proximity because of relative recency of segmentation. These conclusions and the fact that herds were conceived as held in trust for the ancestors, lead us to infer that those who cooperated or oversaw cooperative labor in tending the herd and establishing drinking places for it, were more likely to be related — or at least to claim relationship — than not. (See chapter 3.)

But we have seen that presently homestead clusters (those using a single well) are normally formed on the basis of proximity without regard to descent. This was cited as an indication of the direction of social change among the Herero of western Botswana. Yet well-digging provides even a further indication of social change, for the Herero no longer dig the wells themselves. Instead they hire specialists to do it. These are usually Tswana, but there are also a few Herero. The herdsman contracts with the specialist to dig the well. The latter, in turn, hires four or five others as workers. At the completion of the task, he is paid four to six cattle or about R240 (i.e. $360). Out of this he pays his laborers.

In the case of a drinking well, the cost is borne by the homestead alone. In the case of a livestock well, the several homesteads of the cluster share the cost. If the livestock well is to be pump-driven, there are the additional costs for the equipment and labor to install it, plus the continued expenses for such maintenance items as motor oil which must be purchased from traders. The Herero, therefore, are becoming increasingly dependent on external resources and commercial markets in pursuing their livelihood.

Cattle from the several *ozonganda* or homesteads that use the well come without prompting to the well and congregate there, waiting impatiently for their turn at the trough. (At one watering I estimated the total number of cattle grouped about the well to be

1000–1200.)[3] Fights often break out among the animals as they
jostle one another to get closer to the entrance of the trough section
of the well.

About a dozen men from the homesteads see to the orderly watering of the animals. Armed with their walking sticks (every adult
male carries a homemade walking stick) or with heavy branches,
they walk among the animals, keeping them docile by cracking
troublemakers harshly across the forehead. Three to six men bar the
entrance to the well and, by throwing rocks and sticks and shouting,
keep the animals at a distance of about ten feet from the opening.
This is to allow the animals that have already drunk to leave the
well and to control the number of animals permitted in at any one
time (usually a half-dozen or so) to drink. But even though the number of animals inside the well area is kept low at any one time, fights
still occur at the trough.[4] So two or three men remain within this
area to control the animals. After each group of six or so cattle has
been watered, the animals saunter off to pasture.

Cattle grazing. During the dry season, cattle roam largely untended over the
countryside seeking pasturage. (See Chapter 2 for a description of herding practices.)

Adult sheep and goats prudently wait until most of the larger animals are watered before approaching the well. They are managed by the herdsmen in much the same way as are the larger stock, except of course that more animals are allowed access to the trough at once.

Goats in goat corrals. Management of goats (which consists primarily of watering the animals and corralling them in the evenings) is the responsibility of women and children. (See Chapter 2.)

Kids (and lambs)[5] which have been kept in their corral during the morning watering are provided with drinking water at the homestead itself. This is done around mid-morning and is a responsibility of the women who are assisted by children. A large basin or tin tub is filled and the animals are released to drink. Any adolescents or adults that wander into camp at this time have to be beaten with sticks to keep them from the water, which is solely for the young. This is a tiring exercise, for these animals are exasperatingly persistent and will suffer an amazing amount of abuse before giving up their efforts.

After the morning watering, the smaller animals are not confined. They go to join the herd. Goats, able to subsist on sparser vegetation than cattle, rarely wander far from the homestead. In the early

evening, around five o'clock, the goats return en masse to the homestead accompanying their arrival with a cacophonous announce-
ment of their advent. They are allowed to wander about the camp
for awhile but are corralled before dark.

Cattle begin to arrive at the homestead, if they return at all,
around dark and continue to straggle in for the next hour or two.
They lie about the periphery of the homestead or enter the corral
but, as noted, are not corralled except during the wet season.

Other animals kept by the Herero are donkeys, horses, dogs, and
chickens. Horses and donkeys are kept for transportation. Oxen are
not ridden, although there is some indication that the Herero at one
time used them for riding, yet the practice was short-lived and, according to Buttner (1883:490), was unknown in pre-European
times.

Horses and donkeys are kept in only small numbers, two or three
to each homestead. Though all homesteads have donkeys, horses
are found in about one homestead out of three. It has never been the
practice for the Herero to store hay (Buttner 1883:493), so these
animals must be released to graze, as are the cattle. Both horses and
donkeys are watered with the other livestock at the well.

Dogs are a common sight at all homesteads. They were originally
kept as watchdogs, but they also serve as hunting dogs. Both
Buttner (1883:490,552) and von Francois (1896:273) mention this
as well. But dogs are never used to assist in herding. It is perhaps
their irrelevance to herding activities, the primary concern of the
Herero and the mainstay of their economy, which in part accounts
for their ill-treatment. Although dogs are allowed to feed on the left-
over scraps and the blood of slaughtered animals,[6] they are not
usually fed, except during the rainy season when they are given
some surplus milk. They skulk about a homestead, little more than
skin and bones, forever searching for something to eat. They are
timid around the homestead residents, for they are often kicked and
struck (children delight in tormenting them); but they come to life
at the approach of a stranger, barking and scampering about fur-
iously. A shout or threatening gesture is enough, though, to quiet
them. Nevertheless, they serve their purpose: their initial barking
warns the residents of a stranger's approach.

Children riding a donkey. Herero keep donkeys, horses, dogs, and chickens in addition to cattle, sheep, and goats. (See Chapter 2.)

Though Buttner (1883:490) says that the Herero "don't ever keep chickens" and that "the native Herero don't even like to eat chicken eggs . . . [for] the chicken is an unclean animal to them," it is not uncommon today to find several chickens wandering about a homestead. Like dogs, chickens are not fed or housed. They must fend for themselves. Eggs are eaten,[7] as are the chickens themselves when they die, though they are not killed for consumption.

Cattle, goats, and sheep are also eaten, as is some wild game, whereas horses, donkeys, and dogs are not. The animal most commonly slaughtered for meat is the goat. Today there are few "sacrificial" slaughterings (i.e., the killing of animals for avowed religious purposes), and sheep and cattle (formerly the only acceptable "sacrificial" animals) are often explicitly slaughtered for consumption. This is contradictory to the former practice of the Herero to

A goat being slaughtered for market day in Makakun. (See Chapter 2 and footnote 12.)

reserve such animals (primarily cattle) for religious occasions and to treat them as a ritual rather than as an economic commodity. Such treatment of and attitudes toward cattle have become well known as the "cattle-complex" (Herskovits 1926). Although Schneider (1957) has effectively demonstrated the subsistence use of cattle in societies having the cattle-complex, this does not deny the fact that conceptualization regarding cattle in such societies does not admit their subsistence functions.

The Herero today, however, no longer maintain that cognitive orientation toward their herds that is characteristic of the cattle-complex. That they once did seems clear.[8] For instance, today herds are owned individually by the *omuini* of the homestead, though he gives individual animals, primarily small stock, to other residents. (Individual ownership is not refuted by the fact that animals in a homestead may be owned by several agnates, for they do not own all the animals jointly. Rather, the herd is composed of smaller herds,

Herero hire Tswana, Bushmen, Mbukushu, and others as laborers (see Chapter 2.) Here two Bushmen workers are slaughtering an animal that injured its leg and was unable to graze with the herd.

each owned separately, which are kept together for convenience.) Formerly, according to Wagner (1952:5–6), this was not the case. Cattle, he says, were . . . "consecrated to the ancestors, . . . [and] the individual stockowner was, in a sense, merely trustee of the cattle," which were the property of his sib. The owner . . . "was responsible to his ancestors for the proper care and augmentation of the herds entrusted to him." The Herero were concerned to increase the numbers of *oruzo* cattle—it was their obligation to the ancestors to do so—not just to increase the size of the herd in general. Today, having lost their former intimate connection with the ancestors, the Herero feels his cattle are truly his property and his concern is to increase their total number, irrespective of their formal categories, though vestiges of former customs remain.

HUNTING

Hunting is also a Herero economic activity, albeit of minor importance in comparison to herding. But despite its limited contribution to Herero subsistence, men find it an exciting and psychologically satisfying pursuit, and they discuss the subject with obvious relish.

Rarely, if at all, does a Herero hunt alone. A hunting party may consist of from two to twenty or twenty-five men on horseback, armed with rifles and accompanied by their dogs. A hunting party may stay out for several days, or in the case of a large expedition in search of much game, as long as two weeks.

Dogs are specifically trained for hunting nowadays, though they were not in the past (Buttner 1883:552). Boys, however, learn by trial-and-error. A son is given a gun by his father and he joins a hunting party. He learns by doing.

Just as cooperation in herding activities occurs among nonrelatives, so does hunting. Hunting parties are composed not only of Herero but of non-Herero as well. If someone wishes to go hunting, he will try to interest the men from neighboring homesteads in the venture. These then may be joined by Tswana from the area.

The most active hunting season is during the winter from May to August. Because of cooler temperatures, meat can be kept longer with less change of its rotting. But some hunting is also done during the warmer months. How frequently hunting occurs is not set. It occurs irregularly and is dependent on a combination of whim and need. When meat is desired, yet one does not wish to deplete his cattle assets, he hunts. The Herero say a man hunts "when he is willing," that is, when he feels like it.

But in addition to meat for consumption, Herero also hunt for another reason: to acquire commodities with which to barter. (Herero deny that they hunt for sport, though the sparkle in their eyes and the enthusiasm with which they speak of hunting casts doubt on this.) A man may use the meat and skins of wild game as barter items for supplies such as sugar, tea, salt, tobacco, and so on and therefore does not need to sell his cattle. He may also trade game meat for cultivated crops from a Tswana farmer or take the meat, skins, horns, or whatever to a nearby town and sell it outright to a storekeeper for cash.

The market orientation of the Herero was underscored when I asked informants why, if the Herero prize cattle so much, do they sell them at all? Why not simply hunt wild game and sell that? The answer was simple enough but unexpected: because beef brings a better price than game meat.

Animals hunted, the meat of which may also be eaten, include zebra, eland, gemsbuck, springbok, wildebeest, giraffe, and kudu. Some other animals are hunted but the meat is not eaten; for example, elephant (for tusks and other parts which are sold) and lion and leopard (to sell the skins). The Herero state they will shoot anything. If they cannot consume it, they can sell it.

But hunting, like nomadism, can no longer be indulged in freely. Today hunters must apply and pay for licenses, and the government imposes limits and restrictions on the activity. The Herero deeply resent this interference but are resigned to it.

The previous literature makes slight reference to hunting. Little more is noted than that the Herero occasionally hunted (e.g., Irle 1917:358 and Vedder 1928:182). A bit more detail is available for gathering which is a female activity (see Dinter 1912). For example, Hahn (1869:250) lists the following gathered foods: groundnuts, roots, and wild onions, gum of the *Acacia horrida*, various kinds of wild berries, honey, and mushrooms. Vedder (1938:47) provides a similar list. Apparently wild onions were an important vegetable addition to the diet, for a number of sources mention them, and infant girls were referred to as "little onions" (Vedder 1928:176), underscoring, presumably, the female gathering task.

Today in Botswana gathering is a wet-season activity. During the dry season, vegetables are bought in cans from town stores or acquired fresh through trade with neighbors who grow them, or by growing one's own.

CULTIVATION

Women form cooperative activity-groups in only two instances. One is concerned with the preparation for a wedding feast.[9] The other concerns cultivation, especially during harvest time. If there is a large crop and not enough personnel in one *onganda*, then neighbors—even Tswana neighbors—will help, and they receive some of the crop in payment. Cultivation is, therefore, another example illustrating that proximity and not kinship is the basis for cooperation.

According to previous reports (Hahn 1869:485, Vedder 1928:199, von Francois 1896:170), the Herero were introduced to farming by missionaries. Before that time they are said to have grown no crops (Gibson 1962:617). During the 1950's Gibson (1962:628) reports that a few Herero grew maize but had little surplus. The situation today has not changed substantially. The Herero regard farming with utmost disdain. On the average, about one homestead in each cluster has a field for gardening. That this field is located away from the *onganda,* usually to the east of the huts (i.e., behind them), reflects that cultivation is a foreign activity.[10]

The Herero are unwilling to invest a great deal of effort in cultivation. They will only bother themselves if early rains indicate a lengthy wet season. Consequently, because of the current drought, no Herero has engaged in cultivation for the past three years.

If we take the use of the hoe as the defining characteristic of horticulture and the use of the plow and draft animals for agriculture, then it can be said that the Herero engage in both kinds of cultivation. In neither case are the fields irrigated.

Men clear the land (which requires little labor) and construct a thorn bush enclosure for the field to protect it from livestock. Men also do the plowing in those few cases where plowing is necessary. Six or eight oxen are harnessed to the plow, rather than one or two, for the Herero explain that they do not want to tire the animals unduly.

Even in horticulture, it is the men who do the planting. Women tend the field thereafter and do the harvesting. Planting occurs in late November or early December, after the rains have begun, and harvesting is in April.

Crops are grown primarily for consumption by the cultivators themselves, but if there is a surplus, this is sold or traded to neighbors. No food is specifically grown for sale or trade. Herero say that they cultivate in order to introduce variety into their diets without having to sell cattle to buy foodstuffs at town stores.

The primary Herero crop is maize. Corn is a staple in the Herero diet. A homestead either grows its own or buys it from neighbors or from a store. (In the homestead diagrams in chapter 1 and Appendix F, a small structure near the senior wife's hut is identified as"storage for maize.")

TRADING

Trading (the bartering for, or the buying and selling of commodities and products), though difficult to measure, is the most important of ancillary economic activities because it cross-cuts the other two as well as the primary activity of cattle herding. Indeed, though cattle are still important in themselves, since there exists a lingering identification of the Herero people with their herds, the obvious direction of cattle herding today is an increasing orientation toward a market economy, that is, toward raising cattle for sale and profit.

Though the use of cattle (*ozonzere* and *oruzo* cattle, as well as general cattle) as market commodities is a relatively recent development, trading as a general practice is not new to the Herero. This is not surprising in light of several recent publications which have demonstrated the importance for pastoral nomads of contact with nonpastoral groups in order to acquire items the pastoralists themselves do not produce. Such items include grain products or metal for weapons. (See, for example, Salzman 1970, 1971, 1972).

Though information regarding trade among the Herero of former times is meager, there is enough to suggest that it was a not uncommon practice.

Gibson (1962:622) has stated that he found no reports of extensive trading with the Hottentots nor of any trade with the Tswana before 1895, "when some Herero are said to have acquired horses, guns, and ammunition from them in exchange for cattle," and I have found no contradictory evidence.

The two tribal groups with which the Herero did have exchange relations, as Gibson (1962:622) also points out, were the Ambo and the Bergdama. The most extensive trade apparently was conducted with the Ambo. The Herero acquired axes, weapons, iron for weapons and ornaments, and salt in return for cattle and ostrich eggshells (Gibson 1962:620–1 and references therein; Vedder 1928:183; von Francois 1896:165, 167).

Bergdama subjugated by the Herero became their laborers:

> Apparently in post-contact times the Bergdama acquired the art of forging iron, and served the Herero as smiths (Vedder 1938:28, 43); they are variously called servants or serfs, and were paid in food for their services . . . [Gibson 1962:621].

In addition, calabashes and stone pipes were acquired from the Bergdama (Gibson 1962:621; von Francois 1896:167, 168). In regard to tobacco, Vedder (1928:183) says the Herero "know how to grow it but would rather receive it as a present from others." From whom the present was received and under what circumstances are questions he leaves unasked.

Market places among the Herero were established after the arrival of Europeans. Herero traded sheep and oxen for barrels, wagons (von Francois 1896:168), metal implements, and salt (Vedder 1928:183); pelts and ivory for money, rifles, and whiskey (White 1969:81); and sold butter to white settlers (von Francois 1896:169–70).

Today the Herero have grown dependent on markets for many of their needs. For instance, the characteristic dress of the Herero is no longer the leather apron.[11] Men's clothes are Western-style shirts, jackets, trousers, and hats and are bought ready-made at trading stores. Women buy material for dresses and shawls. (The dresses are the long-skirted, high-necked variety—sometimes called Mother

Two Herero girls. The one on the left wears a long dress, which signifies that she is of marriageable age.

Hubbards—inspired by those of the missionary wives of the turn of the century. The Herero women, however, make their dresses from bright-colored, gaily-patterned material.) Everyday utensils are now all commercial. None of the wooden vessels previously used for holding milk are in evidence. The "wooden milk pails, ladles, funnels, bowls, spoons, and beads" which Gibson (1962:622) "found in every household" in Ngamiland have disappeared. Today milking pails are made of metal, as are all pots, plates, cups, eating utensils, and so on, and are purchased at town stores or from mobile markets. This change to metal containers and utensils is not simply a curiosity to be noted; it is an index of drastic change, for in former times it was forbidden for the "consecrated" milk (see chapter 3) to come into contact with metal. Milk vessels had to be made of wood, and these vessels were never washed. To use metal is an offense to the ancestors.

Variations in Herero dress. The boys wear simple leather aprons until their early teens when they begin to dress in store-bought Western clothes. The two girls in the center are sixteen years old. Within a year they will probably don the adult woman's long dress and so indicate their marriageability. (See Chapter 2.)

Other items upon which the Herero have come to rely, such as soap, salt, tea, sugar, matches, tobacco, and so forth, are also purchased from merchants. Pipes are no longer made of stone but are the common wood and plastic type familiar to Westerners. Nearly all Herero men and many women smoke pipes which are bought at town stores.

Town stores are general stores in the broadest sense. In addition to goods, consisting of food, tobacco, clothes, furniture, tools, and so on, one also finds associated with each establishment a gasoline pump (as often empty as not), a pen for cattle, and a scale for weighing livestock. In addition to these fixed trading centers, there are traveling markets. Actually such a market is nothing more than a goods-laden truck that periodically visits the bush settlements. Makakun is visited once a week. The truck comes from Maun every Wednesday and leaves Thursday afternoon. It starts in the north of Makakun and travels southward, stopping for several hours at fixed locations along its route.

A real "market atmosphere" prevails. People dress up in their finest clothes, for the gathering around the truck is as much a social occasion as it is economic. It is a time for people in the area, Herero and non-Herero alike, to gather together and gossip. Food is cooked in advance and shared in a festive mood. Nubile girls flirt with young men, while the married women argue the quality of a bolt of material and older men sit in the shade of a large tree on chairs they have brought with them and lazily discuss their cattle or the drought.

But the purely economic aspects of the occasion are no less apparent. The truck carries a supply of standard items: cloth, sugar, tea, salt, matches, soap, paraffin for lanterns, and so on. It also brings special orders, such as motor oil or a piece of furniture, placed the previous week. In addition to this, all the area residents bring commodities, such as skins, crops, meat, which they hope to sell or exchange among themselves.[12]

This intra-area trade illustrates the shift from kinship-phrased obligations to share as a way of distributing goods to explicitly economic (market-phrased) exchange.

According to my informants, in former times obligations of mutual aid (including giving food, lending cattle, curing the sick, etc.)

were centered within a patrilineal phratry. The reason always given for this is that phratry members share a common body of ancestors. But because of the loss of cattle as a result of the German war in 1904, the former intimate contact with the ancestors was seen as broken or at least severely weakened—symbolized today by the absence of the *okuruo,* the sacred hearth, at which all ritual that strengthened the bond with the ancestors was conducted (see below). Cattle lost their "sacred" character. So as the Herero struggled in the early lean years in Botswana to reconstitute their herds, they did so in a new context, that is, in a situation in which they saw themselves as divorced from the ancestors.

Some lip service was given to reviving the "traditional ways," but this was never fully achieved. The Herero had grown accustomed to European luxuries and were unwilling to surrender them. If they were to continue to enjoy the material benefits of European civilization, and if they were to acquire enough wealth to purchase more and more European goods, they would have to establish large herds of cattle once again. If, however, they were to use these cattle for the new objective of acquiring European goods, they would have to orient their economic activities to this end (i.e., for sale) instead of along traditional lines of pleasing the ancestors by amassing great herds of ritually important cattle. Thus their *reasons* for keeping cattle changed. No longer were cattle a sacred trust and invested with religious significance. Now they were becoming economic commodities to be used to satisfy needs which developed in response to exposure to exogenous influences. No longer were they only an end in themselves; they had become a means to an end.

This alteration in economic objectives had the effect, in the Herero view, of setting the ancestors at an even greater distance from the people, further weakening the organization of social relations along traditional lines. Since the bond of common ancestors was of diminished significance, it became less important for those who lived near each other and maintained cooperative relations to phrase their interaction in terms of descent. When aid was needed, one turned to one's neighbors because they were neighbors, not because they were seen as related by descent. Tasks, such as well-digging, which required manpower in excess of that which a single homestead might be able to provide, were accomplished through cooperation of neighboring homesteads, without the necessity of invoking kinship and the ancestors. This matter will be covered in more detail shortly. The present juncture is an appropriate point at which to trace the evolution of the practice of selling ritually important cattle—probably the single most important aspect of change in Herero society.

Cattle are the primary economic assets of the Herero. The exchange and sale of cattle, as indicated, are not new to the Herero. But the sale of cattle on a regular basis to acquire cash and other goods and the sale of all categories of cattle, including those that were ritually important and not just general cattle (*ozongombe za ka uriri*), are recent developments.

The previous literature is replete with references to the "sacred" nature of the herds and the reluctance of the Herero to sell cattle. For example, Vedder (1928:206) states that "the oruzo educate its group . . . that all property should be regarded as an ancestral blessing. This blessing implies in the first instance the acquisition of cattle and possessions, nor may such a blessing be disposed of. . . . the Herero regards his possessions in cattle as the best way of pleasing his ancestors." Irle (1917:355) reports that "sacrificial oxen" could not be used as meat or sold, that traders who seized these animals as payment for debts "had to pay with their lives for this frivolity," and that "death befell any Herero himself who seized these animals, slaughtered or sold them."

Yet cattle were sold in the old days, even though, as Buttner (1883:555) says, "cows are only sold to Europeans if some very desirable goods can be gotten in no other way." The key to understanding the seemingly contradictory views (i.e., that the Herero staunchly refused to sell their cattle and, on the other hand, that they often did sell them) lies in Herero cattle categories. *Ozonzere* and *oruzo* cattle simply could not be sold or traded, whereas general cattle could (though the Herero parted with general cattle only with the greatest reluctance). Today all cattle are freely sold, and it is this phenomenon which requires explanation.

All informants unanimously attribute the current common practice of selling ritually important cattle to the desire for European goods. Informants repeatedly declared that it was the desire for supplies, such as sugar and tea, which first induced them to part with their cattle, and that further contact with Europeans aroused their appetites for more and more European goods, which at first were luxuries but soon became necessities. The following excerpts from my field notes are pertinent here.

a) When herds got large, some animals were sold for money. The money was used to buy store goods and supplies. One or two oxen at a time would be sold as money was needed for sugar, shoes, clothes, and the like. Before, the Herero didn't have sugar. But then they tasted it, and liked it, and wanted it. Before, the Herero wore leather apparel. But then they saw and wanted European clothes.

In the early days of cattle selling, general cattle were sold first. If they didn't have any general cattle or if there weren't enough general cattle to bring enough money for what they wanted to buy, they would then sell *oruzo* or *ozonzere* cattle. If they received enough money, they would use some of it to buy a calf to replace an ox that had been sold.

But today Herero sell all cattle indiscriminantly. This is due to the desire to have more and more European things. We want what the whites have. We want clothes and food and trucks. We are making a business out of our cattle.

b) The Herero sell their cattle because of a need for supplies. Before, we supplied all our own needs ourselves. We needed only animal skins. Then after knowing Europeans, we wanted the comforts of European things.

Explanations along these lines were consistently received. In addition, individual informants gave two other reasons: the influence of Christianity and the necessity to brand cattle.

One informant, and only one, said that the British required the Herero to brand their cattle with marks of ownership. They did this, he said, in order to reduce the amount of cattle stealing and to adjudicate more expeditiously disputes regarding cattle and cattle theft. The Herero were opposed to the marking of cattle but were forced to comply. Once the *oruzo* and *ozonzere* cattle were branded, they were defiled and lost their ritual significance. One might as well, therefore, sell the cattle and reap the profits. According to this informant, the marking of cattle broke down the traditional distinctions among cattle categories. In effect, all cattle became general cattle. It is important to note, however, that all other informants questioned about the matter vigorously denied the validity of this explanation. Gibson also casts doubt on this informant's interpretation, for he states (personal communication) that clipping the ears of cattle in distinctive ways has long been a practice of the Herero. We may therefore discount this explanation as a rationalization, one individual's way of assuaging a guilty conscience.

The influence of the missionaries was also cited by some informants as a factor that contributed to the sale of cattle. One informant, who was converted to Christianity in Botswana, said that English missionaries convinced the Herero to sell cattle and to abandon their traditional ways.[13] The conversion to Christianity (referred to by informants as "joining the missionaries"), at first seemed a good idea. The missionaries taught that it was wrong to have many wives, to keep an *okuruo*, to honor ancestors, and to treat cattle as religious items. They taught that cattle are just cattle, dumb beasts that existed for the service of man, that there are not any "sacred" cattle. The Herero gave into this.

But later the Herero decided they had betrayed the ancestors by becoming Christian. They had done, the informant said, a bad thing. They felt irreparably cut off from the ancestors and their former traditions. They no longer felt fit to "consecrate" (*okumakera*, lit., to taste) the milk of the *ozonzere* and *oruzo* cattle. (This alienation and guilt that many elderly Herero feel were mentioned in the introduction.)

None of these factors, alone or in combination, is sufficient to account for the observed change. Further interpretation is required, for other cattle herders faced with similar influences have not found in them adequate inducement to abandon their traditional ways. (See, for example, Hennings 1951 and Schneider 1959).[14]

The explanation is to be found in the fact that the economic foundation of Herero society, their cattle herds, was almost entirely destroyed as a consequence of the German war of 1904. The Herero who fled to Botswana, except for one group, arrived without cattle. The loss of herds and the resultant poverty in which the Herero were plunged led them to hire themselves out to Tswana and others. In other words, the old organization of labor had been thoroughly disrupted. At the same time, the Herero were being subjected to economic influences (which included cattle sale) from their employers and others (primarily Europeans) with whom they were in contact in the new land. When herds were once again established in sufficient numbers to allow the Herero to separate from their former employers, the effects of these exogenous factors influenced the new organization of labor the Herero instituted. Cattle became not only ends in themselves but also means to acquire the new European goods they had been exposed to. This led to the reorganization of other social institutions and behavior more appropriate to the new economic orientation. Descent-ordered units decreased in social importance. Geographical proximity began to replace kinship as a basis for interaction. The loss of ancestors this entailed led to a lapse of religious ritual (which had previously reinforced the former descent-phrased institutions), which is now replaced by secular "entertainments."

The new order, however, is not completely established. Remnants of the old ways remain, chiefly because there are still old men alive who remember how things used to be. When they die, nothing of the old traditions will remain.

CATTLE MARKETS

It is ethnographically useful to complete this chapter with some brief remarks regarding how cattle are sold. In Ngamiland, cattle sales are conducted on an individual basis. Each owner takes a few cattle to a trading store and sells them to the storekeeper at a mutually satisfactory rate. There are no specific market times or areas for the large-scale sale of cattle in Ngamiland as there are in Ghanzi District, though the Ngamiland residents, including the Herero, have petitioned the government to establish a BMC (Botswana Meat Commission) station in the district.

In Ghanzi District markets are held on a regular basis (in June, September, December, and March) and last for a week or so. From the markets cattle are shipped by truck to Lobatse, where the animals are slaughtered and the meat exported.[15]

The Herero receive roughly R6.00–8.00 per hundred pounds from traders for beef on the hoof (the farther from the central processing plant in Lobatse, the ultimate destination of the live animal, the lower the price; thus prices in Ghanzi are higher than in Ngamiland). Hence, a medium-sized ox (about 600–800 pounds) will bring between R36 and R64 ($44–$96).

SUMMARY

This chapter describes the different types of economic activities in which the Herero in western Botswana are engaged, but its main theoretical thrust concerns the effects of the shift in orientation from cattle as sacred trusts to cattle as sale items. When the Herero began to sell cattle regularly, the organization of labor, which invoked kinship and common descent to order the relationships within it, was altered to accomodate this change to a market orientation which included nonkinsmen as significant others. Cattle were formerly conceived as kept in trust for the ancestors by members of a descent-ordered unit. Cattle today are considered to be primarily individually owned and their disposition (sale) is under the control of the herd owner. As items intended for sale, cattle tended to lose their exclusive or sacred nature, eroding thereby the former ideology of which this attitude was an integral part. No longer, therefore, need kinsmen—or individuals considered to be kinsmen (see chapter 3)—be the primary cooperators in the handling of cattle, for the new handling of cattle did not require notions of descent and invocation of the ancestors for its efficient operation. Those near each other cooperate as neighbors without the legitimation of descent because proximity and a common market interest in cattle are sufficient to introduce reliability in interaction. Profit, prestige, and wealth have been redefined in European-influenced terms based on numbers of cattle, and not on numbers of *sacred* cattle, and their conversion potential for other goods at a market place.

Examples (such as watering cattle) are mentioned that support the contention that geographical proximity is a sufficient basis for cooperation. In addition, cooperation based on proximity has extended to ancillary activities, such as cultivation and hunting.

The increasing dependence on a market economy and the nonkinship relations this involves are illustrated by the Herero involvement in trading activities and outside goods available only through markets and the Herero reliance on specialists whom they hire. Significantly, specialists are paid in money or cattle, once again emphasizing the equivalence of the two to the Herero. The use of foreign, commercial utensils, such as metal containers for milk, further underscores the conceived estrangement from the ancestors—and thus from the former traditional ways.

NOTES

[1]Several informants' estimates regarding the relative effort expended on the three subsistence activities were: about 85–88 percent cattle herding, 7–9 percent hunting, 0–6 percent cultivation. Trading activities cross-cut all three.

[2]Some previous literature on division of labor, livestock management, and economic activities generally is: Brincker (1900:68); Buttner (1883:551–5); Hahn (1869:488); Vedder (1928:183); von Francois (1896:199–200, 258–9).

[3]My information on the size of herds is indeed meager. I thought at first this was simply a manifestation of the typical native pastoralist's reluctance to divulge the number of his animals to an outsider. (A visit to the district veterinarian proved fruitless. Though the Herero do avail themselves of modern veterinary services, records do not indicate the tribal affiliation of the herd owner.) But even where I established sufficient trust with an informant, I had difficulty eliciting numbers in regard to animals. I had the same difficulty in regard to number of children. If I asked a Herero how many children he had, I did not get an immediate response. The informant would name his children in order of birth. Just as Herero do not count their children, they do not seem to count their animals. (They know them by sight, however, and can quickly tell when one is missing.) When I pressed an informant, the figure I most often got was 300 head of cattle.

Only one informant, who was considered to be somewhat affluent and thus probably not representative, gave me a breakdown in his livestock holdings. He said he owned between 500 and 600 animals: roughly 4 bulls, 30 oxen, 150 cows, 100 young (male and female calves, and steers), 150 sheep, 130 goats, 12 horses, 10 donkeys.

[4]Being in the trough section of the well during watering can be an unsettling experience to the outsider, for it is not easily remembered that, though these animals are formidable looking (some stand five to six feet tall at the shoulder), a steam-engine charge can be turned aside by a shout and a gesture.

[5]These remarks are based on observations of goat management, for as previously noted goats seem to outnumber sheep among the Ngamiland Herero, and in none of the homesteads in which I resided were there any sheep. It is assumed in this exposition that sheep are treated similarly to goats.

[6]Herero eat all parts of slaughtered animals except the genitals and rectum. They also do not bleed their animals. When I described to them the cattle bleeding common among East African cattle herders and told them of the practice of making a sort of cheese with milk, blood, and urine, they evinced unmistakable repugnance. When, yielding to an urge, I drank the raw blood of a slaughtered animal, I was looked upon as just short of barbaric.

[7]I failed to inquire of the Herero their method of preparing the eggs for consumption, if they are cooked, or if they are simply eaten raw.

[8]Brauer (1925:113–15) provides a neat summary of Herero attitudes and practices which justifies the contention that they once had the cattle-complex.

[9]Whenever an occasion arises, primarily at weddings, when large quantities of food must be prepared, women from neighboring homesteads come together to help the women of the focal homestead with the work.

[10]These comments pertain only to the Herero in Makakun in Ngamiland, for there is no cultivation at the several *ozonganda* east of Maun and, similarly, none at all at Makunda in Ghanzi District. When one considers that Makunda consists of 150 *ozonganda*, one can appreciate the Herero unconcern for farming.

(To my knowledge, no one has speculated in depth on why pastoralists in general hold cultivation in such contempt. This may be because the answer is so obvious: farming requires the setting aside of land for crops that might be otherwise used for grazing.)

[11]For earlier descriptions of Herero appearance, dress, adornment, and demeanor, see Brincker (1900:67); Buttner (1883:552); Hahn (1869:248–9, 256); Hartmann (1897:137); Lambrecht and Lambrecht (1969); Vedder (1928:181–2); von Francois (1896:161–4, 167); and White (1969:36–7).

[12]For example, an elderly woman of the homestead in which I was residing during one of these market days in Makakun had a goat (which was her personal property) killed and butchered. (The slaughtering was done by her BS, who was the only adult male at the homestead at the time, since his father, the *omuini*, was in town and his FyB was away at the cattle post.) Except for the liver, which was given to me, the meat was cooked the evening before the truck was due and was taken to the market area the next day to be sold for cash or traded for other items.

[13]Sillery (1952) and Gibson (1956) both state that missionary activity among the Herero in Ngamiland was negligible. And previous reports (e.g., Wagner 1952:18) attest to the fact that prior to the German war few Herero were converted in South West Africa. Yet Botswana Herero are Christian—if not in practice, then at least nominally; and if not in name, then at least in their overall cosmological orientation. The manner of their conversion, however, was not a subject pursued in depth during fieldwork.

[14]Various passages from Schneider's (1959) article on "Pakot Resistance to Change" illustrate this. The Pakot "object to selling cattle to foreigners largely because the mutual long-term obligation for help and support secured through cattle-sharing and trade are lost in outright sale" (p. 155). "The Pakot like many of the new foods . . . introduced and eat them when they can get them, but they have offered various excuses for not raising them, the favorite being that their cows would dry up if they did so" (p. 154). "Trading areas have been delimited in the reserve in which the traders offer a variety of goods for sale, but the Pakot have taken to few of these" (p. 156). The Pakot "do not envy European ways and have no desire to emulate them" (p. 159). "There seems to be nothing in Christianity to appeal to them, and their own beliefs seem to have been sufficient for their needs" (p. 159). "Their herding life provides all they need and all they want, and they have found almost nothing in Euroamerican culture that will entice them to abandon their old ways" (p. 160). It is to be noted that the Pakot are, and have been, rich in cattle. Unlike the Herero, they did not lose their herds at the same time that they were subject to Euroamerican influences.

[15]This is only a bare outline of the beef business in Botswana but the details of what happens after the cattle leave Herero hands are not pertinent here.

3

Polity, Authority, Order, and Control

LEADERSHIP

Informants claim that at one time there was no leadership beyond the level of the individual homestead, which was headed by the *omuini* or homestead owner. Indirect support for this assertion is provided by the early literature (e.g., Brincker 1899:131; Buttner 1883:550–1; Hahn 1869:247; von Francois 1896:165). From these publications it is safe to conclude that Herero homesteads in prehistoric times were basically nomadic herding units and each politically autonomous due to the nature of the environment throughout most of South West Africa—where rainfall is light and pasturage limited. (See Clark 1959; Esterhuyse 1968; Gibson 1952; Molnar 1966; Mountjoy & Embleton 1967; and Wheeler 1969). Salzman (1967, 1970, 1972) and others (e.g., Johnson 1969) have demonstrated that in areas of limited and unpredictable resources, the character of pastoral nomadic movement tends to be concomitantly irregular and unpredictable. And where adequate pasturage and water are scarce and scattered, herding groups exploiting these resources tend to be small and scattered as well. Given widely dispersed herding units with little opportunity for monopolization of a stable, predictable resource base, there is little likelihood that an

overarching political control can be established. According to Salzman (1967), unpredictable climate and relatively scarce resources
are related to weak, temporary, or an absence of political authority
and to unstable political groupings among nomadic peoples, whereas predictable climate and relatively abundant resources are related
to the emergence of political authority and stable groupings.

The Herero case supports this hypothesis, as is indicated by the
early literature. For example, Buttner (1883:489–90) relates Herero
nomadism, the "nature of the land," and their "anarchic condition,"
though he does not elaborate. Von Francois (1896:165), however, is
much more explicit. He states that the Herero constantly moved
from place to place because grazing and water for their cattle varied
with place and time, and that only "where the whole year through,
nature offers plentiful water and grass, are permanent settlements
found. In these cases, it is not only a single family, or a few, but often several hundred inhabitants who constitute the population of
such a place." He then goes on to say that the "establishment of a
mission, and the advantages which a mission station guarantees,
contribute to the stabilizing of such a settlement."

It is only in terms of this framework that the emergence of the
position of *omuhona* (pl. *ovahona*), a leader with authority beyond
his homestead, is understandable.[1]

The initial step toward achieving *omuhona* status was accomplished by being the first to settle near and utilize a valuable resource, usually water (see Hahn 1869:255). A man who, with his
herd and family, migrated to a well-watered area was considered to
exercise limited control over the resource. He did not "own" the resource itself (though if he invested effort in tapping the resource, for
instance by digging a well, he then indisputably owned the product
of his effort), but he did control to a limited extent access to the resource. Since he was first in the area, he had first claim to the resource. Anyone else wishing to water his herds in the area first had
to ask his permission. By requesting such permission, a later arrival
expressed his recognition of the other's first rights.

If the resource was an adequate one and the *omuini* stayed on for
any length of time and his wealth (herd) grew, so did his reputation
as a successful man. Other Herero, recognizing a good thing, attached themselves to him in one way or another. For instance, they

may have invoked a kinship relationship to him and set up their homesteads nearby. But neither an actual kinship relationship nor common descent was a prerequisite. Newcomers merely asked for fire from his sacred hearth (*okuruo*), demonstrating thereby their recognition of their subordinate position and their willingness to accept his authority as *omuhona*. Gibson (1952:131–2) comments on this:

> Acceptance of sacred fire symbolized acknowledgement of religious and political subjection to the donor. When a man establishes a cattle post or moves his camp to an uninhabited area he carries fire with him as a symbol of loyalty to the chief he leaves. But those settling in the vicinity of an established chief ask fire from him and so acknowledge his political authority and declare allegiance to him.

This raises an important question. To what extent, if any, did the *omuhona* exercise religious authority over his followers? Religious leadership was exercised only within one of the levels of patrilineal segmentation (lineage, sib, or phratry), for it was, and is today, agnatic relatives who were considered to have ancestors in common. (Matrilineal ancestors seem never to have been referred to for social purposes.) Since the area, let us call it a neighborhood, of which the *omuhona* was the head was populated by members of unrelated patrilineages and patrisibs, the *omuhona* would have no claim to religious authority for the entire neighborhood. Vedder's (1928:189) claim that the transfer of allegiance from one *omuhona* to another implied also a change in *oruzo* membership is denied by my informants. They declare that *oruzo* membership is fixed immutably at birth. Yet there are instances when individuals take on secondary *oruzo* restrictions in addition to those of their natal *oruzo*.

The two cases in which new *oruzo* restrictions are assumed concern marriage and child lending. When a bride goes to live in her husband's homestead, she is taken to the *okuruo* fire and there she is smeared with *omaze* (fat from *oruzo* cattle). Thenceforward she assumes the *oruzo* restrictions of her husband. Most informants state that the bride's natal *oruzo* restriction are simply held in abeyance for the duration of the marriage, that she assumes them again if she divorces her husband and returns to her father's homestead.

An unmarried woman. Various visitors to the Herero have remarked on the beauty of these tall, graceful women—and this photograph attests to the validity of such an observation. The long dress is homemade and modeled on the Victorian "Mother Hubbards" formerly worn by wives of missionaries. (See Chapter 2 for a discussion of Herero dress.)

Two Herero girls and a young woman. When women reach an age at which they are marriageable (anytime after the age of sixteen), they don the long dress to indicate their nubility. (See Chapter 3.)

A few say she is no longer a member of her natal *oruzo,* that she retains the new restrictions even upon divorce, and that she only loses them when she remarries and takes on the restrictions of her new husband's *oruzo.*[2] The confusion here concerning whether or not natal *oruzo* membership can be changed and whether the wife permanently or temporarily gives up her natal *oruzo* restrictions at marriage only emphasizes the change that Herero society has undergone and the diminished importance of descent and descent-related traditions as references for present-day Herero behavior. The fat-smearing ceremony is no longer performed, for it must be conducted at the *okuruo* and, as previously noted, all but one Herero homestead in Makakun are without *omaruo.*

When a child was lent to someone at another homestead, it also underwent the fat-smearing ceremony and assumed the oruzo restrictions of the homestead owner in addition to those of its natal *oruzo.* When the child returned to its true parents' homestead, it complied only with its natal *oruzo* restrictions.

It is important to note that both these instances indicate that the assumption of new *oruzo* restrictions is dependent on a *change of residence.* When a wife moves to her husband's homestead, the restrictions change. When, upon divorce, she returns to her father's homestead, she resumes her former restrictions. If her husband dies or if she is divorced but elects to remain in the homestead, her *oruzo* restrictions *do not change.* In childlending it is again the change in residence which occasions the assumption of new *oruzo* restrictions.

It would not be incongruent, therefore, for the same process to obtain on a larger scale (i.e., for groups as well as for individuals). When a homestead moved to a new locality, the neighborhood of an *omuhona,* and the homestead head received fire from the *omuhona's okuruo,* the new residents would be considered *de facto* patrilineal relatives of the *omuhona,* for by taking fire from his they placed themselves under the protection of his ancestors. And herein may lie the origin of phratries.[3]

New groups which settled in an *omuhona's* neighborhood brought with them their various *otuzo* affiliations. And, as it will be argued below, it was more likely neighbors who became kinsmen than kinsmen who became neighbors, it is likely that the several *otuzo* represented in a neighborhood would in time be considered related.

(Eventually myths, such as the one related in chapter 1, would make their appearance to provide a cognitive consistency to existing on-the-ground reality.) That is, at a level more inclusive than the *oruzo*, they would be considered to share ancestors in common. The *omuhona*, then, would exercise religious leadership as a senior phratry member or as the head of the senior *oruzo* in the cluster I am calling a phratry. (The *oruzo* would be senior by virtue of the first-in-area principle.)

The evidence which supports this view is not complete. Neither of the two sources of information upon which we must rely, the previous literature and present-day Herero informants, is very clear on this. Except for Schapera, whose primary ethnographic research interests lay with the Tswana, no previous account lists the member *otuzo* for each of the phratries. (Indeed, besides Gibson and Schapera, no other source even mentions phratries.) And, significantly Schapera comes to a conclusion similar to mine.[4] He comments as follows (1945:28; emphasis added):

> The only reference in the texts [provided by Schapera's informants] to *otuzo* is a very brief and tantalizing statement that certain of them *'are children of one father and work together'*. . . . These allied *otuzo* are grouped as follows:
> a.   onguejuva, otjiporo, okanene, ondjiva;
> b.   onguendjandje, onguanjimi, ombongora;
> c.   ohorongo, onguatjija, ondanga;
> d.   ekoti, otjirungu;
> e.   ojakoto, ohambandarua.
>
> I have been unable to find any reference in the available literature to such a system of affiliation, and I am unable to suggest what is meant here, except possibly that the *otuzo* in each group are derived from a common ancestor, or that *their people are politically related*. In this connection, attention may be drawn to one interesting point. As already mentioned, my informants stated that among the Herero and Mbanderu there were formerly five great chieftainships—those of Tjamuaha, Tjetjoo, Kambazembi, Zeraua, and Kahimemua. Now Maharero's *oruzo* was *ohorongo* . . ., Tjetjoo's *onguejuva* . . ., Zeraua's *ombongora* . . ., and Kahimemua's *ohambandarua*. . . . In these four instances, therefore, we find a correlation between *oruzo* clusters and chieftainship.

There remains the question of Kambazembi. His *oruzo*, according to Dannert, was *onguatjindu*. This *oruzo* is not included in the groups given above. On the other hand, Text I refers on several occasions to the 'village' (*onganda*) of Nguatjindu, of which Kambazembi is named as the head; Vedder mentions an early chief named Nguatjindu, but says nothing more about him. . . . It is mentioned also by Vedder that Kambazembi migrated to Waterberg from the Kaokoveld after the death of Tjamuaha.

The six phratries and their member *otuzo* that I collected in 1973 were:

1.   Ongueuva, Otjiporo, Okanene, Ondjiva, Omuhinaruzo;
2.   Ohorongo, Onguatjija, Otjihaviria;
3.   Ojakoto, Omuko;
4.   Ondanga, Ohambandarua;[5]
5.   Omakoti, Otjirungu, Otjitjindua, Omurekua;[6]
6.   Onguendjandje, Onguanjimi, Ombongora, Osembi (or Esembi), Onguatjindu.

The prominent leaders (in order of descent) of Ongueuva *oruzo* were Seu, Kandjii, Tjetjoo, and Kahaka; of Ohorongo Tjamuaha, Maharero, Samuel (and also the dissident Nikodemus); of Ombongora Zeraua, Manasse, and Michael Tjizeta; of Onguatjindu Kambazembi; and of Ohambandarua Kahimemua. (On phratries 3 and 5 I have no information regarding leaders.) These names reappear repeatedly in the previous historical accounts whenever great *ovahona* and great "priests" are mentioned, along with their geographical locations (see below, including notes 10 and 25).

This view is useful in that it not only helps to explain references in the earlier literature to the *omuhona's* authority but it also aids in understanding why informants say that in former times agnatically connected homesteads were located near each other. This interpretation suggests that homesteads did not become neighbors because they were related but became related because they were neighbors.[7]

In discussing the formation of cooperative groups among the Ndendeuli, Gulliver (1971:192) says: "With indirectly linked neighbors a man sought to establish a working convention of reciprocal assistance. Where such a connection began to be well established, it was associated with the development of the acknowledgement of direct kinship between the two neighbors." In another place (p. 219) he suggests that "it is almost possible to reverse the Ndendeuli ethic [that kinsmen should assist each other], but without distorting the empirical facts, and to say that people who regularly exchanged assistance were kinsmen *because* of that regular assistance."

It is evident that what I am positing here for the Herero—that neighbors tended to be regarded as kinsmen due to shared reliance on a valued resource and the necessity of cooperation—is by no means a totally new idea, though it is one that has yet to receive consistent attention from anthropological theorists. It may well be that in many ethnographic cases the idiom of kinship is introduced after the fact as a convenient method of providing a measure of reliability in the relationships of people who live and work together.

It might then be asked why the Herero do not today employ kinship to order their social relations as they did in the past. The answer, I think, is that the new economy does not require that kind of ideological reinforcement. The reliability kinship once afforded to interaction is not necessary in the more formalized stranger relationships of a market economy.

The use of kinship and descent as references for behavior was congruent with and reinforced by the belief in the ancestors (those who were kin had the same ancestors). And belief in the ancestors depended on the possession of large herds of ritually important cattle. The destruction of the cattle, therefore, led to the weakening of the descent-ordered social organization and the religio-symbolic legitimating system which depended on that particular economic organization. The explicit use of cattle as a market commodity was discouraged in the old economy. One does not share a sacred trust from the ancestors with outsiders (nonkinsmen). One shares the cattle and the labor necessary to maintain the cattle (or at least the control of that labor) with those with whom one shares the ancestors (kinsmen). Therefore, if one is cooperating with someone in the care of cattle, that other person is a kinsmen—that is, he is considered a kinsman whether or not the kin connection can be demonstrated on the anthropologist's genealogical charts.

With the acceptance of a market economy and the sale of cattle, inimical to the old religious ideology, outsiders or "strangers" (Simmel 1950)—that is, nonkinsmen—become important others in regard to cattle. No longer is the cattle economy restricted to kinsmen who share ancestors. In a sense, the herds have become "profane," where once they were sacred, because they are shared with (sold to) nonkinsmen. In exchanging one's property (cattle) for the property (money, crops, etc.) of an outsider, one admits the two are equivalent. One's own property, then, has a ("profane") value that transcends its formerly exclusive ("sacred") value to the owner. The latter, consequently, is sacrificed to the former. And as the former becomes more central to social use, the ideology supporting the latter decreases in importance while a more appropriate ideology replaces it. It is therefore evident that those who cooperate in labor to produce the sale item (cattle) no longer need to be thought of in the idiom of kinship. They can just as well be nonkinsmen or "profane" themselves, just as the herds are. A market economy, as sociology affirms, stimulates such impersonal, stranger-like relationships among the participants.[8]

Hence, today, with the diminished relevance of ancestors and of descent, very little Herero behavior is phrased in terms of descent. Older informants, nostalgic for the former traditions, tend to idealize the past in regard to devotion to the ancestors and, consequently, to conformity to a descent-ordered social structure. It is in the related areas of religion and descent that most drastic change has occurred, in that they have become almost insignificant in present-day Herero society, and it is in regard to these subjects that the data are most confusing and consequently idealized by the Herero.

Though control over a valued resource was a primary consideration, the achievement, and the retention, of the status of *omuhona* also depended on certain personal characteristics. First of all, he should not be too aggressive in his attempt to achieve the position. Lehmann (1955:31) indirectly points this out when he discusses *-hona*, which is the root of *omuhona*. According to him, *-hona* means "to go slowly (to the symbols of high rank)." The *omuhona* should also be scrupulous in his performance of his duties, lest the ancestors be angered and visit disaster upon the living. He must be fair in his adjudication of disputes and heed the advice of his councillors. He must not be overbearing nor seek greater authority than permitted, or his followers will simply pull up stakes and move elsewhere; and he will find himself a leader with no followers.

> The rise of such a chiefdom is thus identical with the possession of the personal characteristics necessary for it, the sufficient number of followers and family members, the sufficient quantity of cattle, and on pasture land. None without the other[s], but only all forms of property together, form the basis of authority of the chief. Should one of them be lost later, all is endangered. If all is lost in war, whether to an enemy or to another chief of his own people, then his former status is no longer useful to the *omuhona*, he has become poor and despised, where possible a servant of another, in any case an *omutjimba*, "poor fellow" [Lehmann 1955:31–2].

Similarly, inheritance of the title was not in itself sufficient to retain the position. If the heir did not evince the proper personality characteristics, he lost his following, despite his wealth and the fact that he was the rightful heir.

Just who was the rightful heir deserves consideration. But it cannot be fully discussed until after religious leadership has been examined, and it is also best discussed within the context of inheritance generally. Therefore we will first consider religious leadership in itself, the contexts in which it functions, and the extent of authority in former times.

Was the position *omuhona*, formerly as it is today, distinct from that of *omurangere* or religious leadership? According to Vedder, it was not. He says (1928:187) that "the chief . . . is omuhona [or] lord, and omurangere [or] priest at the same time." The other early reports refer to the leader as "priest-chief" and thus concur with this view. It is also consistent with the above interpretation regarding the rise of an *omuini* of a homestead to the status of *omuhona* of a neighborhood. According to my informants, in the old days when every homestead had an *okuruo*, each *omuini* or homestead head functioned as *omurangere* for the homestead. It is conceivable, then, that when a homestead was established in the neighborhood of an *omuhona* and fire was secured from his *okuruo*, the *omuhona* functioned as *omurangere* for the neighborhood. Thus, the loci of political authority and religious authority would be identical: in the person of the *omuini* for the homestead and in the person of the *omuhona* for the neighborhood (which then became thought of as populated by members of related *otuzo* of a phratry). If this indeed were the case, and the early accounts provide no plausible alternative, we are justified in speaking of the *omuini-omurangere* and the *omuhona-omurangere*. Hahn (1869:500) comes close to actually stating this when he says that "every family father is priest of his

Gustav Kandjii and Estere, one of his wives. He is the last *omurangere* (a religious leader) in Makunda. (See discussion of homestead C in Chapter 1 and discussion of religious leadership in Chapter 3.)

family and the chief is priest of his whole tribe."[9] Vedder (1928:165–6) also says that the dual aspects of religious and secular leadership were vested in one person and were inseparable. He, too, distinguishes between a "priest of the family" (*omuini-omurangere*) and a "great priest" (*omuhona-omurangere*), the latter having been "conspicuous because of his greater influence as a result of . . . [his] possessions in herds and followers."[10] That is, he was *omuhona* as well as *omurangere*. Similarly, Irle (1917:337) remarks that "old heathen chiefs . . . were also priests of the people."

But there is yet another ethnographic puzzle related to religion and leadership that must be confronted and resolved. This concerns the term *mukuru*. To a man, present-day Herero deny that it refers to anything but God in the Christian sense. Though this is true today, the frequency with which it crops up in the earlier German reports and their repeated assertions that it had other meanings renders my informants' denials unacceptable.

According to these earlier reports, *mukuru* was used in several ways. It referred to the first Herero, the original ancestor who sprang from the *omumborumbonga* tree (Dannert 1906:4; Hahn 1869:489; Irle 1917:489; Vedder 1928:165). It referred to the founder of a patrilineage, though whether to what was identified above as a major or minor patrilineage is not made clear (Vedder 1928:165). According to Vedder (1928:165) it referred to a "father who has just died" (*omuini-omurangere*?) and to the "still living successor of the father." According to Irle (1917:344) it referred to the *oruzo* founder and "to the ancestor who died last, and also to his son who is still living." The same source records that the "chief" (*omuhona-omurangere*?) was called *mukuru*. Finally, Mukuru was the Herero name given to the Christian deity (Irle 1917:345; Vedder 1928:165).[11]

It is not unlikely that the term was used in all these ways. The word literally means "old one," as is attested to by a number of the early sources (e.g., Dannert 1906:3; Hahn 1869:498; Irle 1917:344; Vedder 1928:165). The plural, *ovakuru*, is the term applied to the ancestors. Now, if Kopytoff (1971) is correct in his interpretation, the "ancestors" should be considered deceased elders. His hypothesis is that "ancestor worship," at least among Bantu-speaking peoples, is a misnomer, that just as junior generations seek out and are subject in a more or less degree to their elders, the eldest living members of the society seek out the advice of their elders—who happan, of course, to be dead. And as Cohen points out (1971:207), we are dealing here with one social system, some of the members of which are living, some of whom are dead but nonetheless conceived as interested and active partners in the affairs of the group. The death of a man simply marks his transition from one recognized social status to another within the system. The Herero linguistic evidence supports such a view. It also makes it understandable how there could be a *mukuru* at several levels of the social structure. Since there are a number of levels of patrilineal segmentation, the last deceased elder for each level is the "old one" for the segment at that level (i.e., he is a named and remembered member of a larger, vague class of predominantly unnamed and unremembered *ovakuru*). And the still living elder is referred to as *mukuru* because when he dies he will displace his predecessor as the "ancestor" to whom his group directly appeals. That the original Herero is also referred to as Mukuru is simply an extension of the system to its logical extreme, for *mukuru* in this sense means the ancestor of all Herero, the oldest of the old ones. This is emphasized, according to the early reports cited above, by the Herero belief that their sacred cattle, the ritual that surrounds them, and all their customs were given to them by Mukuru.

The religious leader, whether referred to as *omurangere* or *mukuru*, was clearly the intermediary between the Herero and their ancestors, that is, between living Herero and deceased Herero, for the ancestors were perceived as very real members of, and active participants in, the Herero social system. Phrased differently, we may say that the *omurangere/mukuru* represents the ancestors to the people, and he represents the people to the ancestors. Vedder (1928:165) notes that "he is the representative of the family as well as the ancestral line, and it is his duty in the first instance to keep up the relationship with the dead Ovakuru."

The organization of traditional Herero religion was designed to maintain what the Herero conceived of as their relationship with the ancestors. All ritual had this as its end. A consideration of religious practices and the symbols associated with ritual occasions will make this clear.

All ritual was formerly conducted at the *okuruo* (sacred hearth or ash heap). It was the central symbol of Herero society. It was at the sacred hearth that all important economic, social, political, and religious activities were conducted.

For instance, all "tasting" was performed at the *okuruo*. The verb "to taste" is *okumakera* and the one who performs the tasting is called *omumakere*. It was the task of the *omurangere* to taste the milk from *ozonzere* and *oruzo* cattle each morning and thus make it safe for others to drink. Since these cattle were believed to come from the ancestors, that is, from the realm of the supernatural, they were imbued with supernatural power or energy and referred to as *zera* (sacred or holy). Anything associated with them (such as the wooden pails in which their milk was kept, the wooden spoon with which the milk was tasted) was likewise sacred. This sacred nature, this "*zera* power," had to be neutralized before an ordinary Herero could come into contact with it. To fail to neutralize the *zera* quality of something before coming into contact with it would be like confronting the supernatural head on. The consequences would indeed be dire; death might even result. Mediation was necessary between the natural world of the ordinary Herero and the supernatural world of the ancestors. And it was the *omurangere* who served as mediator. It was through him that the Herero were able to maintain a safe link with the ancestors. Everything coming from the ancestors passed through him and was made safe for the living. And whenever intercourse with the ancestors was initiated, it was through the office of *omurangere*, thus rendering it acceptable to the ancestors. Because the *omurangere* was the vehicle for communication and connection with the ancestors, his very person was considered *zera*.

According to the early literature, the *okuruo* fire burned continually (Brincker 1900:75–6; Irle 1917:346; Vedder 1928:167). It was given to the Herero by Mukuru and, if it went out, could only be rekindled by his mundane representative.

Two sticks, usually called "ancestor sticks," were used. One was called *ondume* (derived from the verb meaning "to cohabit") and represented maleness; the other was called *otjija* (from the verb "to come") and represented femaleness. The stick had a small cavity into which the male stick was placed and twirled to make fire. The sticks represented either Mukuru, the original ancestor, and his wife or just the ancestors in general. The fire was produced by the meeting of the two sticks, just as the Herero are born of the union of the ancestors.

Though the earliest records state that the fire at the *okuruo* must not die out, Gibson (1956:123) reports that at the time of his field-work "there . . . [was] no attempt to keep it burning constantly."

> The fire is kindled in the sacred hearth twice a day, at sunrise and again at sunset, by the chief wife of the priest if she is present, or by her daughter or secondary wife if the chief wife is away. Rekindling of the fire in the sacred hearth at the foot of the bush representing the ancestors gives semi-daily expression to the relationship between a Herero priest and his patrilineal ancestors and also symbolizes acceptance of her husband's ancestors by the woman who tends the fire.[12]

Today all but one of the fires have gone out. If the presence of the *okuruo* formerly was the quintessential symbol of the relationship between living Herero and their ancestors, the absence of the *okuruo* now symbolizes the lack of relationship, the severance of the connection between the people today and their traditional ways. The old traditions were thought of as having been handed down from the ancestors, and the justification for maintaining them was that they were a sacred trust from the ancestors. Religious practices were organized to maintain the reputed connection between living descendants and their deceased ancestors. Most important, the ancestors had given the people cattle, their most prized possession, the source of earthly sustenance, and taught them the proper way to care for them. It was therefore incumbent upon the people to treat their cattle in the traditional manner, the manner prescribed by the ancestors from whom they were a gift. Hence, cattle were invested with ritual importance and were treated in the ritually appropriate manner. When the cattle were lost, the relationship to the ancestors could only be seen as severely weakened (for the currency on which commerce with the ancestors was based had been lost). And when, three decades later, the herds were reconstituted, this was not to please the ancestors but to seek material comfort. (The currency was the same but the commerce for which it was used had changed. In effect, however, the nature of the currency, though still cattle, was perceived as radically changed, for its nature is defined by its social uses.)[13] The explicitly economic value of cattle as a market commodity replaced their former ritual value as the primary orientation of the Herero to their herds. To be sure, this change in economic organization was not felt all at once throughout the rest of Herero institutions. Only gradually were its ramifications felt in the rest of social organization. The religious practices that supported the old organization of labor decreased in importance as the character of cattle herding changed, so that today only the barest traces of the old rituals can be discerned. The old social structure, which emphasized the importance of descent as a conceptual framework for social behavior, is little more than a memory. The ancestors are no longer held to function as active participants in the affairs of the group, for the ritual activity that once tied them to the group is no longer practiced since cattle herding has lost its ritual character. It follows then that the organization of social relations need no longer be phrased primarily in terms of descent because the ancestors, to whom descent is traced, have lost their importance. Only now, seventy years after the destruction of the Herero herds and the first steps toward the new economic orientation were taken, have the effects of the changes diffused throughout Herero society.

Today, except for the limited influence exerted by the last *omurangere,* Herero society as depicted in the previous reports no longer exists in Makakun. Cattle are economic assets and not sacred trusts. The old rites have fallen into disuse. The tie with the ancestors is no longer maintained. By examining some examples of the ritual activity of former times and looking at how they were designed to strengthen the connection to the ancestors, we can appreciate the extent of Herero social change that their absence today indicates.

Two instances, more than any others, heavily underscore the central place of cattle in ritual activities and the importance of ritual in maintaining connection with the ancestors. One concerns the assumption of leadership and the other concerns funeral practices.

There is ample literature on customs surrounding death and burial (e.g., Brincker 1900:89–91; Buttner 1884:386–9; Dannert 1906:48ff.; Irle 1917:339, 352; Vedder 1928:169–70, 184–5, 191; von Francois 1896:201–2). Fortunately, my oldest informant was alive at the time of the last great funeral ceremony, held for Maharero in 1890,[14] and I was able to corroborate the earlier reports and elicit further data to fill in some omitted information. The informant was also present at the ceremony that validated the succession of Maharero's son Samuel to his deceased father's position as *omuhona*.

At a man's death, a number of his cattle of all cattle categories was slaughtered. (A funeral was the only occasion when cattle were killed by slitting their throats. At all other times cattle were suffocated in the sand. Today animals are never suffocated.) He was sewn into the skin of a bull from his *oruzo* cattle and buried within the homestead, near a tree, in the cattle corral, or even in a hut. The skulls of the slaughtered *oruzo* cattle marked the grave and proclaimed the extent of the man's wealth by their number. The homestead was then moved, though usually not to a great distance. The meat from the *oruzo* cattle was eaten by relatives of the deceased.[15] A few of his *ozonzere* cattle were killed, too, but as previously noted (chapter 1), these may not be eaten by Herero. Their carcasses were left outside the homestead. These "sacred" cattle (*oruzo* and *ozonzere*) were said to accompany the deceased on his way to join the ancestors. General cattle were also slaughtered, and these were eaten by anyone.

The meat of the *oruzo* cattle could not be eaten before its *zera* ("sacred") nature had been rendered neutral by the tasting rite. Since the *omumakere* ("taster") was dead and no one had yet succeeded him—and so there was no living person to perform the tasting—the meat was first tasted by the ancestor sticks. Thus, the proper relationship with the ancestors was maintained, despite the fact that the group was temporarily without an *omurangere*.

Today the treatment of the deceased and the conduct of a funeral indicate the lack of that relationship. No longer is the deceased sewn into the skin of a bull and buried in it. Wooden coffins are now used. No longer is he buried within the homestead. Under the encouragement of the Botswana government, the Herero are now establishing cemeteries. Homesteads are not moved. No longer are many cattle ritually slaughtered to accompany the deceased. A few animals are slaughtered, with little or no regard as to the category to which they belong, to provide food for neighbors and relatives who have come to pay their respects. The meat, of course, is not tasted. There are no ancestor sticks, no living *ovarangere*. The meat is unceremoniously consumed.

The rituals surrounding succession to leadership, and their absence today, indicate even more emphatically the changes that have occurred. While the funeral ceremony was carried out, the successor prepared himself to assume leadership. At the sacred fire he pulverized some roots from the upturned bush, rubbed his forehead with them, and threw them into the fire. He then took a piece of root and chewed it. He rinsed his mouth with water, then spat it and the chewed root into the fire. The elders with him at the fire spat water into the flame but did not chew the root.

> This is the first legal act in connection with the assumption of the office of the chief. It is manifest that this act has something to do with the ancestors, although they do not know the exact meaning of this symbolical act [Vedder 1928:188].

The "meaning of this symbolical act" is clear enough in light of my interpretation of what I call the phenomenon of "connectors" among the Herero (more precisely, those acts and objects through which Herero maintain what I have been calling the connection with the ancestors). All through Herero ritual there recurred behavior that symbolized the link between the living people and their ancestors. The sacred fire was probably the quintessential symbol of this sort. It provided a visible sign of the continuity of Herero society. It connected the current living population with their traditions and with their ancestors. It therefore symbolized as well what may be called by the inadequate term "the supernatural." It is fire and hence natural, it is *sacred* fire and hence supernatural, and it is the point of articulation of the two.

The leader in his capacity as *omurangere/mukuru* is also a connector or mediator. He is a man (natural) but a near-ancestor (supernatural), and he mediates between the two worlds—that is, he is a member of both worlds as well as the mediator between them. He provides the connection.

The spray of water from the mouth is a graphic illustration of a connector. The water is spit from a holy (*zera*) person to a common person at nearly all rituals. It connects the supernatural or *zera* realm with the individual receiving the spray of water. During the rite described above, the successor spat water, with a holy root and earth from an ancestor's grave, into the *okuruo* fire. He established a link to the *zera* world. Throughout his later life in his capacity as *omurangere/mukuru* he will spurt water on his fellows, thereby extending the link through himself to other men.

Each day he will perform the tasting ceremony. The *oruzo* and *ozonzere* cattle are *zera*. Men cannot simply drink the milk from such cattle without first neutralizing its supernatural potency. Therefore the leader first tastes the milk each morning and passes it on to others to drink.

Another graphic example of "connectors" can be seen in the next act performed by the new leader. Vedder (1928:188) describes it as follows:

> . . . they take a long thong, fasten it to a branch in the cattle kraal and lead it to the fire. Having reached it, the part of the thong that is too long is rolled up and placed in a little hollow which they cover with the holy milk-pail from which the late father used to drink his sour milk. This being done it serves as documentary evidence that the cattle of the oruzo have henceforth become the possession of the new chief.[16]

Next a cone shell is attached to the hair and hangs over the forehead as a symbol of office. Vedder (1928:188) states that this shell (which he identifies as a mussel shell) is not found in South West Africa but on the beaches of Angola. This custom, like the entire ceremony, is no longer practiced in Ngamiland.[17]

All the trappings and ritual formerly associated with leadership among the Herero have now disappeared. None of the "connectors" is any longer present. The position of *omuhona* is now the lowest level in the state's administrative bureaucracy more than it is the highest level in the indigenous Herero system.

There were other rituals which the Herero used to perform that are no longer extant, and some of these should be mentioned as further documentation of social change. A detailed discussion of the former customs will not be presented, however, since general outlines and the mention of some salient characteristics will suffice for present purposes.

As might be expected, the birth of a Herero was enveloped in ritual.[18] A few months before the birth of her first child a woman returned to the homestead in which her mother lived. Her husband did not accompany her, for he was not permitted to be present at the birth. Elder women, perhaps matrilineal relatives, served as midwives. The birth was announced as follows (Vedder 1928:176):

> When it is a boy the shout is: "ouje, ouje, okauta!", that is, world, world, a small bow" because a future hunter and soldier who will use the bow is born. In the case of a girl the call is: "Ouje, ouje, okaseu, that is, world, world, a little onion!" [because] one is born who will gather wild onions.

The mother and child remained secluded in a special hut constructed for them until the child's umbilical cord dropped off.

> During this period of seclusion the mother has sacred powers which permit her to perform the milk tasting rite, and the milk bowls are brought to her each morning for this purpose. After the child's cord has dropped off it is preserved by the priest-chief in a bag, and the sacred power passes to him [Gibson 1952:169].

After the umbilical cord dropped off, a special rite had to be undergone. This rite occurred at the *okuruo* in the father's homestead. Gibson's summary (1952:169–70) will again suffice:

> When the mother leaves the special hut, she goes to the sacred hearth [of her husband's homestead] where she is sprinkled with water by the chief wife's oldest unmarried daughter. Here also the father presents his child to the ancestors, sprinkles it with water, and rubs both the mother and the child with fat. One of the sheep of the prescribed sort for the *orudo* is slaughtered and its flesh is brought to the sacred fire where the father informs the ancestors of the birth. He sprinkles the meat with water from his mouth, and after this blessing the mother and child may be seen by the group. This appears to be a ceremonial introduction of the child into the father's family, for which the sanction of the patrilineal ancestors must be obtained.

The interpretation offered here suggests that it is more than that as well. The isolation of the mother and child indicates that they are touched by the *zera* world and hence are dangerous to ordinary Herero. A woman who has just given birth and whose child still has its umbilical cord (i.e., its connection with the other world) is *zera* and can perform the tasting. Thus, birth itself seems to be considered (just as death is) a transition from one realm to the other, with the umbilical cord representing the link. Therefore it must be treated by the proper neutralizing rituals.

Today, however, birth is not surrounded by any of the former rites. The woman remains in her husband's *onganda,* is not isolated, and has the baby in her own hut, attended by the other women of the homestead or volunteers from the vicinity. The husband may be present at parturition. The umbilical cord is not preserved. The child is not introduced to the ancestors.

Naming, which occurred about a month after birth, took place at the *okuruo* as well. (The child was taken to the *okuruo* and its forehead touched to that of a calf from the *oruzo* cattle.) Today a father, without ceremony, simply gives the child a name.[19]

The birth of twins was a special event. The parents and the children were considered to be in touch with or have some mysterious connection with the supernatural. The entire family, parents as well as children, was called *epaha* (twins) and was considered *zera.* A special hut outside the homestead was built for the *epaha* family and no one dared approach it. Luttig (1933:73) reports that "the only food the members of the *epaha* family are allowed to eat is meat."[20]

Not long after the birth (the exact time is not specified), either the members of the *oruzo* or the members of the homestead[21] assembled with their cattle, and the *epaha* group left its hut and went to meet them. A ritual fight then occurred. "This ritual battle is explained by Sternberg as the result of the fear of the people (Götterfurcht) when they meet with divine power" (Luttig 1933:74). After the ritual fight, Luttig explains, the father of the twins "blessed" the males present and the mother "blessed" the females.

> During the days which follow, the *epaha* visits the various houses in the village and receives meat and iron-beads from the in-dwellers. No one dares to refuse them this. The father accepts gifts of meat until he is satisfied. He will then ask for cattle, which also are not refused. At the completion of this ceremony, they travel through the country, still clothed in their old skins, and visit various villages where they also receive cattle and iron beads. Upon their return they have become rich people. The twins then receive their names and the old skin attires are discarded [Luttig 1933:74].

The behavior of the group towards the *epaha* family[22] also illustrates the power, and consequently the danger to humans, that emanates from things *zera*. The ritual fight that occurred between the *epaha* family and the group represented the fear experienced by the Herero when confronted directly with the supernatural. Similar ritual fights occurred at other times when the power manifested itself (i.e., when the connection with the ancestors was manifest and thus they were seen as in close proximity to the living), as for example, when the successor to leadership went to the grave of his predecessor for the first time. It symbolized his close connection with the ancestors; and the group in ritual combat threw stones at the successor.

I am suggesting simply that the Herero could not face directly the other world of the ancestors or the force which originates there; that it had to have mediators between them and it which neutralize the supernatural power while providing a connection to it; and that whenever this other world and/or its power revealed itself directly (as in the birth of twins) the Herero reacted with prescribed behavior intended to protect themselves from it and channel it appropriately.

Today mediators are no longer needed because the connection is no longer perceived to exist. As I have previously stated, the connection no longer exists because the new economic orientation of the Herero no longer requires the former legitimation of herding as a ritual activity. The idea of cattle as ritually important is not necessary to the new market economy and is probably even inimical to it.

AUTHORITY

We have seen from the above that religious and secular leadership were combined in one person and were in fact inseparable.[23] Since the religious aspects of leadership are apparent from the preceding section, however, discussion will focus on the secular authority of the *omuhona*. The earlier sources offer the following information.

Hahn (1869:235) says the Herero were divided into a number of independent "tribes" (by this he means the same clustering of homesteads that I have been calling a neighborhood: "Each consists of a more or less large number of villages, of which the chief village in which the chief or *omuhona* resides is called 'ohona'"). On the extent of the *omuhona's* authority he states (p. 254):

> Although the chief is an unlimited master over the life and property of all his subjects, still his power is diminished on account of the custom that everyone can leave his chief and join himself to another. Therefore the chiefs have a reason for not treating their subjects too harshly.

Vedder (1928:189–90) makes a similar point. After stating that "the transfer of [allegiance from] one chieftainship to another cannot be prevented" and that as a result the *omuhona* does not exert "oppressive" leadership for fear of losing his followers, he goes on:

> Consequently the Herero enjoys the greatest imaginable liberty unless he is disturbed or subjugated by external enemies or possesses so little and is so insignificant that his oppression and ill-treatment by some wealthy cattle-owner, is not disadvantages to the latter.
>
> In times of peace it is hardly possible to say what a chief is and what powers are vested in him. He lives in the same way as others of the tribe do. He dresses himself like the others; and yet he is treated with greater respect and his person remains zera or holy. But everyone looks after himself as well as he can and is not very much disturbed by what the chief does or contemplates doing. But the tables are suddenly turned when hostilities arise, as has been exemplified by wars in the past.

Sahlins' (1968:21) terse comments on the authority of "petty chieftains" nicely sum up the Herero case: "The chieftain is usually a spokesman of his group and master of its ceremonies, with otherwise few functions and no privileges. One word from him and everyone does as he pleases."

Von Francois (1896:173–4) offers the following comments:

> As is the case with all nomadic peoples, a resident (governor) does not exist in the political and military sense. The landed omuhona has a certain authority over his next neighbor who has less wealth, for the amount of influence and responsibility over a certain number of caretakers or servants is determined by the size of herds.

> The more animals he possesses, the more subordinate people there are, and because this makes him responsible for the maintenance and feeding of a larger number of people, he takes several wives, has many children and ends up ruling over a large number of people who are dependent upon him for their existence.
>
> When arguments between different werft owners arise over theft of animals, water rights, the beating of servants on both sides, etc., the chieftain is to settle the arguments and punish the wrongdoer.

But in contradiction to Vedder, von Francois (1896:176) says, "special forms of respect, with the chief, for example, are unknown."

It seems clear from these sample passages that the *omuhona* was not a full-fledged chief in the sense of having autocratic authority over, and the unswerving allegiance of, his followers. He had no coercive force and no standing retainers to compel compliance with his wishes. That his followers could simply move away without interference from him is ample illustration of this. It is therefore more accurate to say that they had an incipient chiefdom than to characterize the Herero as definitely having chiefdoms.

But to say that followers could move away implies, of course, that they had somewhere to go. Suitable land had to be available. By the time of the German war in 1904 the availability of open land must have been severely limited (Goldblatt 1971:115ff.). Europeans had settled in ever increasing numbers in Hereroland and thus were restricting Herero movement. It was becoming less easy for the Herero simply to pull up stakes if they felt oppressed by an *omuhona*. Thus, incipient chiefdoms were becoming more and more stable and probably would have evolved into institutionalized chiefdoms had not the war destroyed them.

Contact with non-Herero groups also contributed to the evolution of Herero chiefdoms, as mentioned in the previous literature. Hostile intergroup relations resulted in the need for military leaders. A man who could successfully lead his people in battle against an enemy carried over into times of peace some of the prestige he accumulated. And it was he who then served as spokesman for his group vis-á-vis the former enemy when peace was established. A similar process for the emergence of leadership occurred among the Marri Baluch (Pehrson 1966); the Fulani (Stenning 1959); the Basseri (Barth 1961); and others. Another factor contributing to a stable leadership position is also exemplified by these other pastoral groups. When Europeans enter a tribal area, they are usually hard pressed to deal with the leaderless indigenous population. Because of their presence and the need for negotiation with the native people, a tribal spokesman emerges who represents the interests of the native group. At first the spokesman holds little or no authority within his group; he simply represents the group to outsiders. But gradually he assumes authority because he also functions as a representative of the outsiders to his group. And since Europeans eventually establish their political supremacy, usually through force of arms, in the tribal area, the native spokesman attains authority within his group because he is backed by European power. In return for this backing and his personal benefit, he cedes tribal rights (e.g., in land) to the Europeans. It does not matter that he has no "right" or authority to do so from the point of view of the native population. The military superiority of the Europeans has given him the "right." By his continued exercise of authority whose source lies outside the bounds of his group he gradually attains authority within the group.

A few comments about the rise of the omuhona-ship at Okahandja will suffice to illustrate this. Okahandja is located at the inland termination point of the Swakop River in central South West Africa and is thus the site of a permanent source of water.

Although the first figure of importance at Okahandja for whom we have sufficient historical information was a man named Tjamuaha, a few data exist concerning his predecessors. These are provided by Vedder (1938:135ff.), who attempts to reconstruct the southward diffusion of the Herero from the Kaokoveld in northern South West Africa.

Though in his earlier report Vedder (1928:166) maintains that the Herero entered the Kaokoveld from the north around 1700, in his later work (1938:152–3) he revises this estimate and claims, based on genealogical data, that they entered the Kaokoveld around 1500 and emigrated therefrom around 1750.

Mutjise, for whom Vedder (1938:152) records a birth date of 1730, was Tjamuaha's paternal grandfather and the first to settle at Okahandja (the place at which there would later be erected a monument to his famous progeny). We can safely infer that it was the presence of an ample water supply that first induced Mutjise to settle there when the Herero began migrating south from the Kaokoveld, as it later induced his descendants to remain there.[24]

We have no further information for Mutjise and very little for his son Tjirue, except for mention of some territorial conflict with the Tswana over grazing rights. The following summary is based on Vedder (1938:141–2).

Tjirue allowed his cattle to graze far to the east into the country the Tswana regarded as theirs. Consequently, any Herero cattle they found were confiscated. The Herero retaliated by raiding Tswana herds. For weeks the sporadic fighting continued, eventually ranging as far as the western marshes of Lake Ngami. When the final decisive battle was fought, the Herero, though possessing inferior weapons and suffering great losses, emerged victorious. They had thus succeeded in pushing their boundaries farther east, but to just what location Vedder does not say.

Afterwards—Vedder dates the time at around 1820 on the basis that the aforementioned Tjamuaha participated in the Herero-Tswana battle as a young man—the Tswana chief Tjekeue came to Okahandja, bringing a white ox and a horse (the first, Vedder says, the Herero had seen) as tokens of peace.

It was, however, a Pyrrhic victory for the Herero. They lost many warriors and a substantial number of cattle. Tjirue, who died soon after and was succeeded by Tjamuaha, was left impoverished. In the following passage Vedder (1938:142) describes this period. His comments (as do those of Lehmann 1955 and von Francois 1896) also corroborate what was said previously about the characteristics of an *omuhona*.

> After the war [with the Tswana] was over and the Hereros were able to call the enormous extent of pasturage their own, Tjirue was gathered to his fathers and his son took his place at the sacred ancestral fire. He was not, however, of much account, and thence comes the Herero saying that Tjamuaha was no chieftain at all, but that it was his son who really attained to

that dignity by virtue of his great deeds. In fact he was no chief in the sense that he was the possessor of large herds of cattle, but he was none the less a chief for the simple reason that he was his father's successor to the office of the sacred fire. But still the sacred fire is of no very great importance if the herds of cattle, which are the adjuncts of this fire, are lacking. Then the ancestors have proved themselves weak, for they had not the power to protect the sacred herds from loss and the ancestral fire is not of much account if it fails to help its children to increase their material possessions. Tjamuaha was eager to become rich again at all cost, and we shall be able to recognize this bent of his very clearly later in our story for every means of getting possession of cattle became the same to him. At first he tried lawful methods. He sent a message to his friend, Tjipangandjara, who lived in the Sandveld and begged him to transfer to him some of his numerous followers. Presumably he wanted to use them for the purpose of enriching himself forcibly despoiling other wealthy cattle owners. Tjipangandjara sent him back the reply that he required his people himself, but he was sending his friend a number of oxen as a present; with these he could buy wives and breed children of his own, and then he could soon build up a tribe again, which would not leave him in the lurch, as so many of his people had done when they saw that his father, Tjirue, was reduced to poverty. Tjamuaha accepted the oxen, acted upon his friend's advice, and achieved some measure of success.

After the victory over the Tswana, Vedder goes on (1938:143ff.), the Herero began to spread at a faster rate, having a greater land area they could exploit. And yet, setting up distant cattle posts was no easy task. Besides the danger of stock depletion due to forays by the Bushmen and Bergdamas, intratribal cattle raiding among the Herero was also common. (These frequent raids were confirmed by my own informants.) Considering his subsequent behavior, it is likely that Tjamuaha as well indulged in raiding. We may surmise, therefore, that Tjamuaha managed to acquire enough cattle to justify his status as *omuhona.*

Further, as more people migrated to the area, what I have been calling a neighborhood must have evolved with Tjamuaha as *omuhona,* as it had before around Mutjise and Tjirue. This was only one of several such *omuhona*-led neighborhoods,[25] but it eventually attained a level of prominence that the others never achieved.

This began when, in 1842, Tjamuaha allied himself with the powerful Hottentot leader Jonker Afrikaner. Thus far we have posited control over a valued resource as the single most significant factor in the emergence of an *omuhona*. Such an interpretation is sufficient to account for the early rise of *ovahona* and neighborhoods throughout South West Africa; but to account for the increased political importance of the *omuhona* at Okahandja, we must look to the relationship of the Herero with non-Herero groups, specifically the Hottentots and later the Europeans. To do this, the historical picture must be briefly sketched in.

In their southward migration, the Herero came into increasing contact with the various Hottentot groups which occupied roughly the southern half of South West Africa. Although sporadic fighting had occurred between Herero and Hottentots before, it was not until 1825 that large-scale hostilities commenced.

It was in this year, according to Hahn (1896:238), that a number of Hottentots, attracted by the Herero herds, joined together to attack some Herero and take their cattle. The Herero, though fewer in number and taken by surprise, turned defeat into victory. This battle signaled the beginning of ten years of hostilities (circa 1825–35), during which the Herero established a tentative and precarious supremacy over the Hottentots.

But the Hottentots had by no means given up the struggle. Their need was met by the emergence of one of the greatest tribal military leaders in southern Africa: Jonker Afrikaner, sometimes referred to as the Napoleon of the South.

A group of Hottentots, called Orlams (or Orlaams), under the leadership of Jager Afrikaner (baptized Christian Afrikaner just before his death) had crossed the Orange River into South West Africa from Cape Colony around the turn of the nineteenth century. (Other Hottentots, of course, were already living throughout South West Africa.) The Orlams crossed into South West because of political and economic pressures from the Cape. Jager personally was a wanted outlaw, and he sought safety in South West (Goldblatt 1971:7–9).

At Jager's death a dispute arose regarding succession to leadership. Vedder (1938:179) makes the following comments:

> According to the ancient law of the Namas [Hottentots], the eldest brother was entitled to be chief and many members of the tribe supported his claim. Jonker, however, Jager's younger son, knew very well that his father had chosen him as successor, and he too had his following. As he would not forego his claims, a feud arose which ended in Jonker leaving the tribe, together with his supporters and a small number of stock. In his father's lifetime he had taken a prominent part in some of the raids, and now he became a gang leader such as the Orange River had never yet known. He undertook numerous plundering expeditions on both banks of the river and, in dividing the spoils, he made his chief objective, in the beginning, not the acquisition of property, but the equipment of his men. The greater part of the loot went into the hands of traders, who delivered to him in exchange guns, powder, and shot. With every fresh gun he acquired his strength increased and, as it occurred, the loot increased too and he procured more and more guns with the proceeds of it.

The Hottentots in the north, unwilling to submit to the Herero, sent emissaries to Jonker to request his aid. Jonker replied that he would lend his assistance provided he would be granted the right to settle wherever he chose in their territory. Goldblatt (1971:10) sums up nicely:

> He led his following in a northerly direction and aided the ruler of the Red Nation—a Nama tribe—in repelling the Hereros, who were defeated in three bloody battles in 1835, and driven back from the south to beyond the Aus mountains near the present Windhoek.

For the next several years a state of tension and armed conflict obtained between the Herero, who had been driven back toward the north, and the Hottentots. Jonker had firmly established himself at Windhoek, which the Herero considered their land and were none too pleased about losing.

> Windhoek was old tribal property of theirs and was the gateway to the south, which they did not want to see closed. They were wont to say that wherever the Herero cattle have grazed

is Herero country, and on that ground they laid claim to the southern territories. The Namas were likewise wont to say that wherever the Nama hunter has set his foot is Nama country, and upon this they based their claim to the northern territories [Vedder 1938:182].

Jonker, however, with the aid of firearms, horses, and the availability of large Hottentot fighting forces lured by the Herero wealth in cattle maintained the upper hand. His object allegedly was to exterminate the Herero and set up a kingdom with himself as head.

This was the situation when Hugo Hahn and Heinrich Kleinschmidt, missionaries from the Rhenish Missionary Society (Barmen, Germany), arrived at Jonker's settlement in Windhoek in 1842. They were present on Christmas Eve 1842 when Tjamuaha (and another Herero named Kahitjene) arrived at Windhoek to conclude a pact with Jonker (Goldblatt 1971:15–16; Vedder 1938:198–200).[26]

The Herero were scattered about South West Africa in independent, politically autonomous groupings, and Jonker was conquering them one at a time. To insure his own safety and to protect his herds, Tjamuaha entered into the 1842 agreement with Jonker, whose headquarters were not far away in Windhoek, to refrain from raiding each other. Since intratribal feuding and cattle-raiding were prevalent among the Herero, it was advantageous for Tjamuaha to be allied with a powerful protector like Jonker. While other Herero were losing cattle through raiding and the depredations of the Hottentots, Tjamuaha's herds remained relatively safe. Jonker on his part recognized the military advantage and measure of security afforded by having those Herero living nearest him as allies.

> He wanted to present Tjamuaha's sons with guns as a token of his friendship and confidence and to give Kahitjene one too. He was anxious to train the young Hereros in preparation for times of mutual danger, and Maherero [Tjamuaha's son] ought to be in command of them. Tjamuaha was quite pleased with the idea [Vedder 1938:200].

As Goldblatt (1971:21–2) points out, these Herero became in effect the vassals of Jonker. Even when, two years later, Jonker turned in earnest against the Herero, Tjamuaha remained comparatively safe. Hahn (1829:239–40) states that in 1844 Jonker attacked the Herero "on some ridiculous grounds," fought the "tribes" one by one, and defeated them since they "were under *no* single ruler." That the Herero were continually feuding among themselves was an aid to Jonker's conquest.

And conquest it was, for Jonker initiated an all-out advance against the Herero with the goal of subjugating or destroying them once and for all. And he succeeded. For the next fifteen years or so he established his rule over the Herero. It is unnecessary for present purposes to chronicle the events of this time; Goldblatt (1971) and Vedder (1938) both provide adequate accounts. We need only note that Jonker was able to defeat the several Herero factions and that Tjamuaha allied himself with Jonker against his fellow Herero.

Tjamuaha's alliance with Jonker is economically and politically understandable, as Vedder (1928:158–9) makes clear:

> As Tjamuaha the Chief of Okahandja suffered no other chiefs besides himself, he became a traitor to his own people, for not only did he destroy some of the chieftainships in order to secure grazing for his own cattle but actually voluntarily joined the oppressor Jonker and drove to him the cattle which the latter extorted from the Hereros. Thus the tribe of Tjamuaha was regarded as a vassal of Jonker. The reward consisted of sparing the cattle of Tjamuaha. In order to enable him, however, to protect the herds of Jonker the latter supplied the submissive Tjamuaha with a number of rifles, which action later became disastrous to the Hottentots.

Jonker was often in debt to European traders, and he met his debts by taking cattle from the Herero to give as payment to the traders. "Ultimately," says Vedder (1928:159), "Jonker considered it more expedient to remove his residence from Windhoek to Okahandja, so as to be nearer the riches of the Hereros." With the aid of his Herero allies under Tjamuaha, his Bergdama servants, his Hottentot allies, as well as his own Orlams, he ranged far and wide in raids against the Herero for cattle. Vedder (1938:255) remarks that Maharero, who resided as a hostage with Jonker, often led Jonker's raiders.

How Tjamuaha came to be allied with Jonker has been outlined because it is this alliance and the comparative prosperity it engendered for Tjamuaha's group which aid in understanding how Maharero, his successor, later rose to prominence.

During this period, the mid-1850's, Jonker did not refrain from attacking other Hottentot groups. Conflict among the Hottentots escalated. Finally, in 1858, a peace treaty was signed by all the Hottentot leaders, or kapteins, including Jonker. "The feeling had been gaining ground that the continuous fighting was achieving nothing but misery" (Goldblatt 1971:27).

Goldblatt (1971:27) records the terms of the treaty. Apparently the Hottentot leaders had had enough of Jonker's greed and arrogance, for in their efforts to contain him, they included a clause regarding the Herero. Article iii reads:

> No commando raids are to take place against the Damaras without cause, and any members of the tribe undertaking any raid of their own accord shall be punished.

Most Herero, however, were still under Jonker's thumb—and they were not to get out from under during his lifetime. They were still effectively under his control, despite the treaty. Indeed, considering subsequent events, the treaty terms were more transgressed than honored. Various Hottentot groups raided each other and the Herero as well. But in December 1860, a fatal mistake was made, one which signaled active European entrance into the melee. A party of Hottentots—not Jonker's Orlams—had raided some Mbanderu near Gobabis. On their return, they attacked cattle posts near Otjimbingue and carried off cattle belonging to Europeans, including some owned by a Swede named Charles Andersson (Goldblatt 1971:29).

Andersson and the other Europeans held a council in Otjimbingue in 1860. They planned a retaliatory raid against the Hottentots, but when their property was returned, they relented. The incident, however, and a later altercation between the Hottentots and Andersson (Goldblatt 1971:30) appear to have earned the Hottentots the enmity of Andersson. This enmity was one they could ill afford, for Andersson soon proved instrumental in the Herero's successful attempt to oppose the Hottentots.

The deaths of Tjamuaha and Jonker in 1861 (Goldblatt 1971:29, 31) marked a break between the Okahandja Herero and Hottentot allies. The Herero, especially those under the leadership of

Maharero (who had succeeded Tjamuaha), began to resist the Hottentot domination. The issue was brought to a head at the first major battle of Otjimbingue in 1863. One of my informants described this period as follows.

> The main body of the Herero, those who had moved south, went to war with the Hottentots. The Hottentots had guns, but the Herero had only bows and arrows and clubs. The reason for the war was that the Hottentots came as cattle-raiders to steal Herero cattle. The Herero were at first defeated by the Hottentots because they (the Hottentots) had guns. The Herero became the servants of the Hottentots.
>
> Later the Herero obtained guns. This is how this came about: a man with a load of goods came by selling his wares. He was a German. [Upon subsequent questioning, it became evident that the informant was referring to Andersson.] He asked why the Herero allowed themselves to be so ill-treated by the Hottentots, why they were so subservient. "You should be a strong people," he said. The Herero replied, "But we haven't got guns." The man said, "I want to help you become independent. I will help you get guns."
>
> He went to a place called Otjimbingue. He brought guns from Otjimbingue to sell to the Herero. The Herero bought the guns, got themselves together, and en masse went to Otjimbingue. The Hottentots were angry. They followed the Herero to resubdue them. Another war followed. It was fought for many years. In the end the Herero were victorious and became the lords of the Hottentots. It was during this time that Maharero rose to leadership.

This is a crucial period in Herero history. The Herero established themselves as the single most powerful group in South West. Maharero rose to prominence as a leader and was to become the second most honored Herero folk-hero. (His son Samuel currently holds the highest position in the memory of the Herero.) When present-day Herero in Botswana speak of their history during this period, they are actually referring primarily to the Herero organized around Maharero. This is understandable since it was this group's descendants who made up a large percentage of the Herero who settled in Botswana. What historical material we have, mainly missionary acounts, is also concerned with this group since it was the

Herero in the region where Maharero resided (the Windhoek-Oka-handja-Otjimbingue area) with whom they had most contact. This in itself is not insignificant in explaining the emergence of political authority among the Herero, for, as von Francois (1896:165) points out, the existence of a mission station also contributed to the permanence of a settlement and thus to political authority.

At Jonker's death, Maharero induced the Herero of the Okahandja region to flee. Goldblatt's summary (1971:31–2) will suffice:[27]

> In 1853 the Walfisch Bay Mining Company commenced mining operations a short distance from Otjimbingue, which became the resort of European miners, traders, travellers and hunters. Employment was found at the mine for impoverished Hereros, who were gradually formed into a community under the Chief, Zeraua.
>
> Contact with Europeans at Otjimbingue accustomed the Hereros to the use of fire-arms with which their brethren who accompanied Jonker Afrikaner on his various expeditions had already become acquainted. Soon after the death of Tjamuaha, in 1861, signs of resistance to the Afrikaners began to appear at Otjimbingue. Tjamuaha's sons, Wilhelm Maherero and Kamaherero, at Okahandja, responded to this current by cutting themselves adrift from Christian Afrikaner and escaping to Otjimbingwe.
>
> The realization that the sevants of the Afrikaners had determined to free themselves from their oppressors was the signal for an attack upon Otjimbingwe by Christian Afrikaner in June 1863. The Hereros at Otjimbingwe were assisted by a number of Whites among whom the leading part was played by Andersson. He had on 5 July 1860 bought out the assets of the mining company, and settled down as a business man in Otjimbingwe in the face of objections made at the time by Jonker Afrikaner, who claimed that Otjimbingwe belonged to him.
>
> The attack on Otjimbingwe failed and in the fighting Christian Afrikaner lost his life. In spite of his protestations that he had done nothing to encourage or assist the Hereros, it is clear that Andersson, together with Green played a leading part in the engagement, and he himself later claimed that he had indirectly been the means through which the Hereros had attained their liberty.

These accounts that Maharero's group from the vicinity of Okahandja fled to Otjimbingue, obtained firearms and fortified themselves with the aid of Andersson, and successfully repulsed the pursuing Hottentots at the battle of Otjimbingue in June 1863 are entirely corroborated by my informants and by several published accounts (e.g., Brincker 1899:134; Hahn 1869:241; von Francois 1896:101; Vedder 1928:159, 1938:335–7).

The battle of Otjimbingue, however, was only the beginning. Leadership of the Hottentots went to Jan Jonker Afrikaner, Christian's brother, since Christian's son had not come of age. On the Herero side, Maharero continued to stand at the head of his people in their war of freedom against the Hottentots. Hostilities continued until 1870 when a peace was arranged. The fighting was generally sporadic and consisted chiefly of small skirmishes, although several major battles did occur. During the course of the war, the eastern Herero and Mbanderu rose up and allied with Maharero, increasing his military and political strength; but disagreements with the aforementioned Zeraua led that segment of the Herero to split off from Maharero. For the sake of brevity, I offer the following summary and advise the reader interested in details to consult earlier sources (e.g., Brincker 1899; Goldblatt 1971; Hahn 1869; Vedder 1928, 1938; von Francois 1896; White 1969).

After the battle of Otjimbingue, signaling the beginning of the Herero uprising, the Orlams under Jan Jonker left Okahandja for Windhoek. Jan Jonker refused to admit defeat; he was determined to resubdue the Herero and make them again his servants. A Herero force under an Englishman named Green was mobilized by Andersson and set out against the Hottentots; but Jan Jonker was warned and pulled his forces back.

Though Maharero at this time was a recognized leader by virtue of his wealth and descent, he was by no means chief of the Herero, despite the fact that many of the earlier sources refer to him as "paramount chief of the Herero." This was, in effect, wishful thinking. The Europeans were having difficulty keeping the Herero organized enough to oppose the Hottentots successfully. There were several respected men among the Herero—men of wealth and position and proven ability—but there was no one with whom the Europeans could deal as spokesman for the Herero. No leader's word was binding for all Herero. Indeed, as we have seen, there was no in-herent authority among the Herero to force an individual to loyalty to any one leader. All Herero were free to change their associations, to move from this *omuhona* to that as they saw fit. Raiding and feuds continued among the Herero, working against the unity that would give them strength to oppose effectively their Hottentot foes. So Andersson used his influence to install a "paramount chief." Zeraua was the eldest, and the position was offered to him.

> But Zeraua refused and proposed Maharero. Nobody felt very sympathetic towards Maharero, for it was well known that he and his men had not been responsible for the victory in the bat-tle of the 15th June, but that the Hereros belonging to the mines were the real victors. It was well known, too, that Maharero was avaricious—a characteristic which is not to be admired in a chief; it was noticed as well that Maharero was enervated through having so many wives. This very circum-stance, however, that he had so many wives connected him with all the Hereros of importance, wherever they might be. Maharero was chosen as paramount chief, and the people pledged themselves to obey him.
>
> Andersson had now a man with with whom he could do some-thing. Even if this man had no great ideas of his own, and lacked the energy required of a leader in dangerous times, this defect could be remedied by inspiration on Andersson's part [Vedder 1938:340].

Maharero in reality was not paramount chief and, in fact, the Herero in South West Africa never had a paramount leader; but the Europeans chose someone with whom they dealt as if he were such a chief. For example, von Francois (1896:101) remarks that after the 1863 battle at Otjimbingue, Maharero "won growing influence which extended beyond his herds and pastures. *This was, under-standably, only recognized by the other super- and sub-captains when it suited them*" (emphasis added). And Lehmann (1955:34) says: "A beginning towards a 'paramount chiefdom' among the Herero was made with the temporary appointment of a *omuhona* as common leader of several *otuzo* in the fight against the Hotten-tots. . . . After having achieved its purpose—sometimes even be-fore—the 'paramount chiefdom' dissolved again because it was not an organically developed higher form of statehood."

Soon after the appointment of Maharero as "paramount chief," Andersson managed to have himself named "regent and military commander" of the Herero. Andersson continued in his role as commander-in-chief, directing military operations against the Hottentots, until he was incapacitated in battle on June 15, 1864 at Reheboth. Thereafter, he devoted himself to his business enterprises. It might be well to point out the obvious. Andersson was a trader, not an idealistic romantic fighting for the cause of justice. Goldblatt (1971:32) notes:

> The motive that inspired Andersson was not altogether altruistic. He was interested in the effect of the conflict between Nama and Herero upon his business as a storekeeper, and indeed it was his business interests which brought him actively to the side of the Hereros.

Another passage from Goldblatt (1971:33) illustrates this as well as the practice, begun by Maharero and continued by his son Samuel, of giving over communally held property to outsiders—a practice that was to cause resentment among the Herero population and that would later contribute to the Herero-German war:

> There is also a record of an agreement (26 December 1866) between Andersson and Kamaherero, whereby Kamaherero made a grant to Andersson of certain waterholes and rights of grazing etc. for services rendered by Andersson during the Freedom War. There is a suggestion that Andersson threatened to shoot Kamaherero if he had refused.

On July 4, 1867 Andersson died on a trip to Ovamboland. Under his stern leadership, the Herero had been able to inflict considerable damage on the Hottentots. But Jan Jonker had far from given up, though he was experiencing other difficulties.

The Hottentots were quarreling among themselves, and some groups even went over to the Herero. In fact, Maharero in June 1866 had concluded a separate peace with one of the most powerful Hottentot people, the so-called Red Nation.

And Maharero's strength had increased by the addition of the eastern Herero and Mbanderu who rose up against Jan Jonker and the Hottentots near Gobabis. These eastern Herero and Mbanderu had not participated in the war until this time. The Hottentots in the area had been led by a relatively peaceful man, but at his death Jan Jonker began to incite the Hottentots, who already had a growing number of adventurers in their midst, to violence against the Herero and the European traders to enrich themselves. He spurred them on with visions of a rich empire encompassing all of South West Africa under Hottentot rule.

> All superfluous Hereros and Mbanderus were to be killed; all the Europeans were to be driven out of the country; then the Hereros were to be forced to resume again their former servitude. Jan Jonker was to be the master of the country, and Frederick Vlermuis [as eastern Hottentot leader] the second man in the empire, and this was to stretch from the Orange to the Kunene. Naturally all the tribes which had been subdued were to pay regular tribute, and from this they would live comfortably without working.
>
> The Hereros and Mbanderus heard all this loud talk. It seemed to them that the time was not exactly ripe for trying to carry out plans of that kind, when there was in Otjimbingue a man like Maharero keeping a careful eye on the Afrikaners and dealing them heavy blows whenever it was necessary. They got together, therefore, and before the inhabitants of Gobabis realized it, a Herero rebellion had broken out. Many of the Orlams lost their lives, and many of them lost all their stock [Vedder 1938:351].

Jan Jonker was considerably weakened. He had been bested by the Herero under Maharero and by the Herero and Mbanderu in the east. Moreover, the Hottentot forces were not unified; some had made individual peace treaties with Maharero. Jan Jonker was growing desperate.

In December 1867 he unsuccessfully attacked Otjimbingue. The Herero pursued but did little damage. Jan Jonker escaped westward to Walvis Bay where he raided the whites and made off with a large amount of booty.

Maharero, too, was experiencing difficulty. Vedder (1938:359–60) says:

Zeraua's and Maharero's people could not agree any more, and
Zeraua left and went to live on the Omaruru River. He left
Maharero to defend himself unaided against the Namas and
Jan Jonker, and that meant that he was very much weakened.
Besides that, there was not sufficient grazing for the immense
number of cattle he had. In the district of Otjimbingue the veld
was bare, and the beginning of the new year, 1868, did not bring
with it the long expected rains. Maharero looked round for the
cause of his misfortunes. His witch-doctors told him: 'Your
father Tjamuaha is angry with you in his grave at Okahandja.
You have deserted him and have not made any sacrifices. Instead of this you have been listening to the missionaries.
Tjamuaha must now be propitiated, and that can only be done
by your people.'

So Maharero returned to Okahandja and resumed his residence
there.

During the year 1868, both Maharero and Jan Jonker marshaled
their forces. In November they met outside Okahandja. The ensuing
battle was a decisive victory for the Herero (Vedder 1938:362). To
be brief, this Hottentot defeat led the way for a peace treaty. A
meeting was arranged, and in 1870 Maharero and Jan Jonker, with
other Nama leaders in attendance, met in Okahandja. (See Goldblatt 1971:44ff. for details).[28]

The terms of the 1870 peace treaty were pointedly unfavorable to
Jan Jonker. He was confined to Windhoek, and the influence he had
once wielded was severely limited. Maharero, considered the Herero
paramount chief by Europeans, felt that Jan Jonker was now his
subject and held Windhoek only as a grant from him. The other
Herero, though not recognizing Maharero as supreme, were willing
enough to let him continue in his delusion. First of all, he *was* indeed
a rich and powerful man. He had many cattle and many followers
dependent on him, and he was connected through marriage to
prominent families throughout Hereroland.[29]

But perhaps the most important consideration for the Herero in
allowing Maharero to strut about as if he were a petty king was that
his settlement lay closest to Jan Jonker's and could act as a buffer if
fighting broke out again. Vedder (1938:404) remarks:

The difficult times were past and the cattle were no longer in danger. Those of the chieftains who did not live on the border were devoting all their efforts to increasing their stock. Maharero, however, lived right on the border and so he had to take upon himself its entire protection. The other chiefs left, therefore, to him the regulation of all political relationships amongst the allies, for they did not like this man at all, and, rich though he was, they regarded him as far too greedy for a paramount chief.

It is therefore not difficult to understand why Maharero became a powerful leader. It was his group which stood, face-to-face, so to speak, with the Hottentots to the south. His importance in military encounters would contribute to his authority. Tjamuaha, his father before him, had amassed a great deal of wealth and with it personal status that he passed as a legacy to Maharero, who had grown up in Jonker Afrikaner's camp and knew the Hottentots well. It was Maharero who, bitter about his treatment at the hands of the Hottentots, was one of the first to break away from their grip at Jonker's death. He had grown accustomed to the use of firearms and was trained by the Hottentots. It is not unlikely that other Herero would rally around him when they sought to free themselves. And Maharero, apparently no less ambitious and avaricious than his father, had strengthened his political position through judicious marriages. He might count on affinal allies to support his claims or at least not to dispute them too vigorously. And, not the least important, from the time of the missionary Hahn through that of the German occupation (from 1884 on), the Otjimbingue-Okahandja region, in which Maharero lived and which was first settled by Mutjise, his great-grandfather, was a center of European activity. When the outsiders sought a native leader to turn to as a representative of his people, Maharero was at hand. It was most likely the backing Maharero received from the Europeans which was the most important factor that supported his claim to leadership (as it later was for his son Samuel).

It would be unnecessarily tiresome to chronicle in detail the European incursion in South West Africa and the effects of contact with Europeans on political authority among the Herero. To some extent Lehmann (1955) has done this. For a more comprehensive account the reader is advised to consult one of the several histories of South West Africa, of which Goldblatt's (1971) is perhaps the most concise and least biased against the Herero.

Nevertheless, a brief resumé of the salient facts is in order to support the interpretation proposed here. I suggest that the European colonization of South West Africa (which began in earnest during the ten years' peace after 1870) affected Herero political authority in two major ways.

First, it strengthened the authority of the various *ovahona* within their neighborhoods. This was the effect produced by Europeans' occupying open land around these neighborhoods and thus limiting Herero freedom of movement. It tended to confine homesteads to the neighborhood and hence kept them within the sphere of the *omuhona's* authority. Before European settlement, more open land was available, and a disgruntled *omuini* could simply pack up his few belongings and move his herds and his dependents to a new area. The existence of this option, as previously asserted, was crucial in checking the development of coercive authority of *ovahona*. But European occupation of such land and their acquisition of large tracts for mining (see Goldblatt 1971:115ff. for a summary of this acquisition of land by Europeans) tended to confine the Herero to neighborhoods. (The importance of "social circumscription" has been emphasized by Carneiro [1970] in his theory of the origin of the state.)

Though this process unfolded gradually over time, it can be illustrated by an occurrence in 1900, after South West Africa became officially a German possession. Samuel Maharero (the son of Maharero and his successor as *omuhona* at Okahandja) and Michael Tjizeta (at the time the *omuhona* at Omaruru) were persuaded by the German authorities to agree that "those Herero living in Samuel's country remain Samuel's people, " and "those living in Michael's country remain Michael's people" (quoted in Lehmann 1955:38). This is an explicit articulation in concrete terms of a process that had been slowly progressing for some years. It may even be seen as the formalized culmination of that process. Thus, one is led to the opinion that Herero political organization in South West Africa in the years immediately prior to the German-Herero war is best characterized by the term "incipient chiefdom."

Second, the European presence contributed as well to an "incipient paramount chiefdom." Two things are clear from the ethnographic and historical sources: 1) that Herero political organization never developed a full-fledged paramount chieftaincy, and 2) that the tendency toward paramountcy originated as a result of conflict with Hottentots and was strengthened by contact with Europeans.[30]

We have already seen how Maharero came to prominence during the war with the Hottentots from 1863 to 1870. In 1880 he again asserted his leadership when renewed Herero-Hottentot hostilities broke out. During the course of the war, Maharero accepted the "protection" of Germany. His alliance with the Germans strengthened his claims to leadership (since he was supported by German troops), but his dependence on them facilitated the German plan to subjugate the Herero. The Germans planned to use the Herero to subdue the Hottentots and then to turn on the Herero and disarm them. (See Goldblatt 1971:108ff. for details.)

Before the time of the German occupation, however, other Europeans, notably W. C. Palgrave from Cape Colony, sought to install a paramount chief (Maharero) among the Herero in order to facilitate negotiations for land rights (Goldblatt 1971:53–71). This is amply described by Lehmann (1955) and therefore will not be repeated here.

I shall, however, present in some detail an account of the events leading to the Herero-German war.[31] I do so for several reasons. 1) Such an account by describing the means employed by the Germans to establish their supremacy illustrates the political fragmentation of the Herero in South West Africa. 2) The war was the most important factor in determining the course of Herero social change since it destroyed the economic foundation of Herero society. 3) It was the defeat of the Herero in this war that led to their flight to Botswana where my fieldwork was conducted. Considerable time in the field was spent attempting to elicit information regarding Herero settlement in Botswana. Since the details of that settlement are not available anywhere else, an account will be presented here. For this, some understanding of the events surrounding the war is necessary.

Though Bismarck had established South West Africa as a German territory in 1884, it was not until 1889, when Captain Curt von Francois arrived with a small military force to protect German mining interests that the German occupation began in earnest (Goldblatt 1971:111).

Before this, however, Maharero had been persuaded to agree to a protection treaty (one reason for this was that he feared, with little basis, a Boer invasion). For this he was chided by his enemy Hendrik Witbooi, who had by now become the most powerful Hottentot leader. Soon after the German-Herero protection treaty, many Hottentot groups made similar pacts with the Germans—except, that is, for Hendrik Witbooi.

Hendrik had the foresight to see what was happening, that the "protection" treaties would result in subjugation by the Germans (this foresight is apparent in a letter he wrote to Maharero which is in part reproduced in Goldblatt 1971:112–3). Because of this realization, he had repeatedly tried to conclude a peace with Samuel Maharero after Maharero's death in 1890. (It was not until November 1892 that he was successful and the last Herero-Hottentot war was brought to an end.)

Von Francois settled his force first outside Otjimbingue and then in October 1890, the month and year of Maharero's death, he established himself at Windhoek, causing ill-feeling among the Herero, who considered it their territory. But, as Goldblatt (1971:113) records, "Von Francois, very soon, made up his mind as to the requirements of the situation. South West Africa was to become settled by Whites."

Seeing that an alliance between the Herero and Hendrik could lead to resistance to the Germans, von Francois attacked Hendrik as a first step in his plans to attack each of the Hottentot groups, subdue them, and then disarm the Herero. "His object was to confine the Natives to reserves and have the rest of their land as Crown land" (Goldblatt 1971:113–4).

In the end, this is what would eventually happen in South West Africa; but it was not to be as easy as von Francois envisioned, and he would not be the one to do it.

In short, von Francois failed. He failed at the outset in his campaign against Hendrik. Hendrik succeeded in capturing von

Francois' horses, and with them attacked and destroyed the German communication line to the coast in 1893.

> The effect of all this was increasing distrust of the Home Government by the White people of the Territory and at the end of 1893 Major Leutwein was sent out to investigate the situation, shortly afterwards replacing von Francois, who, however, remained in the country until 24 April 1894 [Goldblatt 1971:114].

Where von Francois failed, Leutwein, a skilled military commander and shrewd—some might say unscrupulous—manipulator of people and of situations, succeeded. Leutwein had only a small number of men, but, according to Goldblatt (1971:120):

> Leutwein did, however, possess an instrument which, together with the small military force, enabled him, step by step, in the course of a number of years to bring about a transfer of the greater part of the land from the Natives to the White man. His plan, carried out with consummate skill and complete cynicism, was to obtain the assistance of various tribes in subduing other tribes, and to enlist the aid of the leaders of one tribe in destroying other leaders of the same tribe. The age-old principle of *divide et impera* which Leutwein himself professed to be employing [sic].

After establishing a temporary armistice with Hendrik, Leutwein was presented with a situation among the Herero that allowed him to establish German authority over them by supporting Samuel in his contest for power. The matter of succession to Maharero's position is an involved one, and I will elaborate more fully in a later discussion of inheritance and succession. For present purposes, Goldblatt's (1971:122ff.) summary, from which I quote liberally, will suffice. Though the following excerpts are rather lengthy, their appearance here is justified because a) they provide an understanding of the political disunity of the Herero, and b) they illustrate how, with European backing, an incipient paramount chiefdom began to emerge among the Herero.

> No sooner had Leutwein returned to Windhoek with his men than an opportunity arose to establish his hold upon the

Hereros. According to Herero custom, Tjetjoo, the son of Kamaherero's eldest sister, was entitled to the succession. He, however, waived his rights and Nicodemus then became entitled to the succession. But apparently through the mistaken impression of von Francois that the succession went to the eldest son of the deceased chief, the German authorities treated Samuel as the legitimate chief.

While the armistice with Hendrik was still in force, a dispute arose between Samuel and the wealthy and influential old Riarua, the chief advisor of Kamaherero and the commander-in-chief of the Herero forces. Samuel was worried and left Okahandja for Osona, from where he complained to Leutwein and asked for assistance.

'Such a favourable opportunity,' says Leutwein, 'of interfering in the affairs of the Hereros would never again offer itself, and I gladly assured Samuel of my assistance.'

Leutwein, thereupon, went to Osona with a small force. He took Samuel's side and effected a settlement which ended in Riarua's being relieved of his arms and ammunition.

Leutwein's suggestion that Samuel should agree to a German garrison being established in Okahandja, to support his chieftainship, was gratefully accepted by Samuel. Thus, with a clever stroke Leutwein succeeded in effecting the occupation of Okahandja by a military force, of making Samuel dependent on him, and of creating a division in the ranks of the Hereros of southern Damaraland [p. 122].

The German governor soon found additional opportunities to capitalize upon Herero political fragmentation and intratribal disputes in order to entrench white control in Hereroland.

Another circumstance which favoured Leutwein was a dispute between Samuel Maharero and Nicodemus, the stepson of Riarua who, as previously mentioned, had claims to the chieftainship. Nicodemus tried to enlist the support of the German Government, but Leutwein preferred to leave the dispute unsettled, thereby ensuring that the split between the two would be perpetuated.

Wasting no time, Leutwein proceeded to deal with a case in Omaruru where a White man who had murdered a Native had himself been killed by one of Manasse's men, in excess of instructions given by the Herero Chief of Omaruru. Leutwein

took Samuel with him in order to demonstrate his support of
Samuel's paramountcy, but Samuel had not been recognized as
Paramount Chief by Manasse, and this action of Leutwein's
only served to intensify a cleavage which already existed between them.

Manasse was afraid that he might be taxed with the guilt in
the matter of the White man's death, and adopted a submissive
attitude towards Leutwein. 'To sift the truth in the matter of
the killing was not,' said Leutwein, 'as important as to exploit
politically the awkward situation in which Manasse found himself.' This Leutwein did by requiring him to cede to the German
Government the Bergdama settlement at Okombahe [pp.
123–4].

Other incidents illustrate how German support led to the growth
of the authority of certain Herero leaders and created further divi-
siveness and discontent.

Turning his attention now to the eastern Hereros where
Tjetjoo, Nicodemus and Kahimemua refused to recognize the
eastern boundary which had been agreed upon between Leutwein and Samuel, Leutwein took Samuel with him for a friendly
chat with these chiefs. A situation which threatened to lead to
fighting ended peacefully—although from the point of view of
these chiefs, not happily.

Leutwein secured the recognition by Nicodemus and Kahimemua, of Samuel as Paramount Chief. Nicodemus was thereupon appointed by Samuel as chief of the eastern Hereros and
Kahimemua as chief of the 'Mbanderus (close relatives of the
Hereros), but the latter was to be subordinate to Nicodemus.
An alteration was made to the eastern boundary which had
been agreed upon between Leutwein and Samuel, the boundary
now running along the middle line between the Seeis River and
Nosob River. Leutwein then went north, where on 21 August
1895 he agreed with Samuel and the son of Kambazembi, the
powerful Chief of the northern Hereros, as to the northern
boundary of Hereroland.

Still intent upon exploiting the differences amongst the
Hereros and playing one against the other, Leutwein made use
of the habit of the Hereros to graze their cattle wherever grazing was found to be necessary. He wished to stop trespassing,

and brought Samuel into the matter, by agreeing with him that
Leutwein should be entitled to impound all trespassing cattle,
Samuel to receive half and the Government the other half. But,
as Leutwein remarks, this would result in an increase in
Samuel's cattle, so, instead of the cattle being divided, they
were to be sold and the proceeds divided. The cattle would be
sold by public auction to White purchasers. [The reason Leutwein did not want Samuel to have the cattle was that the more
cattle he had, the more land he would require for grazing; and it
was Leutwein's objective to deprive the Herero of as much land
as he could.]

In this way he concentrated upon Samuel the anger of the
chiefs whose people had their cattle impounded, and at the
same time he ensured the passing of Herero cattle to the
Whites.

Soon afterwards there arose the inevitable trouble through
the impoundment of trespassing cattle, and a conflict
developed between the Hereros who owned the cattle and the
Whites upon whose land the cattle trespassed.

Matters came to a head at the beginning of 1896 at a meeting
held by Leutwein with the Hereros at Okahandja. The Hereros
wanted: 1) the eastern boundary to be shifted to include the
Seeis River; 2) that punishment for trespassing should be
meted out jointly by Samuel and Leutwein.

In regard to the second point no change was made, and in regard to the first point, as Leutwein felt it was merely a matter
of shifting the border of Hereroland about 8 km, he agreed to it.

But a more important reason for hs agreement was the fact
that this shifting of the border benefited the western Hereros,
i.e. the Okahandja Hereros under Samuel, as against the eastern Hereros under Nicodemus. As a consequence Nicodemus
claimed that Gobabis should be given to him.

'Now,' says Leutwein, 'an excellent opportunity again offered itself to apply the *divide et impera* principle. Okahandja's
wishes were granted and those of Nicodemus refused. The result was that three months afterwards the Okahandja Hereros
were on our side against Nicodemus' [pp. 125–6].

In March 1896, Nikodemus, Kahimemua, and some Khauas Hottentots rebelled against the Germans. They were defeated by Leutwein with the aid of Samuel and the western Herero.

. . . Kahimemua and Nicodemus were taken to Okahandja, court-martialled and shot. Leutwein saw to it that two leading members of Samuel's Council formed part of the tribunal which condemned the two Herero leaders.

. . . .

After the execution of Nicodemus and Kahimemua (13 June 1896) Leutwein returned to Windhoek. He says that he himself would have pardoned Kahimemua, but that Samuel insisted upon his execution.

The echoes of these executions, which aroused deep emotions at the time, are still heard amongst the 'Mbanderu of whom Kahimemua was chief [p. 126].

Thus, Leutwein was skillfully establishing German domination of the Herero and setting up Samuel as his puppet "paramount chief" of the Herero. But it was not long before Samuel did an about-face and turned against the Germans in the brief but catastrophic Herero rebellion of 1904.

The following summary of this period is based on my informants' testimonies. Most of the accounts are brief and simplified:

Maharero's brother's son [i.e., Kavikunua's son] Nikodemus made an attempt to seize power from Samuel. Nikodemus was assisted by an ally named Kahimemua. Samuel reported their attempt to the Germans. The Germans sought out Nikodemus and Kahimemua, arrested them, and executed them. Samuel continued as leader.

The German war then followed. The Germans wanted the Herero to pay taxes and to register their guns. The Herero refused. Thus began the war. It was also true that the land Samuel was selling to the Germans was land the Herero wanted back, so they attacked the European settlers while the German forces were away dealing with the Hottentots. When they returned, they defeated the Herero in battle. They captured many, but some, with Samuel, escaped to Botswana.

Another informant says:

The Germans were disrespectful about Herero traditions. They would destroy their sacred hearth, take away the upturned bush, and put out the fire. They would shoot Herero cattle in the field for meat. The Herero were angry at the German contempt for their way of life, so they went to war.

But others gave more involved accounts, such as the following:

At first the Germans were good to the Herero. They co-operated with the Herero. They helped them in the war with the Hottentots. But after the war, the Germans changed.

The Germans said, "Your guns are all defective. Bring them to us and we will fix them and make them right."

Some did give up their guns, but others hid theirs. At this time Samuel was leader, for Maharero had died. Samuel turned in his guns.

But three groups refused to cede their arms: those of Otjiseu, Nikodemus, and Kahimemua. Samuel and the other Herero who had given up their guns wanted to take these three to task for their delinquency and prepared to bring them to trial. So all three left the area. They went to a place near Gobabis to settle. But there they met up with some Germans who were camped nearby. The German captain asked, "Why have you come here? You are not supposed to be here. Where is your leader Samuel? Did he send you?"

The Herero were annoyed. They said, "Don't ask such foolish questions."

All this while, the German had a big knife [a saber?] and was harassing a Herero with it, poking him in the chest and stomach. So the Herero shot and killed him.

This precipitated a battle between the Herero and the Germans in the camp. The Germans were defeated, but they managed to send a report of the matter to German headquarters at Okahandja (this was also the place where Samuel lived).

Nikodemus and Kahimemua were not themselves personally present at this battle when the Herero met and fought the Germans. When Samuel heard of the matter, he sent Nikodemus' younger brother and Kahimemua's younger brother (both of whom had remained with Samuel) to call them back. Nikodemus came back in good faith but was imprisoned by Samuel at Okahandja. Kahimemua refused to return. Samuel and the Germans went out to fight Kahimemua's and Otjiseu's people [the Otjiseu-group to which the informant refers was headed by Tjetjoo, the senior member of Otjiseu lineage at the time]. There was a big battle. There were many deaths on both sides. But Samuel and the Germans finally won. Kahimemua was caught. To avoid possible future trouble with these groups, Samuel and the Germans took Tarauhota, Kandjii's son as hostage [Tarauhota was actually Kandjii's grandson and Tjetjoo's son].

There then followed a great meeting of Herero and Germans to judge who had provoked whom near Gobabis and who was at fault for starting the fight. A German presided at this judgment. The general feeling was that the Germans had ill-treated the Herero and provoked the encounter. But Nikodemus' younger brother and Kahimemua's younger brother stood up and said that for what they had done they should be executed. Yet the Herero consensus disagreed with this. The Germans, however, thought this was a good idea, saying, "See, even their own brothers acknowledge their guilt and want them punished." So they took Nikodemus and Kahimemua and hanged them. And the remaining guns were taken from their followers.

But Kahaka [a son of Tjetjoo] refused to relinquish his arms. He wanted to continue the fight against the Germans and expel them from the land. But no one would go along with him. So Kahaka left South West Africa and went to Botswana.

Now the Herero were like helpless women. They had no guns and could not fight the Germans. They were subject to all sorts of abuses and indignities at the hands of the Germans. When the Germans found a Herero woman alone, they would shoot and kill her for sport. When asked why, they would respond that they thought it was an animal, claiming that the three-pronged hat looked like an animal's horns and that the leather apron looked like an animal's skin. But they would also shoot Herero men when they found them in the pasture with the cattle. And they would shoot Herero cattle for meat. And they made light of Herero beliefs and customs. They purposely destroyed the sacred fire when they came upon it.

The Germans also tried to force the Herero to buy European goods and clothes, though the Herero at that time did not want them. One time some Germans brought some goods to the Herero, left them, and went away. They wanted to see if the Herero would take them. They did not. When the Germans came back, they said the Herero had to pay for the goods anyway. So the Herero paid, even though they did not take the goods.

Then the German commander called the Herero to a meeting. He said he wanted all Herero castrated. But, the German leader conceded, just as a herd of cattle needs some bulls, so did people. So he would not castrate the men of Samuel's group.

At this time Samuel's German friend secretly informed him that the Germans intended to kill him as a demonstration of their authority. They could then say, "We have made you nothing. We have taken your land. We have taken your genitals. And here is the head of your leader, too, whom we have killed."

So the Herero people held their own meeting. They reckoned it would be better that they die, that they lose their heads instead of their genitals. They held a war council and decided to fight the Germans. But they had only bows and arrows. So they employed various ruses to steal firearms and ammunition.

They would go to a German police station, taking some people with them and claiming they had stolen cattle. When the Germans came outside to talk to the people, some Herero would sneak inside the station and steal guns. Or they would take cattle to a trading store, ostensibly to sell them. When the trader came out to examine the cattle, some Herero would slip inside and steal guns.

But they were defeated in the war and some fled to Botswana, while others were subdued by the Germans.

As far as can be determined from other sources, the above account, though erroneous in minor detail, is generally accurate.

Goldblatt gives several reasons for the uprising. He reproduces (1971:133–4) a letter written by Samuel, which was never before published in its entirety, in which Samuel recounts the reasons for the war: 1) whites often killed Herero with impunity; 2) whites pressured the Herero to accept goods on credit and then confiscated cattle in payment of these debts, often in excess of the debt; 3) the justice system favored the whites; 4) imprisoned Herero were maltreated and often killed by their jailers; 5) German soldiers, especially a certain officer, made repeated attempts to take his (Samuel's) life.

Goldblatt's analysis (1971:134–8) concurs, and he adds further causes. He blames the war on: 1) the credit system of the whites; 2) the unfair administration of justice; 3) the growth of white trading and farming during 1900–03 (often whites would simply occupy some land without bothering to acquire it through legal procedures); 4) the Germans wanted to confine the Herero to reserves and in 1902 Otjimbingue was declared such a reserve, the first for the Herero, and plans were being made for others at Okahandja and Gobabis.[32]

Not cited by Goldblatt as a direct cause of the war, but mentioned in my informant's account above, was the Herero's fear of having their firearms confiscated. The Germans had ordered Herero guns registered, and the Herero were afraid this was the first step toward confiscation. The Herero in the east under Tjetjoo at first refused to comply with the order. A German military force, accompanied by Samuel, visited Tjetjoo and persuaded him to comply (Goldblatt 1971:131).

Not long after, the German forces moved south to suppress an uprising among a Hottentot group. It was while they were gone that the Herero rising occurred. On January 12, 1904 the Herero-German war began.

It began with the killing of 123 Germans. It is to be noted that the Herero directed their hostility toward the Germans only. Samuel had ordered that "the men do not lay their hands on Englishmen, Basters, Berg Damaras, Namas and Boers" (quoted in Goldblatt 1971:135). According to Goldblatt, it was understood that missionaries were not to be harmed either. (Nevertheless, contrary to Samuel's wishes, seven Boers and three women were killed, in addition to the Germans, in the fury of the uprising.)

The war was brief. The Herero were thoroughly defeated at the battle of Waterberg in August 1904 (Lehmann 1955:40, Vedder 1928:161–2). Goldblatt (1971:131) succinctly records the events:

> When it became evident that practically all the Hereros (by far the greatest tribe in the territory outside Ovamboland) had risen in revolt, large military forces were sent out from Germany.
>
> The Hereros, although showing great resistance, were unable to match the military strength of the Germans. The fighting took place under difficult conditions. The German soldiers had freedom of movement; the Hereros however moved about with their wives and children, and, worst of all, with their vast herds of cattle which they would under no circumstances abandon even in retreat.

The result was catastrophic. They were utterly defeated at Waterberg and many were killed, but most escaped by fleeing in the direction of Bechuanaland which was the only way in which they could avoid encirclement. Some also fled north-wards into Ovamboland, and others took refuge in parts of the country which were not accessible to military troops, and where the means of livelihood were very sparse. The retreat into Bechuanaland was across hard, cruel, and waterless country. Many more lost their lives in trying to cross this 'Sandveld' than in actual battle.

Among those who escaped to Bechuanaland was Samuel Maha-rero. According to Wagner (1952:3) some 2000 Herero managed to cross the border. With their entry into the new land, another phase of Herero history commences.

For present purposes, those Herero who remained in South West Africa need not be considered further; for the Herero of South West prior to the German war and the Herero who fled to and flourished in Botswana as a result of that war form one historical line and are treated as such herein.

Though the history of Botswana is well documented (especially by Sillery 1952, 1965; other works on Botswana include Munger 1965 and Young 1966, in addition to those cited elsewhere in this study; Phenane 1974 has compiled a bibliography of historical sources), almost no mention is made of the Herero, how they in-fluenced or were influenced by historical developments, or what their precise relationship was to the numerically and politically dominant Tswana peoples.[33] Consequently, after a few very brief notes on Botswana, the early days of the Herero in their new land will be presented based almost entirely on my informants' accounts. This will lead to a consideration of the *omuhona* among the Herero today, with which this section on political authority will be con-cluded.

The first European visitors to the Bechuanaland territory in the first decade of the nineteenth century were missionaries. Other mis-sionaries, such as Robert Moffat and David Livingstone, soon fol-lowed. Traders and entrepreneurs came next. The Boers tried to get a foothold. But eventually, after urgings from missionaries, and in part in response to the German occupation of South West Africa to the west and the threat of the Boer trekkers and the Transvaal to the east, Bechuanaland was brought under formal British protection on January 27, 1885—a bare four months after Germany first granted its official protection to South West Africa.

The Bechuanaland Protectorate remained in existence until September 30, 1966, when it was granted its independence as the Republic of Botswana, a member of the British Commonwealth (Botswana Information Services, n.d.).

The bulk of the population consists of Setswana-speaking peoples, though other tribal groups (such as Kgalagadi, Bushmen, Mbukushu, and, of course, the Herero) reside in Botswana as well. There are eight principal Tswana tribes, each with an hereditary chief: Ngwato (the largest), Ngwaketse, Kwena, Kgatla, Tawana, Lete, Tlokwa, and Rolong. Each tribe traditionally occupied a separate territory. The Tawana, who occupy Ngamiland, the northwestern district, are the group with which the Herero have had most contact, though mention will briefly be made of the Ngwato chief Khama (or Kgama), the grandfather of Sir Seretse Khama, the present (and thus far the only) President of Botswana.

Stevens describes the country (1967:1–2) saying:

> Larger than the British Isles, Botswana is bounded by South Africa, South-West Africa, Zambia (at a point on the map) and Rhodesia. The country is a tableland at a mean altitude of 3,300 feet and with elevation up to 5,000 feet, and is estimated to cover some 220,000 square miles. The regional differences of climate, soil and vegetation are considerable. Most of the west and south-west consists of Kalahari sand-veld and is largely uninhabited, although it is not desert in the strict sense it includes many large tracts of savannah. Everywhere water is in short supply. The 1965 census places the population at 542,104, of whom 3,900 are Europeans. The population is concentrated in the sub-tropical to temperate eastern region, which is better watered and straddles the railroad to the north. Essentially it is a livestock country which has raised the economy above the bare subsistence level.

In the same volume Henry (1967:161) makes the following comments:

In the south and west, there are vast areas, amounting to more than half the entire country, of undulating scrubland: the Kalahari desert. In the south-west of the area, real desert conditions exist. Rainfall, highest in the northern regions, varies between twelve and twenty-seven inches a year.[34]

In the northwest, in Ngamiland district, is found the Okavango swamp, "the largest swamps in Southern and Central Africa" (Henry 1967:161). Here is a potential water supply that has never been exploited in this thirst-ridden country. The swamp teems with wildlife, malaria, and tsetse fly.

Howe (1973:20) sums up:

> Botswana: Pop. 650,000, spread over area larger than Texas. Multiparty democracy under southern Africa's elder statesman, President Sir Seretse Khama. New mineral discoveries offer potential prosperity. No coastline but short frontier with Zambia. Shares South Africa's currency. Moderate, pro-Western regime. Armed forces: negligible.

The governmental structure differs little from that instituted by the British under their system of "indirect rule." Under the Minister of Local Government and Lands are the District Commissioners, one for each of the nine districts, assisted by a District Council. The District Commissioner is the representative of the national government. Local leadership is provided by community headmen (such as the Herero *ovahona*) or hereditary chiefs (such as are found among the Tswana).

Botswana's primary economic occupation is livestock. It exports beef to England, Switzerland, the Middle East, Zambia, South West Africa, and South Africa.

Currently Botswana is experiencing a severe drought which is damaging its cattle industry considerably. Church, writing of the "West African Drought Pattern" (1973:95), says:

> Since 1951 there is evidence of the southward displacement of climatic zones in the northern hemisphere, and of a northward shift in the southern hemisphere, with a consequent tendency to reduced rainfall along the southern Sahara and northern Kalahari fringes. The equatorial rain belt had been narrowed, although intensified near the Equator. These changes

have been under way for twenty years, and are not likely to change or disappear immediately; indeed, they may be part of a 200-year process. Changes in oceanic circulation may be the cause of new tracks of monsoonal air masses.

Necessarily frail marginal environments have become more hazardous to nomadic pastoralism, catch crops and flood retreat cultivation. Water resources are not good, whilst well development has often caused vegetation and soil degradation around water holes. Ever more people, livestock, and crops compete for apparently diminishing resources, often in remote and landlocked areas. Livestock will have to be limited in these areas, and some people resettled. Pastures need more management, and ranching should be tried in places.

The largest concentration of Herero (according to my informants) is in western Botswana, that part of the country hit hardest by the drought. As a result, Herero settlements that have been in areas for years are breaking up and their inhabitants moving to new locations. The oldest Herero settlement in Botswana, that in the area of Makakun (or Makakung), is only a shadow of what it used to be. To understand the Herero settlement in Botswana, we must focus upon its development.

As a consequence of the Herero defeat by the German forces at the battle of Waterberg in August 1904, Samuel Maharero[35] and a group of Herero fled South West Africa for what was then Bechuanaland. But this was not the first group of Herero immigrants to the British Protectorate. Gibson (1956:111) reports:

> A handful of Herero had already migrated into Ngamiland about 1896 and had been permitted to remain by the Tawana who were in political control of the area. According to my Herero informants, an agreement between Chief Letsholathebe of the Tawana and certain Herero chieftains had been made, when the Tawana were occasionally raided by the Makololo and Matabele (this would probably have been in the 1860's), providing that either tribe could take refuge in the country of the other should the need arise.

Indeed, one of my own informants was about seventeen years old during this migration and was a member of this party. It is from his recollections that the following account is drawn.

The informant, Friedrich, lived at the time in Okahandja, part of the group of which Samuel was the leader since his father's death in 1890. Friedrich's father had grown dissatisfied with conditions under the Germans. He decided to pull up stakes and take his family elsewhere in search of a new life:

> The Germans had brought a big, comfortable chair for Samuel. My father said that Samuel and the Germans were getting too friendly. Eventually, he predicted, there would be trouble and ultimately war. He advised that we leave before the trouble began.

The family's cattle had been lost due to rinderpest. But there was a European named Stanley leaving at that time with a large herd for the Transvaal. Since Friedrich's group was without cattle to support itself on a long trip, they hired themselves as herdsmen to Stanley. Moreover, as Stanley's herdsmen, they would avoid the difficulties they might otherwise encounter trying to cross international boundaries by themselves.

They drove the herd to the Transvaal but soon found life with the Boers no more congenial than with the Germans. Many Herero had accompanied Stanley to the Transvaal but most died of hunger there, and only a few, Friedrich and some relatives, managed to flee to Botswana.[36] (Friedrich said that all the other Herero who went to the Transvaal perished there.)

Khama (the current President Khama's grandfather) was at the time chief of the Ngwato at Serowe in Botswana. Friedrich's small group went to him, explained that they were badly treated by the Boers, and asked if they could settle there. Khama sent them to Tsau.[37]

The group, with just two cows, settled in the area of Tsau on the western side of the Okavango delta. Being poor, they had no choice but to go to work for the Tswana.

Friedrich's group was the first Herero group to settle in Botswana. Later, but still before the German war, five additional families came and settled near Tsau, for they had heard there were already some Herero there. These five families included Kahaka, the grandfather of Kaekurama, the present *omuhona* at Makakun.[38] The

Tswana allowed these Herero to settle in the area around Tsau, Makakun, Nokaneng, and Nakalatswi. Then the Tswana came to Friedrich's father and asked him to act as leader for the group. Friedrich's father declined. He said:

> Kaekurama's father is my elder, my *honini* ["father's elder brother"]; go ask him. Besides, I have become Christian and it would not be really proper for me to be *omuhona.*

Later, after the war, more Herero came. Apparently they left South West Africa in scattered groups, for another of my informants, named Levi, who was about six years old at the time of the German war and whose group came because of the outbreak of violence, did not travel in the company of Samuel. According to Levi, his family awoke one morning and decided to "take their blankets and run." The route they took was through Gobabis, Mamuno, and Ghanzi to Tsau. They, too, had heard of the Herero settlement there.

In this group were Levi, his father, his mother, his father's elder brother's son, and his father's sister's son. They had no cattle, but his father had a gun, so they were able to hunt along the way.

The group that fled with Samuel had gone farther east. According to Goldblatt (1971:148) these Herero had in 1907 entered into contracts as mine workers for a Transvaal mining company.[39] Schapera says (1945:7):

> Samuel himself was subsequently induced by a labour agent to move with some of his people into the Transvaal, where he made his home in the Nylstroom District. He returned to Bechuanaland in 1922, and settled at Mahalapye, in Ngwato Reserve, as a subject of Chief Khama. He died there the following year, and was buried at Okahandja in South West Africa, beside the graves of Maharero and Tjamuaha. His son Friedrich . . . succeeded him.[40]

But the Herero throughout Botswana were in difficult straits. Though a few, like Kahaka, came with cattle, most Herero had none. Friedrich says:

> Kaekurama's [grand]father brought many cattle. Other Herero came later, after the war. There were many people and

only a few cattle. Some worked for the more fortunate Herero; but there were many people and not enough other Herero to hire them. So they were forced to work for the Tswana.

My family did some herding for the Tswana, too. We received milk and the use of bulls for stud in return for our labor. We made an arrangement for a calf as payment at the end of a year's work. But sometimes the Tswana owner was sympathetic and would take pity on us and we would get two calves. We milked cows, took the milk and made butter and *omaere* [a cheese-like product], which the Tswana didn't make; and then we sold these to the Tswana for money. We then used the money to buy more cattle.

It sometimes took eight, ten, or twenty years, but in this way the Herero built up their herds and gained economic independence.

The following is paraphrased from the account of another informant, Gustav.

During the German war, Gustav's group fled South West Africa. They were afraid of being killed by the Germans. In Gustav's group were Gustav, his father, his mother, his elder brother, and a number of other people with whom they were traveling. Some of the people were related; some were not.

Some people came with cattle, but many died along the way from lack of water. Gustav's group lost all its cattle on the journey.

They came from Okandjerzu in South West, to Mamuno, to Kalkfontein, to Ghanzi. When Kahaka heard they were coming, he sent two men with an ox to feed them and lead them to his settlement. When they arrived, they met Friedrich's people there. They did not have to ask permission of the Tswana to settle there since Kahaka had already received permission to settle, and he could admit additional Herero.

They went to work for the Tswana. In payment they received a cow after a year. The Herero who were already settled there, and could afford to, gave some cattle as gifts. The newcomers worked to build up their herds. They were interested in building their herds not selling the animals.

A more complete account is provided by Joas, an individual who, unlike the others so far quoted, was born in the new land.

The Herero fled from South West Africa after the Herero-German war and came to Botswana. Many Herero perished along the way in the desert. They didn't know the way and they didn't know where to find water. Those few cattle they managed to bring with them for the most part died.

So the Herero went to work for the Tswana in order to make a living. They cut wood and sold it to the Tswana. They worked as servants for the Tswana. They herded cattle for the Tswana. In return they were paid meagerly. They were given some milk in return for their labor. At first they were not given animals as payment.

After a number of years of service, at least two but perhaps more, depending on the particular Tswana owner, the Herero herdsmen might be given a female calf. From this, through Herero expertise in cattle management, they began to build their herds by using the Tswana owner's bulls for stud.

As his herd increased in size, maybe as few as five animals, the Herero would separate somewhat from the Tswana and devote himself to caring for his herd. He would remain, however, still under the dominion of the Tswana and dependent on him because he would not have a sufficient number of animals to support himself and his family. For this reason and also to avoid incurring the wrath of the Tswana and risking possible conflict, he would take some of the Tswana-owned animals and look after them for him. The Herero were not yet strong enough to set up independently and be entirely separate from the Tswana.

When I was born in 1917, this was the position of the Herero; they were beginning to separate but were still economically tied to the Tswana.

Meanwhile, Herero women worked in the Tswana fields. They were given a little corn in payment. But instead of consuming the corn, the Herero sold it to buy sheep and goats. Thus the herds continued to grow.

Then as the herds grew to sufficient size to support the Herero independent of any reliance on the Tswana, the Herero began to break away completely and set up their separate homesteads. They would return Tswana cattle and no longer serve as herdsmen for them. At this time, with enough cattle, people formed together into homesteads, so that they needn't

fear reprisal from the Tswana, since they had sufficient numbers and a firm base of wealth from which to draw resources.
[According to the informant, the Herero people as a whole had
effected this complete separation by 1934.]

This eventual separation was not the result of an organized
effort on the part of the Herero people as a whole but was effected through individual Herero making their separation. It
was the cumulative result of individual action.

With separation from the Tswana and the setting up of
homesteads, the Herero began to reinstitute their traditional
ways.

Since, however, the economic foundation upon which the old ways
were based had drastically changed as a result of the 1904 war and
the exigencies of life in the new land, the attempt to reestablish the
former traditions was never fully successful. Herero social institutions were already weakened because they were dependent on the
possession of ritually important cattle, and the Herero had lost
their cattle after the war. Herero participation in European-and
Tswana-dominated interaction, which included cattle sale for the acquisition of other goods, served to undermine further the old ways.
Thus when the Herero reorganized themselves around the new
herds that they had slowly amassed, they began to incorporate this
major new element, the sale of cattle, which was inimical to the old
system in which sale was prohibited.

Today the Herero are prosperous cattle herders once again. In the
phenomenally short time since their entry into the new land, these
displaced pastoralists, by serving as herdsmen for others and perhaps through stealing cattle on the side (Gibson, personal communication), have become economically independent of their former
Tswana employers and have proved themselves cattle herders par
excellence. They now hire Tswana workmen and others as herdsmen
and laborers. They are thought by European and black African alike
to be the wealthiest single group in Botswana. A Herero sits on the
Tawana Land Board in Ngamiland, a board whose task it is to ap-
portion land to applicants. They exude an unmistakable air of confidence and self-assurance and, according to volunteered information from non-Herero (especially Tswana and Kgalagadi), are well
respected by their fellow citizens.

The position of *omuhona,* however, has undergone change. No longer are *ovahona* leaders by virtue of being the first to utilize a valued resource. No longer do followers and dependents cluster about them in neighborhoods. Though they are still called *ovahona* by the Herero, they are simply community headmen appointed by the state administration as its local representatives. They need not even be Herero, though in communities whose population is largely Herero (as in Makakun and Makunda), they are. Elsewhere Herero live under headmen from other tribes. For example, the small Herero community of Dauga, east of Maun, has Letsholathebe II (a Tawana hereditary chief) as its headman.

When the Herero first came to Botswana, it was under British rule, with several district commissioners under a high commissioner for the entire territory. Beneath the district commissioners were the Tswana chiefs, each of whose territory corresponded more or less to the British districts. Local-level tribal affairs were by and large left in the hands of the chiefs. Thus, when the Herero entered Botswana, it was the chiefs and not the British who granted them permission to settle. (For a complete account of the administrative structure, see Sillery, 1952.)

Just as the British had the Tswana chiefs to deal with as spokesmen for their people and just as these chiefs were responsible for maintaining order and control within their groups, the Tswana chiefs appointed Herero headmen to function similarly for their people. The situation today is much the same, except that after independence the bureaucratic structure was altered slightly so that the headman stands in a position intermediate between the local populace and the District Commissioner, to whom the headman reports once a year. (See also British Information Services 1966 and Kuper and Gillett 1970.) It is not surprising that these headmen were those who had been important *ovahona* in South West Africa. They had already held the title once. This was not a prerequisite for leadership in the new land, however, and is evident by the fact that the headmanship in Makakun was first offered to Friedrich's father and that only after he declined was if offered to Kahaka (the only individual in Makakun at the time who had been an *omuhona* before).

Other evidence is available for the contention that the nature of omuhonaship has changed. The most significant, perhaps, is the fact that the *omuhona* is no longer *omurangere* or religious leader. He is considered an entirely secular leader and need not have an *okuruo* to be recognized. The only *omurangere* remaining in Makakun is not the *omuhona*. And neither of the two *ovahona* interviewed is an *omurangere*. The fact, however, that Friedrich's father refused the headmanship because he was Christian suggests that the divergence of the two roles occurred as a gradual process.[41] (It also supports the interpretation that in former times the two forms of leadership were viewed as inseparable.)

Though in the past the headmen in Botswana may have served as "representative mediators" (Loffler 1971), by representing the larger political entity to the Herero and also representing the interests of the Herero to the dominant power, there are indications that the *ovahona* are becoming purely government representatives at the local level. They are seen by the people as acting for the government and not for them. The primary indication of this trend is the formation of village councils in several communities to petition the government directly for desired services and facilities (such as schools).[42]

Another datum which supports the view that the position of *omuhona* today is totally dependent on, and defined by, exogenous factors was reported to me by one of the *ovahona* interviewed. Until now the headmanship has passed patrilineally. For example, Kaekurama, the *omuhona* at Makakun is Kahaka's grandson (SS), Richard Kambura, the *omuhona* at Makunda, is the great-great-grandson (SSSS) of Katjiova (reported by Schapera [1945:1] as the headman of Makunda in 1940), and Raseuaka, the *omuhona* at Mahalapye, is Samuel's great-grandson (SSS). The government policy has been to appoint as headmen individuals descended in the male line from previous headmen. This tended to foster Herero acceptance of the individual as well. Now, however, the decisive factor in the appointment of a headman is becoming a command of English (the language in which official forms are completed), and no one with less than a Standard Seven education, no matter what his standing within the community, will be eligible. This effectively excludes all but younger men, since middle-aged and elderly Herero have had little or no formal education.[43]

This policy seems a curious one at first, especially when it is recalled that the government provides a scribe for each headman to do the necessary paperwork. Yet it may be interpreted as a useful maneuver in the Botswana government's discouragement of "tribalism." Since the central government is attempting to erode local and ethnic allegiances, the appointment of local headmen on the basis of criteria other than those associated with the tribal or ethnic identity of the appointee obviously furthers this aim. By diverting attention, for example, from notions of descent to level of education, the government is emphasizing the importance of factors that are nationally determined and controlled at the expense of those that are locally defined.[44]

Finally, the presence of a village policeman illustrates that the *omuhona* is an official of the government more than he is a spokesman for his people. Each community has a policeman, and he is in the service of the *omuhona*. He is normally not an original member of the community, nor is he necessarily even a member of the same tribal group which he polices.

The headman handles minor legal cases, such as cattle stealing, disorderly conduct, abusive language, and so forth. More serious crimes, such as murder, are referred to the District Commissioner. The headman decides whether the case is to be tried by himself or by the District Commissioner. All cases, however, first come to the attention of the *omuhona*, either through a complaint from the aggrieved party or through a third party. The *omuhona* then sends the village policeman to investigate. When the accused is apprehended by the policeman, he is brought to the *omuhona* for trial. The trial is held under a large tree and anyone may attend. The aggrieved party and the accused each have an opportunity to be heard. They may call witnesses on their own behalf or to discredit their adversary. The *omuhona* alone decides guilt or innocence, passes judgment, and allots sentence; but either party may appeal the decision to the District Commissioner.

Cattle stealing is the most common offense. Typical punishment is a fine, equal to the value of the stolen cattle, paid to the owner and an additional fine of twenty-five percent of this value paid to the government. If the criminal is unable to pay, he is sentenced to six to twelve months in prison.[45]

INHERITANCE AND SUCCESSION

What the early literature on inheritance and succession lacks in clarity it makes up for in quantity (see especially Dannert 1906; also Vedder 1928:187, 192, 194, 195; and von Francois 1896:171, 177, 201–2). Gibson's (1956:132) remarks will suffice to summarize traditional inheritance practices and those obtaining in Botswana during the period of his fieldwork.

> After the death of a rich man his herds and goods are distributed among his relatives, and his sister's sons are eligible (after his brothers) to inherit his widows and to share in his estate. Formerly the cattle were divided into two classes: the sacred cattle which descended to his sons and the other cattle (which often were more in number) which descended to his *ovasia*, "sister's children". . . . In Ngamiland, however, this pattern has undergone alteration to bring it into line with Batawana law and custom. Jealous sons who desired to deprive their patrilateral cross-cousins of their inheritance challenged the custom of inheritance by the sister's child in the Batawana tribal courts, with the result that the courts directed the sister's children to turn over their portion of the inheritance to the sons of the deceased. This change is still not considered proper by most Ngamiland Herero, but they feel powerless to attempt to reinstate the former custom. Formerly a sister's child ranked next after the younger brother of a deceased in the administration of his estate, and in the absence of a younger brother the sister's son divided the inheritance.

It should be pointed out as well that the early German literature speaks of the *eanda* inheritance and the *oruzo* inheritance (the former passing to uterine relatives and the latter to agnatic relatives of the deceased). Today, however, informants deny there is any inheritance within the *eanda*. (And they claim there never was. The frequency with which it is mentioned in the earlier literature, however, casts doubt on this. It is likely that present-day Herero have simply forgotten it since it no longer exists.)

Inheritance by the ZS (*omusia*) is still practiced, but informants claim that this individual inherits because he stands in the particular genealogical relationship of ZS and not because he is in the same *eanda.* That many Herero are as likely to forget their *eanda* as not lends credence to this assertion. This is further pointed up by the fact that the ZS is the only uterine heir. No longer do the deceased's other *eanda* relatives (e.g., his MB; see Vedder 1928:187 and von Francois 1896:202) inherit.

The *oruzo* inheritance, however, is still conceived of as patrisib property. (This is probably due to the fact that patrilineal inheritance receives support in the courts, while matrilineal inheritance does not.) This is illustrated by the manner of its administration. Elders of the same patrilineage in which the deceased was a member gather at the deceased's homestead.[46] It is they who oversee the proper distribution of the inheritance.

Whereas the previous literature speaks simply of "sacred" cattle as the *oruzo* inheritance and "secular" cattle as the *eanda* inheritance, the current situation is not as clear-cut. The bulk of the *ozonzere* and *oruzo* cattle passes to a man's son, but a few are given to his ZS by the administrators to show their generosity and to engender good will. (The number, informants say, is very small, but I could not elicit a standard figure.)

The *ozongombe za ka uriri* (general cattle) go primarily to the ZS, but he then gives perhaps twenty percent to the deceased's son. He, too, does this as a gesture of generosity and to create good will. For the same reasons he gives some cattle to each of the deceased's *ovazamumue* (consanguineal relatives), if he can do so without diminishing his inheritance too greatly. This inheritance by the ZS is the ideal; but informants confide that increasingly the deceased's son is claiming even general cattle as his own, as Gibson points out in the passage above.[47] It is not difficult to imagine that when the influence of the elder Herero passes with their deaths, the custom of inheritance by the ZS will soon follow.

All personal property of the deceased (e.g., clothes, firearms, the homestead itself) is inherited by the eldest son. Money in a bank is considered personal property and goes to the son, but money not deposited in a bank is distributed among lineage-mates.

Succession to leadership is a much more difficult subject to untangle since, as we have seen, the roles of *omuhona* and *omurangere* are now distinct. The former is a political appointment which has in

the past passed from father to son with the approval of the government[48] but which is now becoming contingent upon other criteria,
especially education, so inheritance is not a decisive factor. In addition, the title of *omurangere* is simply passing away with the elders,
and the *omaruo,* with which religious leadership is associated, are
dying out. Thus, there are no present rules of succession to be
enumerated since no one is succeeding to the position. We must
therefore rely on earlier sources to understand succession to leadership.

These sources agree that leadership, religious and secular, remained within the *oruzo* and thus passed to an agnate. But there is
disagreement in the previous literature regarding just which agnate, a brother or a son, was the rightful heir.

Though Vedder (1928:188, 1938:146–7) claims that omuhona-
ship, along with the trusteeship of the sacred fire, passed from
father to son, others (notably Dannert 1906:53ff.) claim that it
passed to the deceased's younger brother(s) and then upon his
death to the eS of the deceased eB. That this second view is the correct one is amply demonstrated in the literature dealing with the
dispute between Samuel and Nikodemus (also known as Kambaha-
hize) over succession to Maharero's position and is corroborated by
the ethnographic situation as Gibson found it in 1953. Both sources
of evidence will be briefly outlined.[49]

When Maharero died in 1890, a dispute arose regarding who
should succeed him. Schapera says (1945:7):

> His oldest son, Uaita (general known by the baptismal name of
> Wilhelm), had been killed while fighting against the Hottentots
> in 1880—a loss that was deeply mourned by all the Herero,
> since he was of outstanding ability and good character. Samuel,
> the second son, had then come to the fore as Maharero's assist-
> ant in dealing with Europeans, but he was vain, pleasure-seek-
> ing, and, as Vedder says, 'very much addicted to liquor'. More-
> over, he was not the senior member of his *oruzo,* being inferior
> in status to the sons of Kavikunua, Maharero's elder brother.

Kavikunua was deceased (he died before his father Tjamuaha)
and so his eldest surviving son Nikodemus was next in line to

inherit. He renounced Christianity, so that he might become custodian of the *okuruo* (Dannert 1906:61), and laid claim to the omuhona-ship as the rightful heir according to Herero tradition.

> However, the attempt to make this inheritance law count was unsuccessful since the German govenment imposed the inheritance law of the homeland by proclamation and made Samuel, Maharero's son, his successor [Dannert 1906:55].

Von Francois (1896:172) mentions the European contribution, which he claims was at first unwitting, in establishing Samuel as successor.

> . . . because the mission and the German government promoted Samuel's ascendancy, perhaps half unknowingly, Nikodemus moved back to Ovambandyeru resentfully.
>
> The addressing of a letter, which we directed to Samuel soon after Maharero's death, may have contributed greatly to Samuel's elevation.
>
> According to our narrow European conceptions, we considered him his father's successor without further ado at that time, thus we addressed the letter: To the chief of the Herero, Samuel Maharero. This was considered recognition by the German government.

Nikodemus, however, along with Kahimemua and his Mbanderu, joined the Khauas Hottentot rebellion against the Germans. The rebellion was put down in short order and the two dissident leaders were executed. Meanwhile, as noted above, Kahaka (of Otjiseu lineage) indignant at Samuel's assertion of authority and complicity with the Germans, especially in disarming Tjetjoo, emigrated to Botswana. His father Tjetjoo remained in South West and participated in the 1904 war, but he later died during the flight to Botswana.

But before this Samuel had been declared paramount chief by the Germans. My eldest informant who was present at the time said:

> There was a great feast. The Germans came and brought beer. They came to give their approval to Samuel's succession. They recognized him as *omuhona* of his people.
>
> Many cattle were slaughtered but only *ozongombe za ka uriri* because all people, even Hottentots, were invited to come and eat.[50]

From the Herero point of view, as pointed out above, Samuel was "paramount chief" in name only and, in any event, his tenure was not a long one. Schapera (1945:7) sums up:

> Samuel's appointment as paramount was not welcomed by other leading chiefs, and by no means all of them accepted his authority. He alienated them still further by selling tribal land to Europeans, and by helping the Germans to disarm Tjetjoo and the others in the east. But when, at the beginning of 1904, he issued secret orders for a universal rising against the Germans, all the Herero sided with him. After considerable fighting, they were decisively defeated at Waterberg. . . .

But Samuel, though he became *omuhona* and was considered by the Europeans to be the paramount political authority among the Herero, did not inherit religious leadership for his patrisib. He was Christian and therefore ineligible to tend the *okuruo*. So the title of *omurangere* passed to Kavezeri, a younger brother of Maharero (Schapera 1945:6).[51]

This set a precedent for the separation of religious and secular leadership that is still prevalent in Botswana today. When Gibson did his fieldwork in the 1950's, this separation was evident in their respective succession practices. Whereas the omuhona-ship, under the influence of the Tswana, passed from father to son,[52] as it had from Maharero to Samuel, religious leadership was in the first instance adelphic, as was the case when it passed from Maharero to Kavezeri. Gibson (1956:125) reports:

> The office of priest descends successively to younger brothers of a deceased priest, in theory passing through all of the living male descendants of former priests by their great wives in his generation before returning to the eldest son of the senior line in the next generation.

Today, for the reasons related to economic organization given above, *ovarangere* will soon entirely disappear from Herero society. *Ovahona*, though radically changed in character since they are now part of the state's judicial-administrative structure, will remain as long as that structure is not altered.

SUMMARY

I have attempted to describe the divergence between religious and political leadership throughout this chapter. The disappearance of the former role is interpreted as due to the new economic orientation of the Herero and the transformation of the nature of secular political leadership. Previous notions of Herero leadership depended on descent criteria; and notions of descent were dependent on, and reinforced, the former manner of resource exploitation. With a redefinition of the Herero relationship to their resource and the reliance on new resources from outside Herero culture, the religious ideology associated with the former relationship became inappropriate. Examples of how former ritual reinforced the old relationship are mentioned, and their absence today is interpreted as due to the redefined relationship.

In addition, Herero political leadership no longer relied on the old religious ideology to legitimate authority, for political leaders were utilizing a new resource, the state, from which they drew their authority. In order to understand this aspect of change, considerable historical material is introduced to trace the development of leadership among the Herero.

In the Herero conception of things during pre-contact times, it seems that those who maintained order and conformity (i.e., those who exercised political authority) had the sanction of the ancestors by virtue of their (the leaders') being senior lineage or sib heads and thus representatives of the ancestors (i.e., they were religious leaders as well). What analysis suggests is that those who exercised political authority because they controlled a valued resource, and thus created dependency in their followers, then legitimated this authority by reference to descent and the ancestors.

But, as long as land was open and available, the authority they exercised was limited, for their followers could simply move out from the leader's sphere of influence ("neighborhood," in geographic terms) if they felt ill treated. The influx of Europeans and the resultant scarcity of land this influx produced made it less feasible for an individual to move out of a neighborhood whenever he felt like it, for there was no place to go. Hence, I suggest, authority roles grew stronger and this influenced the rise of "incipient chiefdoms."

How exogenous factors—the German state administrative apparatus and the European presence generally—contributed to the rise of incipient paramountcy in leadership among the Herero is also outlined. This development was cut short by the 1904 war when the Herero were forced to flee to Botswana.

There they encountered an already existing state administrative structure. Their adaptation to this political system, seen as an exogenous source of energy, is described and interpreted as the basis for local Herero leadership as it appears today.

NOTES

[1]Previous discussions of leadership and authority and political organization as a whole are far from enlightening and often create more confusion than clarity. They also frequently contradict each other. Hence, I do not attempt here to cover all possible aspects of these subjects, particularly since they are no longer relevant to modern Herero society. What is relevant to a discussion of overall change, however, is included. For earlier accounts, see Dannert (1906:56ff.); Hahn (1869:253–5); Lehmann (1955); Vedder (1928:187–90); von Francois (1896:173–6).

[2]Based on the fact that when asked her *oruzo* a woman always replies with the name of her natal *oruzo*, if she remembers it, I conclude that the majority view (i.e., that a bride only temporarily cedes her natal *oruzo* restrictions) probably reflects the custom of former times.

[3]I do not entertain the speculation that the new arrivals would take on the *oruzo* affiliation of the *omuhona*, for this would require observing its restrictions, either in addition to their own or in place of their own. And they would have to make alterations in the types of livestock they could and could not keep and make changes in the food taboos they observed.

[4]I had some difficulty obtaining Schapera's paper. It was only after I had completed my fieldwork and drawn these conclusions regarding the origins of Herero phratries that I obtained a copy of his article.

⁵Ohambandarua is given as Kahimemua's, and thus an Mbanderu, *oruzo*. I met several Herero, however, whose *oruzo* was Ohambandarua. I have no explanation for this except to speculate that intermarriage between Herero and Mbanderu led to a diffusion of the sib to both groups.

That Schapera only obtained information regarding five clusters of *otuzo* and I obtained six, that there is disagreement over Ohambandarua as being originally Herero or Mbanderu, and that Kambazembi and Zeraua's respective *otuzo* are given by my informants as belonging to the same phratry I attribute to the passage of time and the decreased importance of descent for behavior in Herero society today. I do not consider these to constitute a refutation of the interpretation offered here.

⁶Omurekua is the name of an *oruzo* which, as far as I know, is not reported in any of the previous literature. Gibson (personal communication) reports that he found the patrisib Omurekua among the Himba of Angola during his research there in 1973.

⁷Gibson (personal communication) expresses skepticism about this interpretation. He prefers the Herero explanation—that is, that phratries are the result of segmentation—because of its simplicity and because it applies to lineages and sibs as well as to phratries. He adduces his finding basically similar phratry groupings among the Himba of Angola as evidence contradictory to my interpretation. The other objections he raises—for example, that he, Schapera, and I all found, with some differences, similar phratry groupings of sibs; that most sibs within a phratry have similar myths; and that there is some correlation of *oruzo* restrictions for sibs in the same phratry—may be explained by the fact that the Herero from whom the present-day Herero in Botswana are descended were from the same general area in South West Africa (the Okahandja-Otjimbingue-Windhoek region) and by the fact that Gibson, Schapera, and I all worked among the Botswana Herero. One would therefore expect our findings to be similar. Needless to say, this subject requires further exploration.

⁸It is taken as a given in this work that the Herero formerly considered their cattle to be "sacred" property. I do not consider why this might have been. My analysis of the Herero situation, however, suggests a possible answer to the larger question of why property among pastoralists (and perhaps among other peoples) is considered sacred. I hypothesize that the "sacred" nature of animals is a reflection of their exclusivity. That is, where, as in the Herero case, herds are considered the exclusive property of certain kinsmen and are overwhelmingly the primary resource upon which

the group relies, they are defined as "sacred." And where, as is the case
with camels among the Bedouin, the condition of exclusivity does not obtain, animals are not defined as "sacred." Corelatively, the conduct of raiding will vary with the exclusivity/nonexclusivity of the animals for which
raiding occurs. Where the animals are "sacred" or exclusive property, raiding can result in human fatalities; where the animals are not "sacred" or
exclusive property, raiding is less likely to result in death. These hy-
potheses, however, require cross-cultural investigation and are beyond the
scope of the present study.

[9]This is an example of the confusing terminology that abounds in former
accounts. From the context of the entire article, I take Hahn's use of family here to refer to a homestead or the core agnatic relatives of a homestead
and tribe to refer to what I have been calling a neighborhood. Elsewhere
Hahn uses tribe to refer to an *oruzo*.

[10]Vedder (1928:166) names seven such "great priests": "Maharero at
Okahandja, Zeraua at Otjimbingue, Kukuri at Otjosazu, Kandjii and
Kamareti and Kambazembi at Waterberg" for the Herero proper and
Aponda for the Mbanderu. These were all *ovahona* as well.

[11]The use of the term to mean "God" may be the result of missionary influence. According to Irle (1917:342) and Vedder (1928:164), the missionaries among the Herero did not hear the name Ndjambi, which was then
taken to mean "high god," until 1871. Up until that time, they had been using *mukuru* in their proselytizing to refer to the deity. (Present-day Herero
say they use Ndjambi to refer to God as the giver of rain.)

[12]In previous reports (e.g., Vedder 1928:168), it was the daughter's obligation to tend the fire (she was known as *ondangere* in this capacity), and
the senior wife of the *omurangere* took over the duty when the daughter
was not present.
  The only *omurangere* left in Makakun during my stay there said his
okuruo was tended by his senior wife or his daughter and that it did not
matter which so long as it was done. According to him, the procedure for
tending the *okuruo* is as follows. The fire is kindled anew each morning by
his wife or daughter. Matches, formerly forbidden, are used. (Informants
say they lost their ancestor sticks when they came to Botswana, though
Gibson [1956:123] reports that they still had them in 1953. I interpret their
statement as support for my view that the old ways, symbolized by the ancestors and their representations, began to be discontinued with the loss of
cattle at the time of the flight to Botswana.) The *omurangere* is present for

the kindling. The fire is started before the cattle go to pasture in the morning and then is allowed to burn out. But it must be rekindled in late afternoon or early evening before the cattle return.

For more detail concerning former practices related to tending the *okuruo,* see Brincker (1900:74); Dannert (1906:4–5); Hahn (1869:500–1); Irle (1917:346); Vedder (1928:167–9); von Francois (1896:193).

[13]Calling cattle currency is not so far-fetched as it may at first appear. Indeed, Schneider (1974) even makes a case for considering cattle to be a form of money among East African cattle herders.

[14]Irle (1917:350) claims the "death sacrifice" was not made for Maharero, yet my informant was an eyewitness.

[15]At first the informant said that the *oruzo* cattle could only be eaten by the "old men" of the deceased's *oruzo.* However, I went through the terms for *ovazamumue* (consanguineal relatives) and the informant said yes, all *ovazamumue* could eat the meat. Then I asked if *ovakue* (affinal relatives) ate it, and he said they did since in the old days, because of FBD/MBD marriage, affinal and consanguineal relatives overlapped and were generally the same people. (This is a point on which all informants agreed: in former times when, it is asserted, marriage to the preferred marriage partner—*omuramue,* a cross-cousin—was the statistical norm, affines and consanguines were the same people.)

[16]It was this act, so apparently explicit in its meaning, that first suggested to me the idea of "connectors." Other behavior then began to make much more sense in this light.

[17]It might be well to include here for the ethnographic record the eyewitness account of Samuel Maharero's succession that my informant gave.

Milk from the *ozonzere* cattle was brought in calabashes to the *okuruo,* around which were gathered the younger brothers of Maharero, Samuel's father. These men took the milk and poured it into wooden plates. Each person around the *okuruo* then tasted it. Each took only a little sip, for the tasting of milk was not meant for nourishment. Samuel took his father's chair and sat in it. He also put on his father's favorite hat, even though it was tattered, and his father's shoes. The old men at the fire chewed the ashes from the *okuruo,* then took water into their mouths and spat it upon Samuel. Then Samuel performed the rituals described above. From this point on, Samuel was *omuhona.* (This is a loose paraphrase of the informant's account.)

My informant did not mention, as Schapera does (1945:6), that Kavezeri, a younger brother of Maharero, "succeeded Maharero as custodian of the 'sacred fire'," since "Samuel, who succeeded Maharero as chief, had been baptized, and was therefore ineligible to act as tribal priest."

He did mention, however, that present at the *okuruo* were several men, including Kavezeri, who stood in the relationship of *injangu* ("younger brother") to Maharero. Those remembered in addition to Kavezeri were Tjinjonge, Kararaimbo, and Kaijata. These became Samuel's council; they advised him on the proper way to handle his duties as *omuhona*.

[18]For more information on customs concerning birth, see Brincker (1900:76); Dannert (1906:19); Gibson (1952:169–70, 1959a:36); Irle (1917:356–7); Vedder (1928:175–6); von Francois (1896:196–7).

[19]A child was born during my stay in Makakun. Goats were slaughtered to provide meat for an informal celebration, but no ritual was conducted.

For information on naming, see Brincker (1900:77); Buttner (1884:387); Dannert (1906:20–1); Gibson (1952:170); and Vedder (1928:190).

[20]Other sources for information on twins include Brincker (1899:77–9); Dannert (1906:20); Irle (1917:357); and von Francois (1896:197). It should be mentioned that Luttig's book on the Herero is a summary of previous literature, for Luttig did not himself conduct research among the Herero.

[21]The literature is unclear about which group is meant, and I failed to make inquiries on this point during research (though it is doubtful whether the Herero could supply this information today). I suspect that what I have been calling a neighborhood may be closer to the reality.

[22]The birth of twins nowadays, needless to say, receives no ritual attention. Friends and neighbors drop by the homestead and bring gifts of animals, but informants say they do this out of happiness and to offer "support for the new big family." None of my informants had ever heard of the treatment accorded the *epaha* family that is described in the earlier literature.

[23]At least this seems to have been true until Christianity began finding converts among the Herero. But converts before the time of the German war in 1904 were few (as pointed out above). Other references on the influence of Christianity are found in Brincker (1895:210); Hahn (1869:485); Irle (1917:345, 357); Vedder (1928:201–3); von Francois (1896:161).

[24]Some previous literature has already been cited to support this interpretation; but it might be well to add further evidence from Vedder (1938:174), who lists sites already settled by the Herero around 1820: "Then Kandjizei, the father of Kdjiharine, later of Omburo near Omaruru [both on the Omaruru River], came into the country, and likewise Kaneena, the son of Kuaiima, who settled in Osona [on the Swakop River] near Okahandja. Oseu, the father of the mighty chief Kandjii made his appearance and lived for a considerable time between Okahandja and Windhoek [besides this region being a drainage area for four rivers (Swakop, Kuiseb, Olifant, Nossob) Windhoek itself is the site of a famous hot spring] . . . . Kavarikotjiuru, an uncle of Tjirue's came in, too, and settled at the hot springs of Windhoek. Mungunda, who was one of the same family, chose the hot springs of Otjikango [later named New Barmen by the German missionaries] as the site for his kraal. On the east, the Mbanderu encroached upon their brothers, the Hereros. Epako (Gobabis) was in their possession and their cattle grazed in the bed of the Nosob River."

Later, Omaruru (first under the *omuhona* Zeraua, succeeded by Manasse or Okosondje) and Waterberg or Otjozondjupa (of which Kambazembi was the *omuhona*) would become well known Herero settlements.

[25]Some of the other most frequently mentioned *ovahona* and their areas of influence are: Zeraua (and later Manasse) of Otjimbingue and then Omaruru, Kambazembi at Waterberg (Otjozondjupa), Tjetjoo (and his son Kahaka) in the east near Gobabis.

[26]Jonker later turned against Kahitjene, without any interference from Tjamuaha, and stole his cattle. Soon after, Kahitjene was killed by some Herero with whom he had a dispute over inheritance rights. See Brincker (1899:133-4); Hahn (1869:240-1); Lehmann (1955:32-3); and Vedder (1928:158-9, 202-25, 249-50).

[27]Goldblatt (1971:31) says that Maharero (or Kamaherero) had a brother named Wilhelm and implies that they made certain decisions together. No other source mentions this brother; the only similar references are to Wilhelm Maharero, Maharero's son, later killed in battle against the Hottentots. (My informants confirmed that Wilhelm was Maharero's son.)

[28]Included among the Herero *ovahona* who signed this treaty were Maharero, Zeraua, and Tjetjoo; Kambazembi was absent (Goldblatt 1971:46).

[29]At one point, Vedder (1938:326) says that Maharero had more than 60 wives. Brincker (1900:83) gives the number of wives as 42, an Schapera (1945:8) mentions two other sources that claim the number was 30 and 12.

[30]See the quotation from Lehmann on p. 147 regarding the first point. Von Francois, regarding the second point, attributes the rise of a "paramount chief," as he says (1896:174), "more to the machinations, practices and insinuations of the immigrant merchants and missionaries rather than to a naturally evolved system instituted by the natives."

[31]In addition to my field notes, this account relies on Goldblatt (1971).

[32]Lehmann (1955:37) is inclined to emphasize the ceding of land by Samuel as the cause of the war: ". . . Samuel Maharero had angered his followers by his large debts. He promised them to recover the land he had sold at the first opportunity. This developed into a dangerous situation, culminating in the Herero uprising."

[33]Ethnographic information on the Tswana, thanks to Isaac Schapera, is voluminous (see, for example, Schapera 1938, 1943a, 1943b, 1947, 1952, 1970).

[34]Langdale-Brown and Spooner (1963) estimate the mean annual rainfall for northern Botswana to be about eighteen inches, although the level may reach as much as 27 inches in the extreme northeast. The rainy season lasts from mid-October to mid-April, but actual rainfall is erratic and unpredictable.
The following figures are excerpted from a table provided by Langdale-Brown and Spooner (1963:27). They show the mean monthly and annual rainfall in inches for 1921–50 for Maun in Ngamiland: January, 3.96; February, 3.38; March, 3.30; April, 1.02; May, 0.18; June, 0.02; July, 0.00; August, 0.00; September, 0.03; October, 0.55; November, 1.70; December, 2.89; annual, 17.03.
Despite repeated efforts, I have been unable to obtain more recent meteorological statistics from the Botswana Weather Bureau.

[35]Samuel died in Botswana in 1923 and is buried with Tjmauaha and Maharero in Okahandja where a memorial was erected in their honor. The inscription reads: "Here lie three chieftains at rest. They ruled the country for the good of the Herero people, but now they are dead. They were chiefs indeed." (Since I did not have an opportunity to visit the tomb while I was in South West, the inscription is quoted from White 1969:60. A photograph of the memorial appears in Vedder 1928, facing page 180.)

[36]In this group were Friedrich, his father, his mother's father, his sisters, his father's sister, the four children of another of his father's sisters (who had died in the Transvaal), and his mother's brothers (Friedrich could not recall their number).

[37]Friedrich implied that Khama granted them permission to settle in Tsau. This could not have been the case since Khama's authority did not extend to Ngamiland, where Tsau is situated. Sekhoma (or Sekgoma) Letsholathebe, the brother of Moremi II, was at the time chief of the Tawana during the minority of Moremi's son Mathiba. (The current Tawana chief, Letsholathebe II, is the grandson of Mathiba.) Sekhoma was the only one who could grant anyone permission to settle at Tsau. I assume, though Friedrich did not say so, that Khama sent them to Sekhoma, and Sekhoma allowed them to reside at Tsau. (The British did not even enter the picture, though Bechuanaland was a British Protectorate, for they recognized the chief's authority in such matters.)

[38]The informant referred to the individual who emigrated from South West to Bechuanaland as "Kaekurama's father." According to other accounts, quoted above, the individual in question was Kahaka, Kaekurama's grandfather (FF). The reader will recall that Kahaka was Tjetjoo's son and the leader of the Otjiseu-group who, rather than cede his arms to the Germans, left South West Africa. Schapera's (1945:11–12) informants confirm that the individual in question was actually Kahaka. He was later joined, after the 1904 war, by a group led by his half-brother Tarauhota (their father Tjetjoo died during the flight through the desert). Kazoninga, Kaekurama's father, became the next *omuhona* for Makakun. ("Owing to persistent refusal to obey the orders of the Tawana chiefs, Kazoninga was ultimately sent to prison in 1938. He died there shortly afterwards" [Schapera 1945:12].)

[39]On the fate of Samuel's Herero in eastern Botswana I have no new information. My fieldwork was conducted in the west, in Ngamiland, principally at Makakun but also near Maun, and even at Makunda in Ghanzi District. Gibson (1956:111–12) provides the following notes: "It is uncertain how many Herero reached Ngamiland in their flight from the Germans. Some under Samuel, son of the famed Chief Maharero, stayed only a few years in Ngamiland and then moved on to the east, finally settling in Mahalapye, where the chief of the Ngwato offered them land. Others eventually established settlements at Rakops on the Botletle River and at Makunda in Ghanzi District. But a larger portion, members of both Herero

and Mbanderu tribes, remained in Ngamiland and settled in two distinct areas where they still maintain their tribal separation to a large extent. The number of Herero now in Ngamiland is estimated at about 6,000."

[40]Friedrich's successor was Lotof, and Lotof's was Raseuaka, the current Herero *omuhona* near Mahalapye.

[41]Since the position of *omuhona* has been divorced from the traditional notion of descent and the headman is not necessarily a lineage head at the same time he is the local-level representative of the government, none of the role conflicts described by Fallers (1955) for African headmen is apparent among the Herero.

[42]For example, there exists in Makunda a Village Development Council. The Council collected contributions from the community residents and sent them to the Ghanzi District authorities as a donation toward a hospital they want to build in the area. (The school in Makunda was built by the people of the community, who now—to indicate the kinds of changes going on—have a local Parent-Teachers Association that meets regularly.) (For a recent treatment of the place of Village Development Councils in local-level politics in Botswana, see Vengroff, 1975.)

[43]Of the eleven informants questioned on the extent of their formal education, five had had less than six years of formal education and six had had none at all. My nineteen-year-old interpreter, however, had nearly finished his secondary education and was preparing to enter a university. His is an atypical case, for few Herero seek higher education. The use of education, they say, is in gaining wealth. Since they already have wealth (their herds), they do not seek an extensive education.
On Botswana's "brigade" educational system, see, for example, Henderson (1974) and Ulin (1974).

[44]The published sources for this manner of viewing the relationship of the local community to central authority and the kinds of demands each makes on its constituents are Cohen (1969a and 1969b). In Cohen's (1969a:661–2) terms, incidentally, Botswana is an inchoate state.

[45]For previous literature on legal procedure, see Dannert (1906:6–8); Hahn (1869:490); Vedder (1928:195–6); von Francois (1896:174–5).

[46]Though, as previously mentioned, many Herero today no longer know the name of their lineage because they have forgotten the name of its

founder, they nevertheless know who among living Herero are their line-age-mates.

[47]Gibson (1956:112) also says: "Living under Tawana and British au-thority has introduced some changes into Herero life, the most far-reach-ing being the nonrecognition of matrilineal inheritance under Tawana tri-bal law."

[48]The position of headman is "semi-hereditary in the male line with ap-proval of the Tawana tribal authority" (Gibson 1959a:3).

[49]This evidence is drawn from a number of sources, the most detailed be-ing Dannert's (1906:53ff.); but Schapera's (1945:7) much briefer account is far more lucid.
The view of inheritance as adelphic was also confirmed by my eldest informant.

[50]When asked why Samuel, and not one of Maharero's brothers, suc-ceeded Maharero, the informant replied that he thought this was due to missionary influence, since the missionaries favored direct inheritance by a man's son.

[51]Kavezeri, whom Irle (1917:347) calls "the oruzo successor of Maha-rero," may have been an adopted son of Tjamuaha.

[52]Kazoninga's yB Taave served as *omuhona* for Makakun until Kae-kurama, Kazoninga's son and the present *omuhona*, came of age. (I do not show Taave in the genealogical chart for Otjiseu lineage [Fig. 8, ch. 1].)

Concluding Remarks

REVIEW

To summarize briefly, this study has attempted to demonstrate several points: 1) that Herero society has undergone, and is still undergoing, extensive social change; 2) that the adoption of the practice of selling formerly "sacred" cattle accounts for most of the alterations in Herero institutional activities and in patterns of social behavior generally; 3) that the adoption of cattle sale as a regular practice was due to exogenous stimuli after the Herero were defeated in war by the Germans in 1904 and were forced to flee their homeland; 4) that changes in Herero political organization in historic times were likewise the result of exogenous influences, first in South West Africa where contact with the immigrant Europeans tended to strengthen local native authority and, secondly, in Botswana where Herero incorporation into an established state system rendered local authority subordinate to, and dependent upon, an already established foreign power structure. In order to demonstrate these points, I have examined several aspects of Herero social organization.

The configuration of Herero homesteads in 1973 was found to differ considerably from that reported in the early German literature and even from that reported by Gibson as typical for 1953. The changes in spatial organization appear to be the result of the absence of the *okuruo*, the former focal point in homesteads. In former times the *okuruo* was also the symbolic focus of Herero society, in that all important ritual which strengthened the relationship of the Herero with their ancestors was conducted there. The "ancestor cult" of the Herero was dependent upon the keeping of ritually im-

192

portant cattle, which were conceived of as having been handed down from the ancestors. Considerable space in this study was devoted to demonstrating that the practice of selling ritually important cattle has led to a weakening of this tie with the ancestors. The rituals which formerly expressed that tie, or "connection" to the ancestors, have been gradually discarded as cattle sale increased. Consequently, the *okuruo* where these rituals used to be performed is disappearing as well. Thus, cattle sale was interpreted as responsible for changes in homestead configuration. This is expressed diagrammatically in Figure 13.

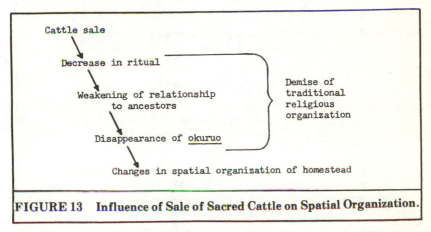

FIGURE 13   **Influence of Sale of Sacred Cattle on Spatial Organization.**

The occurrence of a minimum of descent-phrased behavior among present-day Herero was also interpreted as the result of cattle sale. Since in former times cattle were seen as ritually important and as held in trust for the ancestors, those persons or groups which shared responsibility for cattle phrased their cooperation in terms of descent, that is, they asserted they had ancestors in common. Today the emphasis on cattle raising as a business divorced from the ancestors does not require the support of descent. The impersonal relationships between "strangers" (nonkinsmen) in a market economy introduce outsiders as significant participants in activities involving cattle that were once considered exclusive.

Since Herero cattle have now become "profane" exchange commodities (i.e., they have lost their exclusive or "sacred" character because of their use as marketable assets), there is no need to confine management of the herds to kinsmen. The discussion in chapter

2 of cattle management practices demonstrated the cooperation of nonrelatives in herding tasks among present-day Herero.

Just as cooperation in the care of cattle is no longer confined to relatives, cooperation in other activities, such as hunting and cultivation, also occurs primarily among nonrelatives. In secondary economic activities neighbors cooperate with neighbors with little reference to descent, since descent is no longer a referent for cooperation in the primary economic pursuit. (See Fig. 14.)

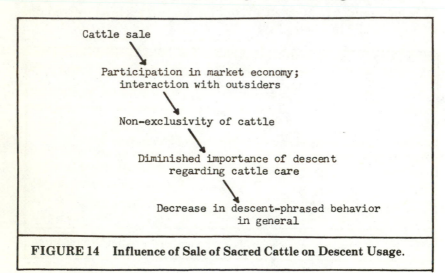

FIGURE 14   Influence of Sale of Sacred Cattle on Descent Usage.

This decrease in descent-phrased behavior generally further weakened the former relationship with the ancestors; for common descent is traced from common ancestors. The fewer instances in which common descent is invoked, therefore, the fewer occasions there are to refer to the ancestors. If there are few instances in which the ancestors are called upon, there is little need for religious spokesmen or mediators between living Herero and their dead. Thus, the role of religious leader begins to disappear. The breakdown of traditional religious organization is consequently interpreted as due to cattle sale. (See Fig. 15.)

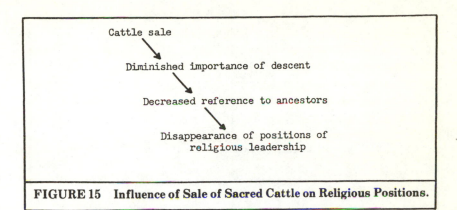

FIGURE 15   Influence of Sale of Sacred Cattle on Religious Positions.

The foregoing diagrams (Figs. 13–15), which attempt to illustrate the primary importance of cattle sale in influencing other changes in Herero social organization, may be combined to suggest the overall process of change as interpreted in this work (see Fig. 16).

Though most of the changes in the organization of social relations among the Herero can be attributed to the adoption of cattle sale, the practice of selling cattle is interpreted as due to stimuli from outside Herero society. Exposure to European goods and to the sale of cattle to acquire these goods during the years of impoverishment in Botswana after the Herero-German war was seen as providing the conditions which led the Herero to begin selling their ritual cattle when they had reamassed large herds. Thus, the ultimate source of Herero social change was found to be exogenous.

The effect of exogenous influences on the Herero was most clearly seen in the realm of political authority. Though political leaders seem to have arisen originally because of their control over a valued resource (a dependable source of water), their authority was very limited. Intertribal conflicts, especially with the Hottentots, may have added to a leader's prestige, but that prestige was apparently not significant in adding to his authority in times of peace. It was not until Europeans began settling in South West Africa that political organization began to change significantly.

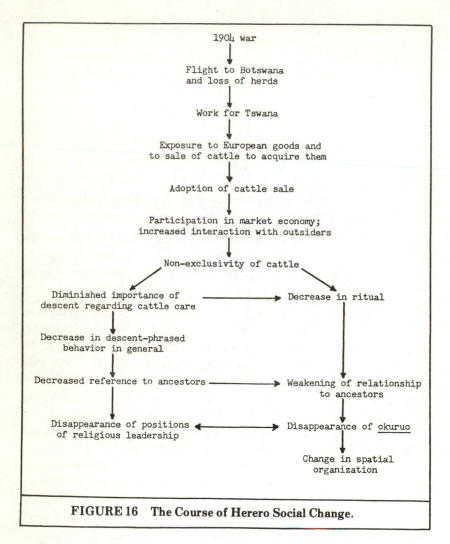

FIGURE 16   The Course of Herero Social Change.

The influence of the European presence was felt in two ways. First, as whites settled in open areas, they contributed to a leader's authority by limiting available land to which his dependents could move. Followers would put up with a leader's assertion of authority because they had little choice. There was nowhere else to go.

Second, the Europeans made repeated efforts, for various reasons, to install a paramount chief among the Herero. The German colonial administration came closest to success in this endeavor by making Samuel Maharero its political puppet. Samuel's paramountcy was never realized, however, for the Herero rebelled against the Germans in 1904. Samuel and some two thousand other Herero escaped to Botswana, and the remaining Herero in South West Africa became virtually prisoners of the Europeans.

The Herero who fled to Botswana came in small and scattered groups and were allowed by the Tswana chiefs to settle in their territory. Botswana was at that time administered by the British, but tribal matters within the several districts of the country were by and large left in the hands of the Tswana chiefs. The Herero who

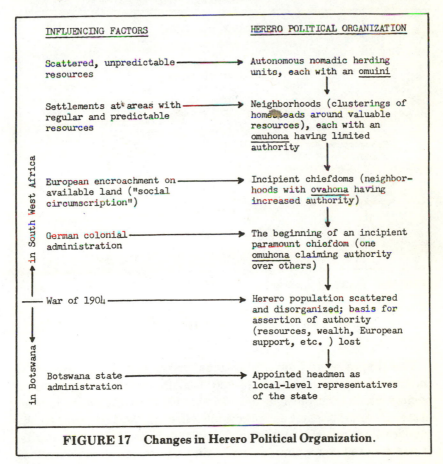

FIGURE 17 Changes in Herero Political Organization.

came to Botswana came as cattle-poor refugees. They had little choice but to accept their incorporation into the state structure in a subordinate position. Herero leaders became dependent on the state, through the Tswana chiefs, for any authority they possessed. The authority of local Herero headmen today is still held by grace of the state and is not due to indigenous factors.

Figure 17 is an attempt to depict the evolution of Herero political authority as interpreted here.

Figure 18 illustrates the articulation point (the 1904 war) of the two major endogenous changes which are interpreted as results of exogenous influences.

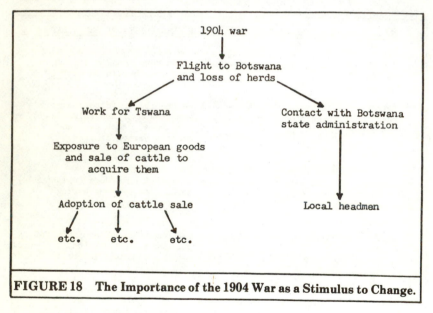

FIGURE 18   The Importance of the 1904 War as a Stimulus to Change.

NEED FOR FURTHER STUDY

The Herero went from a traditional tribal society, comprised of independent settlements possessing ritually important cattle, to a society which is currently deeply immersed in the affairs of a nation-state. Herero society has successfully accommodated itself to the modern sociological situation in which it finds itself. In other words, it has adapted to its new environs. But adaptation implies the loss of some things (those with limited survival value) and the addition of others to meet the new environmental conditions, social and physical. What has been lost, what has been transformed, and what has been added? These are the questions which this study has attempted to answer.

Unfortunately, all the information that might be helpful is not available. There are several reasons for this. The primary reason of concern to the anthropologist is that in many cases the knowledge has passed out of Herero memory. Even the eldest living Herero no longer know some of the old ways, beliefs, traditions; or their memories are so confused and contradictory as to be almost useless. The young people, of course, know even less. They are often even unaware that their people previously had different customs (if we take the point of view that the old ways are no longer as adaptive as they once were, it is then not surprising that the young people have failed to learn them).

Another problem is the absence of data from what may be called the macro-perspective. The Republic of Botswana discourages "tribalism." The government is trying to turn the people from local allegiance to loyalty to the state above all else. One consequence of this policy is that such records as population statistics, school attendance figures, use of veterinary services, and so forth, do not identify subjects by tribe, so such useful data as the number of Herero living in Botswana, the number of Herero children in school, the number of Herero cattle sold to traders, the number of Herero cattle inoculated against disease, the contribution of Herero cattle to Botswana's beef export, and so forth, are not available.

Some gaps in the data, however, are due to the short period of field investigation. If I had been able to stay among the Herero for a longer time, more quantitative data could have been collected and certain areas of social organization, such as kinship terminology and marriage practices, could have been more intensely studied.

And it is perhaps only a slight exaggeration to say that the older literature on the Herero, especially that written in the nineteenth century, raises more questions than it answers—leaving more gaps regarding what Herero society was once like.

Nevertheless, there was enough information to accomplish the overall objective: to trace the course of social change among the

Herero. It was the purpose of this study to describe in broad perspective the transformation of Herero social organization, to record the social change that has occurred and the conditions under which it occurred.

Unless immediate steps are taken to conduct further research among the Botswana Herero to record additional detail in the transformation of traditional ways, the data will be lost to us forever. Despite their sometimes faulty memories, the primary sources for this information remain elderly Herero, approximately seventy years old or older. There are only a few of them now; soon there will be none.

REMARKS ON THE STUDY OF CHANGE

I have tried throughout this study to avoid a mechanistic interpretation of social change. I have attempted to avoid reifying aspects of social organization and giving the impression that social institutions are doing things to people. I tried to emphasize that people doing things with each other produce institutional changes. This statement appears truistic so explicitly expressed. But such statements need to be made occasionally. All too often descriptions of social change leave the reader with the impression that mysterious forces are at work in a society, setting into motion sequences of events in which people are manipulated like puppets.

This study has tried to demonstrate that social change among the Herero was not mysterious, that people were the manipulators of a situation. Man is an opportunist. If we can identify the opportunities and constraints latent in any particular situation, we are more likely to be able to understand social change; for social change is the product of people choosing alternatives. Social change results from how people choose to adjust to new situations.

This point of view is not unlike Barth's (1967) argument that studies of social change should focus on the cumulative result of individual adjustments to changing conditions—measurable as frequencies of alternative allocations of time and resources—rather than on differences in the morphology or form of institutions at different points in time. He suggests (p. 633) that "a social form is . . .

the epiphenomenon of a number of processes" and that "analysis . . . [should concentrate] . . . on showing how the form is generated."

The present work was intended to show how the Herero responded to changing conditions, how the Herero by adopting a foreign strategy for making a living changed their society. Though this was a study of one particular society, the interpretation employed here has implications for the study of social change in general. If Cohen's theory, as outlined in the beginning of this work, is applicable in the Herero case, the suggestion is that it may apply in other cases. And if the present study has helped to confirm proffered generalizations about the workings of human society, it serves as more than just another contribution to the ethnographic record.

*

Glossary

eanda (pl. *omaanda*)   Matrisib.

ohambo (s. *ozohambo*)   Cattle post.

okumakera   To taste.

okuruo (pl. *omaruo*)   Sacred hearth.

orutjandja   Flat, open area; basin or pan.

oruzo (pl. *otuzo*)   Patrisib.

Otjiherero   Language of the Herero people.

omaze   Fat from *oruzo* cattle.

Omuherero (pl. *Ovaherero*)   Herero person.

omuhona (pl. *ovahona*)   Leader of a neighborhood, community headman.

omuini (pl. *oveini*)   Owner.

omumakere   Taster; one who first eats a bit of food that is *zera* in order to neutralize its supernatural power and thus render it safe for ordinary persons to eat.

ovondjuo   Persons residing in a single house (*ondjuo*).

omurangere (pl. *ovarangere*)   Leader of religious ritual.

omusuko (pl. *ovasuko*)   Concubine.

ondjuo (pl. *ozondjuo*)   House, hut; matrilineage.

onganda (pl. *ozonganda*)   Homestead; patrilineage.

ozongombe (s. *ongombe*)   Cattle.

zera   Sacred; taboo; dangerous because imbued with supernatural power.

*

Map II: South West Africa

Place Names

1. Waterberg
2. Omaruru
3. Okahandja
4. Otjimbingue
5. Windhoek
6. Gobabis
7. Rehoboth

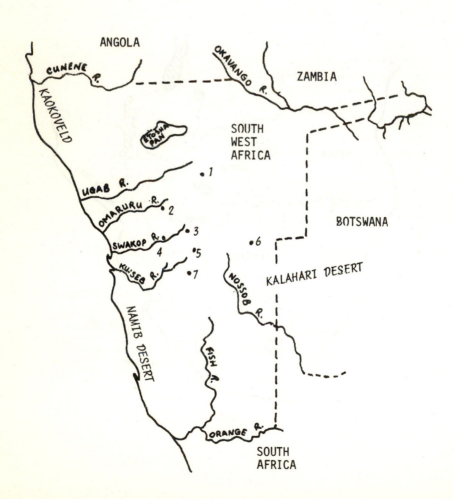

Map III: Botswana

Place Names

1. Mamuno
2. Makunda
3. Charles Hill
4. Kalkfontein
5. Ghanzi
6. Sehitwa
7. Toteng
8. Maun
9. Dauga

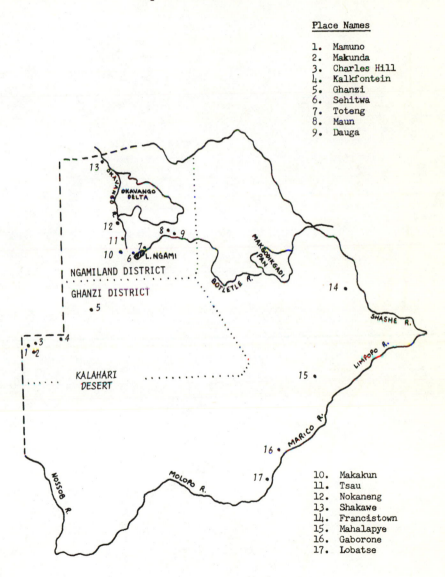

10. Makakun
11. Tsau
12. Nokaneng
13. Shakawe
14. Francistown
15. Mahalapye
16. Gaborone
17. Lobatse

APPENDIX B

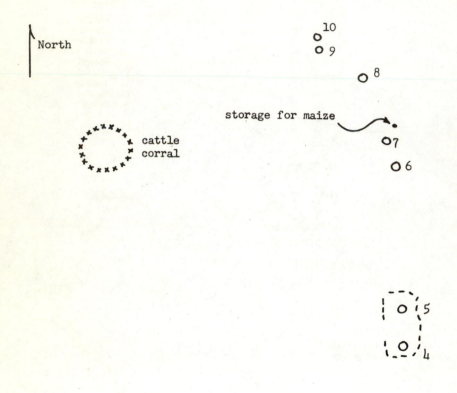

Diagram of Homestead F

Key to Diagram of Homestead F

Number	Identification
1	Hut of yB and yBW.
2	Storage hut for hut 3.
3	Hut of *omuini* (ego), W, and children.
4	Storage hut for hut 5.
5	Hut of Z (unmarried).
6	Storage hut for hut 7.
7	Abandoned hut (formerly hut of Z who has now married and moved away).
8	Hut of ZS (son of woman in hut 5).
9	Storage hut.
10	Storage hut.

Diagram of Homestead G

North

cattle
corral

Key to Diagram of Homestead G

Number	Identification
1	Storage hut for hut 2.
2	Hut of *omuini* (divorced) and child.
3	Hut in construction for Z (unmarried) and ZC.

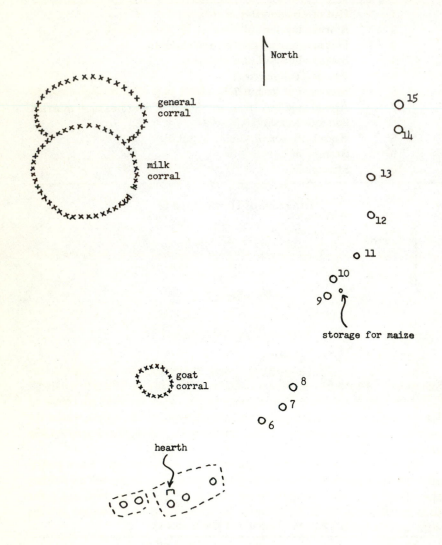

Diagram of Homestead H

Key to Diagram of Homestead H

Number	Identification
1	Hut of *omuini*, W, and children.
2	A secondary hut for *omuini*, W, and children.
3	Storage hut for hut 4.
4	Hut of yB, yBW, and children.
5	Abandoned hut.
6	Hut of FB and FBW. (FBS and FBSW and children moved away.)
7	Storage hut for hut 6.
8	Storage hut for hut 6.
9	Storage hut for hut 10.
10	Hut of M.
11	Hut of Z (unmarried).
12	Abandoned.
13	Abandoned.
14	Abandoned.
15	Abandoned.

APPENDIX C

List of Otuzo (Patrisibs)

The table on the following page summarizes my eldest informants' responses to the question, "Is this a Herero *oruzo*?" Column 1 lists names which appear in previous sources as those of Herero *otuzo*. The final question (not shown on the table, since its results are incorporated in the table) was, "Are there any other *otuzo*?"

According to Gibson (pers. comm.) the Ambo do not have patrisibs. My informants' identification of certain *otuzo* names as Ambo, therefore, must be interpreted as meaning, "the term does not refer to a Herero sib, so it must refer to something in a foreign group, such as the Ambo."

List of Otuzo (Patrisibs)

Alleged otuzo names in earlier sources	Respondents:								
	1	2	3	4	5	6	7	8	9
Ongueuva	Yes	Yes	Yes	Yes	Yes	Yes	Yes	Yes	Yes
Otjiporo	Yes	Yes	Yes	Yes	Yes	Yes	Yes	Yes	Yes
Okanene	Yes	Yes	Yes	Yes	Yes	Yes	Yes	Yes	Yes
Ondjiva	Yes	Yes	Yes	Yes	Yes	Yes	Yes	Yes	Yes
Omuhinaruzo	Yes	Yes	Yes	Yes	Yes	Yes	Yes	Yes	Yes
Ohorongo	Yes	Yes	Yes	Yes	Yes	Yes	Yes	Yes	Yes
Onguatjija	Yes	Yes	Yes	Yes	Yes	Yes	Yes	Yes	Yes
Otjihaviria	Yes	Yes	Yes	Yes	Mbanderu?	Yes	Yes	Yes	Yes
Ojakoto	Yes	Did not know it	Yes	Yes	Yes	Yes	Yes	Yes	Yes
Omuko	Yes	Yes	Yes	Yes	Mbanderu?	Yes	Yes	Yes	Yes
Ondanga	Yes	Yes	Yes	Yes	Yes	Yes	Yes	Yes	Yes
Ohambandarua	Yes	Yes	Yes	Yes	Yes	Yes	Yes .	Yes	Yes
Omakoti	Yes	Yes	Yes	Yes	Yes	Yes	Yes	Yes	Yes
Otjirungu	Yes	Yes	Yes	Yes	Yes	Yes	Yes	Yes	Yes
Otjitjindua	Yes	Yes	Yes	Yes	Yes	Yes	Yes	Yes	Yes
Omurekua	Yes	Yes	Yes	Yes	Yes	Yes	Yes	Yes	Yes
Onguendjandje	Yes	Yes	Yes	Yes	Yes	Yes	Yes	Yes	Yes
Onguanjimi	Yes	Yes	Yes	Yes	Yes	Yes	Yes	Yes	Yes
Ombongora	Yes	Yes	Yes	Yes	Yes	Yes	Yes	Yes	Yes
Osembi (Esembi)	Yes	Yes	Yes	Yes	Mbanderu?	Yes	Yes	Yes	Yes
Onguatjindu	Yes	Yes	Yes	Yes	Yes	Yes	Yes	Yes	Yes
Onguangoro	Not Herero?	Yes?	Did not know it	Yes	Mbanderu?	Mbanderu	Mbanderu	Mbanderu	Mbanderu

List of Otuzo (Patrisibs)

Alleged otuzo names in earlier sources	Respondents: 1	2	3	4	5	6	7	8	9
Onguazembi	Not Herero?	Did not know it	Yes?	Did not know it	Mbanderu	Ambo	Ambo	Ambo	Ambo
Ongandjira	No?	Ambo	Ambo	Ambo	Ambo	Ambo	Ambo	Ambo	Ambo
Ojombonjova	No?	Ambo	Ambo	Ambo	Ambo	Ambo	Ambo	Ambo	Ambo
Ojojakoli	No?	Ambo	Ambo	Ambo	Ambo	Ambo	Ambo	Ambo	Ambo
Ojokasema	No?	Ambo	Ambo	Ambo	Ambo	Ambo	Ambo	Ambo	Ambo
Onguahonge	No?	Ambo	Ambo	Ambo	Ambo	Ambo	Ambo	Ambo	Ambo
Otjizamatjinge	No?	Ambo	Ambo	Ambo	Ambo	Ambo	Ambo	Ambo	Ambo
Ojarutuu	No?	Ambo	Ambo	Ambo	Ambo	Ambo	Ambo	Ambo	Ambo
Onguarangua	No?	Ambo	Ambo	Ambo	Ambo	Ambo	Ambo	Ambo	Ambo
Ondjombore	Did not know it	Lineage	Lineage	Lineage	Did not know it		Inquiry not made		
Onguagemba	No?	No	No?	No	No				
Onguahavetju	No	No	No	No	No				
Okahuri Munyungu	No	No	Place name in S.W.A.	Place name in S.W.A.	Place name in S.W.A.				
Onguakavero	Not Herero?	Did not know it	Did not know it	Did not know it	Mbanderu?	Mbanderu			

APPENDIX D

Oruzo Proscriptions and Prescriptions

The table on the following pages summarizes the data supplied by my informants concerning the *oruzo* restrictions for each Herero patrisib. Column 1 lists the names of patrisibs. Column 2 shows what is *izera* (proscribed or tabooed) for each patrisib. Column 3 lists the prescribed cattle for each patrisib. The horizontal lines separate phratries.

Oruzo Proscriptions and Prescriptions

Name of Oruzo	*Izera*		*Oruzo Cattle*	
Ongueuva	a.	Ondumbu cattle	a.	Ombonde
	b.	Ondovazu sheep	b.	Orukueja
			c.	Ombatoona
			d.	Ondorojeo
			e.	Ekuara
			f.	Ondorozu
			g.	Ongombe
Otjiporo	a.	Ondumbu cattle	a.	Ombambi
			b.	Ondjandja
			c.	Eo
Okanene	a.	Ondumbu cattle	a.	Ombaue
	b.	Ondovazu sheep		
	c.	Ohungu cattle		
Ondjiva	a.	Ondumbu cattle	(Same as Ongueuva)	
	b.	Ondovazu sheep		
Omuhinaruzo	a.	Ondumbu cattle	(Same as Ongueuva)	
	b.	Ondovazu sheep		
Ohorongo	a.	Ohungu cattle	a.	Ondumbu
Onguatjija	a.	Ongonga cattle	a.	Ombiriona
			b.	Ondovazu

| Otjihaviria | a. | Ombuindja (steinbok) | a. | Ombiriona |
| | | | b. | Ondovazu |

| Ojakoto | a. | Ondovazu sheep | a. | Ondaura |
| Omuko | a. | Ongombe jao komangoti (neck of cattle) | a. | Osaona |

| Ondanga | ? | | a. | Ondanga |
| Ohambandarua | a. | Ondovazu sheep | a. | Ondaura |

Omakoti	a.	Tripe	a.	Ondumbu
Otjirungu	a.	Tripe	a.	Ondumbu
Otjijindua	?		?	
Omurekua	?		a.	Orupera (or otupera)

Onguendjandje	a.	Ondumbu cattle	a.	Osaona
	b.	Ondovazu sheep	b.	Ondjandja
Onguanjimi	?		?	
Ombongora	a.	Ongonga cattle	a.	Ombongora
Osembi (Esembi)	a.	Ondumbu cattle	a.	Ombahiona
	b.	Eraka (tongue of cattle)		
Onguatjindu	a.	Ombua ondorozu (black dog)	a.	Orukueja
			b.	Ondovazu

APPENDIX E

List of Omaanda (Matrisibs)

The table below summarizes some of my informants' responses to the question, "Is this a Herero *eanda*?" The responses of all informants are not shown, since all responses were identical.

Omaanda names in earlier sources	*Respondents:*			
	1	*2*	*3*	*4*
Omuekueuva	Yes	Yes	Yes	Yes
Omuekuenombura	Yes	Yes	Yes	Yes
Omuekuatjivi	Yes	Yes	Yes	Yes
Omuekuauti	Yes	Yes	Yes	Yes
Omuekuendjata	Yes	Yes	Yes	Yes
Omuekuendjandje	Yes	Yes	Yes	Yes
Omuekuahere	Yes	Yes	Yes	Yes
Omuekuatjiti	Yes	Yes	Yes	Yes
Omuekuenatja	Yes	Yes	Yes	Yes

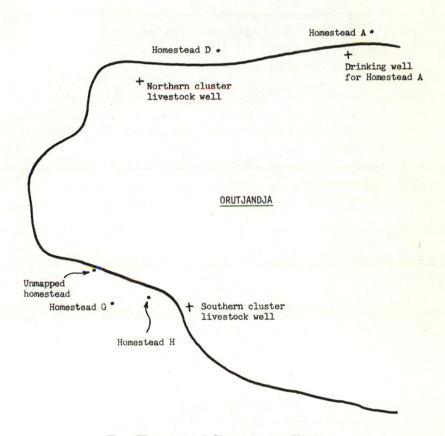

Two Homestead Clusters and Wells

APPENDIX G

Map of Herero Makakun

A rough map of the Herero community in Makakun appears on the next page. The following notes pertain to that map.

- = homestead verified by ethnographer.
* = unverified homestead on map drawn by informant.
―――――― = Land Rover tracks
A - - - -
B - - - - = transect surveys.

1. Southern *orutjandja* cluster (homesteads G, H, and one other).
2. Northern *orutjandja* cluster (homesteads A, D, E, F).
3. Homestead B.
4. Homestead C.

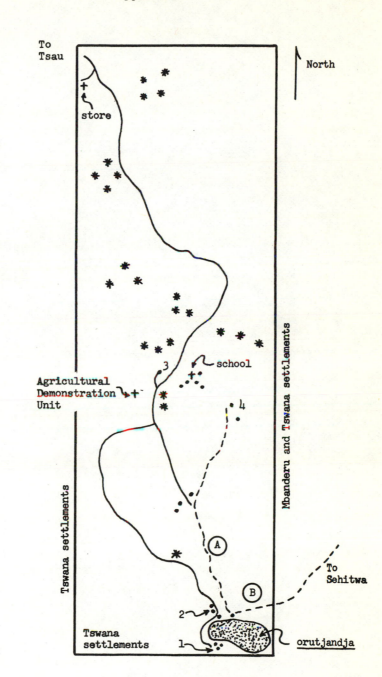

MAP OF
HERERO
MAKAKUN

To Tsau

North

store

Agricultural
Demonstration
Unit

school

3

Mbanderu and Tswana settlements

Tswana settlements

4

A

B

To Sehitwa

2

orutjandja

1

Tswana
settlements

Bibliography[*]

Barth, F.
  1961   *Nomads of South Persia.* Boston: Little, Brown.
  1967   "On the Study of Social Change." *American Anthropologist* 69:661–9.

Bates, D. G.
  1971   "The Role of the State in Peasant-Nomad Mutualism." *Anthropologist Quarterly* 44:109–31.

Botswana Information Services
  n.d.   *Botswana in Brief.* Gaborone: Botswana Information Services.

Brauer, E.
  1925   *Züge aus der Religion der Herero. Ein Beitrag zur Hamitenfrage.* (Features from the religion of the Herero. A contribution to the Hamite question.) Leipzig: Institut für Völkerkunde. Reihe I: Ethnographie und Ethnologie, Bd. 7.

Brincker, P. H.
  1895   "Das Zaubergift der Bantu." (Bantu sorcery poison.) *Globus* 68:210–11.
  1899   "Die Eingeborenen Deutsch-Sudwest-Afrikas nach Geschichte, Charakter, Sitten, Gerbrauchen und Sprachen." (History, character, customs and language of the natives of German South West Africa.) *Mittheilungen des Seminars fur Orientalische Sprachen* 2:125–39.
  1900   "Charakter, Sitten und Gebräuche speciell der Bantu Deutsche-Sudwest-Afrikas." (Character, customs, and specific usages of the Bantu of German South West Africa.) *Mittheilungen des Seminars fur Orientalische Sprachen* 3:66–92.

*English translations of the German works were used in the preparation of this study, though all page numbers cited refer to the original German publications. The English translations have been made by Gordon D. Gibson and his co-workers for the Human Relations Area Files of Yale University.

British Information Services
  1966   *Botswana.* London: British Information Services.

Buttner, K. G.
  1883   "Die Viehwirtschaft der Herero." (Herero cattle management.)
          Das Ausland 56:489–94, 529–33, 550–56.
  1884   "Die Herero und ihre Toten." (The Herero and their dead.) *Das
          Ausland* 57:386–9.

Carneiro, R. L.
  1970   "A Theory of the Origin of the State." *Science* 169 (no.
          3947):733–8.

Church, R. J. H.
  1973   "West African Drought Pattern." *The Geographical Magazine*
          45:905.

Clark, J. D.
  1959   *The Prehistory of Southern Africa.* Baltimore: Penguin Books.

Cohen, Y. A.
  1968   *Man in Adaptation: The Cultural Present* (second edition
          1974). Chicago: Aldine.
  1969a   "Ends and Means in Political Control: State Organization and
          the Punishment of Adultery, Incest, and Violation of Celi-
          bacy." *American Anthropologist* 71:658–87.
  1969b   "Social Boundary Systems." *Current Anthropology* 10:117–26.
  1971   *Man in Adaptation: The Institutional Framework.* Chicago:
          Aldine.
  ms.   *Inside Culture and Boundary Culture: A General Theory of
          Human Social Organization.* In preparation for publication.

Dannert, E., Jr.
  1906   *Zum Rechte der Herero, inbesondere Über ihr Familien- und
          Erbrecht.* (On the law of the Herero, especially about their fam-
          ily and inheritance.) Berlin: Reimer.

Dinter, K.
  1912   *Die Vegetabilische Veldkost Deutsch-Sudwest-Africa.* Oka-
          kandja, South West Africa.

Esterhuyse, J. H.
  1968   *South West Africa, 1880–1894.* Cape Town: C. Struik.

Estermann, C.
1956–60   *Etnografia do Sudoeste Angola* (3 vols.). Lisbon: Ministerio do
          Ultramar.

Evans-Pritchard, E. E.
1940   *The Nuer.* New York: Oxford University Press.

Fallers, L.
1955   "The Predicament of the Modern African Chief: An Instance
          from Uganda." *American Anthropologist* 57:290–305.
1965   (Orig. 1956) *Bantu Bureaucracy.* Chicago: University of Chica-
          go Press.

Faris, J. C.
1969   "Some Cultural Considerations of Duolineal Descent Organiza-
          tion." *Ethnology* 8:243–54.

Forde, C. D.
1950   "Double Descent among the Yako." in A. R. Radcliffe-Brown
          and C. D. Forde, eds., *African Systems of Kinship and Mar-
          riage.* London: Oxford University Press.

Fox, R.
1967   *Kinship and Marriage.* Baltimore: Penguin Books.

Geoghegan, W. H.
1969   "Decision Making and Residence on Tagtabon Island." Work-
          ing Paper No. 17, Language-Behavior Research Laboratory,
          University of California, Berkeley.
1970a   "A Theory of Marking Rules." Working Paper No. 37, Lan-
          guage-Behavior Research Laboratory, University of California,
          Berkeley.
1970b   "Residential Decision Making among the Eastern Samal."
          Paper presented at the American Anthropological Association
          Annual Meetings, San Diego, California.
1970c   *Natural Information Processing Systems: Formal Theory and
          Ethnographic Applications.* Ph.D. thesis, Stanford University.

Gibson, G. D.
1952   *The Social Organization of the Southwestern Bantu.* Ph.D.
          thesis, University of Chicago.
1956   "Double Descent and Its Correlates among the Herero of
          Ngamiland." *American Anthropologist* 58:109–39.
1959a   "Herero Marriage." *The Rhodes-Livingstone Journal* 24:1–37.

1959b   "Levels of Residence among the Herero." Paper presented at
           the American Anthropological Association Annual Meetings,
           Mexico City.
1962   "Bridewealth and Other Forms of Exchange among the
           Herero." in P. Bohannan and G. Dalton, eds., *Markets in
           Africa*. Evanston: Northwestern University Press.

Goldblatt, I.
1971   *History of South West Africa*. Cape Town: Juta & Co.

Goodenough, W. H.
1956   "Residence Rules." *Southwestern Journal of Anthropology*
           12:22–37.

Goody, J.
1961   "The Classification of Double Descent Systems." *Current
           Anthropology* 2:3–25.

Gulliver, P. H.
1971   *Neighbours and Networks*. Berkeley: University of California
           Press.

Hahn, J.
1869   "Die Ovaherero." (The Ovaherero.) *Zeitschrift der Gesellschaft
           für Erdkunde zu Berlin* 4:226–58, 481–511.

Hartmann, G.
1897   "Das Kaoko-Gebiet in Deutsch Sudwest-Afrika auf Grund
           eigener Reisen und Beobachtungen." (The Kaoko region in Ger-
           man South West Africa on the basis on some trips and observa-
           tions.) *Verhandlungen der Gesellschaft für Erdkunde zu Berlin*
           Bd. 24, pp. 113–41.

Henderson, W.
1974   "Brigades, Government, Enthusiasm and Development: A Cri-
           tical Review." *Botswana Notes and Records* 6:179–88.

Hennings, R. O.
1951   *African Morning*. London: Chatlo & Windus.

Henry, H. G.
1967   "The Economy of Botswana." in R. P. Stevens, *Lesotho, Bots-
           wana, Swaziland*. New York: Frederick A. Praeger.

Herskovits, M. J.
1926   "The Cattle Complex in East Africa." *American Anthropolo-
           gist* 28:230–72, 361–80, 494–528, 633–64.

Howard, A.
1963   "Land, Activity Systems, and Decision-Making Models in Rotuma." *Ethnology* 2:407–40.

Howe, R. W.
1973   "Downriver to Armageddon." *World* 2:18–23.

Irle, J.
1906   *Die Herero.* Gutersloh: C. Bartelsmann.
1917   "Die Religion der Herero." *Archiv für Anthropologie N. F.* 15:337–67.

Izmirlian, H., Jr.
1969   "Structural and Decision-Making Models: A Political Example." *American Anthropologist* 71:1062–73.

Johnson, D. L.
1969   *The Nature of Nomadism.* Chicago: University of Chicago Press.

Keesing, R. M.
1967   "Statistical Models and Decision Models of Social Structure: A Kwaio Case." *Ethnology* 6:1–16.
1970   "Kwaio Fosterage." *American Anthropologist* 72:991–1019.

Kopytoff, I.
1971   "Ancestors as Elders in Africa." *Africa* 41:129–42.

Kuper, A., and S. Gillett
1970   "Aspects of Administration in Western Botswana." *African Studies* 29:169–82.

Lambrecht, F. L., and D. Lambrecht
1969   "Victorian Fashions at the Edge of the Kalahari." *Natural History* 78(3):48–50.

Langdale-Brown, I., and R. J. Spooner
1963   "Land Use Prospects of Northern Bechuanaland." Forestry and Land Use Section, Directorate of Overseas Surveys, Tolworth, Surrey, England.

Leach, E.
1962   "On Certain Unconsidered Aspects of Double Descent." *Man* 62:130–34.

Lehmann, F. R.
1955   "Das Häuptlingtum der Herero in Sudwest Afrika." (The chief-
        tainship of the Herero in South West Africa.) *Sociologus*
        5:28–43.

Loffler, R.
1971   "The Representative Mediator and the New Peasant." *Ameri-
        can Anthropologist* 73:1077–91.

Luttig, H. C.
1933   *The Religious System and Social Organization of the Herero.*
        Utrecht: Kemink.

Molnar, T.
1966   *South West Africa.* New York: Fleet Publishing Co.

Mountjoy, A. B., and C. Embleton
1967   *Africa: A New Geographical Survey.* New York: Frederick A.
        Praeger.

Munger, E. S.
1965   *Bechuanaland.* London: Oxford University Press.

Murphy, R. F.
1964   "Social Change and Acculturation." *Transactions of the New
        York Academy of Sciences* 26:845–54.

Murphy, R. F., & J. H. Steward
1956   "Tappers and Trappers: Parellel Process in Acculturation."
        Economic Development and Cultural Change 4:335–55.

Murdock, G. P.
1940   "Double Descent." *American Anthropologist* 42:555–61.
1949   *Social Structure.* New York: The Free Press.

Nimkoff, M. F., and R. Middleton
1960   "Types of Family and Types of Economy." *American Journal
        of Sociology* 66:215–24.

Oliver, S. O.
1962   *Ecology and Cultural Continuity as Contributing Factors in the
        Social Organization of the Plains Indians.* University of Cali-
        fornia Publications in American Archaeology and Ethnology,
        vol. 48, no. 1. Berkeley: University of California Press.

Ottenberg, S.
   1968   *Double Descent in African Society: The Afikbo Village-Group.*
          Seattle: University of Washington Press.

Pehrson, R. N.
   1966   *The Social Organization of the Marri Baluch* (compiled by F.
          Barth). New York: Wenner-Gren, and Chicago: Aldine.

Phehane, J. Taetji
   1974   "History of Botswana: Sources of Information." *Botswana
          Notes and Records* 6:19–28.

R. A. I. (Royal Anthropological Institute of Great Britain & Ireland)
   1951   *Notes and Queries on Anthropology.* London: Routledge and
          Kegan Paul.

Sahlins, M. D.
   1968   *Tribesmen.* Englewood Cliffs, N. J.: Prentice-Hall.

Salzman, P. C.
   1967   "Political Organization among Nomadic Peoples." *Proceedings
          of the American Philosophical Society* 111:115–31.
   1970   "Nomadism as an Adaptive Mechanism." Paper presented to
          the McGill Faculty Seminar on Human Ecology.
   1971   "Adaptation and Political Organization in Iranian Baluchis-
          tan." *Ethnology* 10:433–44.
   1972   "Multi-Resource Nomadism in Iranian Baluchistan." *Journal
          of Asian and African Studies* 7:60–8.

Schapera, I.
   1938   *A Handbook of Tswana Law and Custom.* London: Oxford Uni-
          versity Press.
   1943a *Native Land Tenure in the Bechuanaland Protectorate.* Alice,
          South Africa: Lovedale Press.
   1943b *Tribal Legislation Among the Tswana of the Bechuanaland
          Protectorate.* London: Lund, Humphries. (Revised version
          published as Schapera 1970.)
   1945   "Notes on Some Herero Genealogies." *Communications from
          the School of African Studies,* New Series No. 14. Cape Town:
          University of Cape Town.
   1947   *Migrant Labour and Tribal Life.* London: Oxford University
          Press.
   1952   *The Ethnic Composition of Tswana Tribes.* London: London
          School of Economics.

1970   *Tribal Innovators: Tswana Chiefs and Social Change, 1795-1940*. New York: Humanities Press. (Revised version of Schapera 1943b.)

Scheffler, H. W.
1966   "Ancestor Worship in Anthropology: or, Observations on Descent and Descent Groups." *Current Anthropology* 7:541–51.

Schneider, D. M.
1962   "Double Descent on Yap." *Journal of the Polynesian Society* 71:1–24.

Schneider, H. K.
1957   "The Subsistence Role of Cattle among the Pakot and in East Africa." *American Anthropologist* 59:278–300.
1959   "Pakot Resistance to Change." in W. R. Bascom and M. J. Herskovits, eds., *Continuity and Change in African Cultures*. Chicago: University of Chicago Press.
1974   "Economic Development and Economic Change: The Case of East African Cattle." *Current Anthropology* 15:259–76.

Sillery, A.
1952   *The Bechuanaland Protectorate*. London: Oxford University Press.
1965   *Founding a Protectorate: History of Bechuanaland, 1885–1895*. The Hague: Mouton & Co.

Simmel, G.
1950   "The Stranger." in K. H. Wolff, trans. and ed., *The Sociology of Georg Simmel*. Glencoe: The Free Press.

Stenning, D. J.
1959   *Savannah Nomads*. London: Oxford University Press.

Stevens, R. P.
1967   *Lesotho, Botswana, and Swaziland*. New York: Frederick A. Praeger.

Steward, J. H.
1955   *Theory of Culture Change*. Urbana: University of Illinois Press.

Ulin, R. O.
1974   "The Brigades of Botswana Eight Years Later." *Botswana Notes and Records* 6:189–96.

Van Horn, L.
1972   "Double Descent and Subsistence among the Herero of South
        West Africa and Botswana." *Anthropological Journal of
        Canada* 10:2–15.

Vedder, H.
1928   "The Herero," in *Native Tribes of South West Africa.* Cape
        Town: Cape Times Limited.
1938   *South West Africa in Early Times.* London: Oxford University
        Press.

Vengroff, R.
1975   "Networks and Leadership in a Development Institution: the
        District Council in Botswana." *Political Anthropology*
        1:155–74.

Viehe, G.
1902   "Die Omaanda und Otuzo der Ovaherero." (The *omaanda* and
        otuzo of the Ovaherero.) *Mittheilungen des Seminars für Orien-
        talische Sprachen* 5:109–17.

von Francois, H.
1896   *Nama und Damara, Deutsche-Sud-West-Afrika.* (Nama and
        Damara, German South West Africa.) Magdeburg: G.
        Baensch.

Wagner, G.
1952   "Aspects of Conservatism and Adaptation in the Economic
        Life of the Herero." *Sociologus* 2:1–25.

Wheeler, J. H., Jr., *et al.*
1969   *Regional Geography of the World.* New York: Holt, Rinehart
        and Winston.

White, J. M.
1969   *The Land God Made in Anger.* New York: Rand McNally.

White, L. A.
1949   *The Science of Culture.* New York: Farrar, Strauss and Giroux.
1959   *The Evolution of Culture.* New York: McGraw-Hill.

Young, B. A.
1966   *Bechuanaland.* London: Her Majesty's Stationery Office.

*

Index

†